a break from all the work and they finally gave her permission to come over Saturday afternoon and stay until Monday morning.

With Julie added to the mix, I had Mark covered. Al told me he also liked girls and there were still plenty to get him hooked up with as well. If I really got lucky Al might hit it off well enough with one of the girls to allow me to bow out of at least one relationship. I doubted it, but hope springs eternal. These were the thoughts in my head as I finished up my work for the week and went out on Friday night with Bobbie.

With my parents staying at the hotel for the weekend, I was ready for the sleep over. What I was not ready for was how to deal with Bobby and all the other girls. Although she did not say it, I could tell that she was getting tired of sharing me with them. I certainly sympathized with her feelings, but I still had no idea how to get myself out of those relationships. The girls I was involved with were a lot like me. We all hated drugs, smoking and did not use alcohol. That made them a bad fit for 99% of the boys available in their respective age groups. I mean, it was not like they could just go out and find another me.

I really enjoyed spending time with each of my girlfriends and that left me somewhat unwilling to just drop them even if the opportunity presented itself. However, I also knew that my situation was un-sustainable and could not go on for much longer. The only relationship I was sure about was the one with my cousin. She did not trust boys, liked girls enough to have sex with them and was apparently sexually satisfied with the regular intercourse we had together. I would never quit on her. I knew that she would probably move on someday, but until that time came I treasured our moments together.

Bobbie and I went to a concert in Tampa, then had a late dinner in at my the hotel where myu dad worked. My folks were already staying there for the weekend, but they were up in the suite. Bobbie and I talked for a while, then went back to my house. We planned to take a swim and found Ingrid and Laura already in the pool. They were naked, so we took off our clothes and joined them. Laura swam over to me and began making out. Before Bobbie could react, Ingrid saw my situation and took action.

My cousin swam over to Bobbie and gently caressed her body from behind. Ingrid rubbed her back, them moved her hands around to touch and massage Bobbie's breasts. Bobbie looked scared, but was afraid to insult or upset my cousin by rebuffing her. Instead, she allowed Ingrid to come around to her front and make out with her. After a while we switched partners and it really turned me on to watch Ingrid make out with Laura while I did the same thing with Bobbie.

As we were getting out of the pool, Ingrid started drying off Bobbie. After both of them were dry, she took Bobbie by the hand, picked up their clothes and lead her to the bedroom. I knew that was the last I would she of Bobbie for the night and I was fine with that. As much as I liked being with Bobbie, I knew she was exactly what my cousin liked and needed. If Bobbie could be a bit more open to the idea, the two would be a terrific match and take some of the pressure off my situation.

Laura and I went to my bedroom and had sex. Afterward, we made out for a while then fell asleep together. I woke up around three in the morning to someone climbing into bed with me. Laura was gone and I assumed had gone back to her own bedroom to sleep, but Bobbie was there getting into bed with me. She was naked and held me tightly and basically said that she wanted forgiveness for whatever she did with Ingrid. I told her that she had nothing to be forgiven for and reminded her of my own bisexual nature.

I knew that Bobbie felt guilty, but I told her that she needed to give herself permission to enjoy sex with other people just the way I did. This was the Age of Aquarius and free love for goodness sake! I knew it was a stupid excuse, but hoped that it would be good enough to help Bobbie to stop being such a sexual prude. There was no reason that all of us could not get along, love one another and have sex as a group or individually without feeling any sort of guilt based on puritanical morales that were outdated and ineffective when it came to making people happy.

Bobbie and I had great sex that night. I could smell Ingrid all over her and just thinking about what the two had done together made me all the hornier. Likewise, Bobbie smelled Laura all over me and I think that turned her on as well. Once we got going I was surprised at how long we did it. My penis was numb and had been stuck into both her holes numerous times before I finally shot my load. Her much freckled body was already a super turn on for me, so everything else was just a bonus which kept me going for what seemed like all night.

By the time I woke up in the morning Bobby was in the shower. She had some work to do with Ingrid and from the voices I heard downstairs, Diane was already at the house. I joined them for breakfast, then went to shower and dress so that I could finish all my errands for Ingrid before it was time for Mark, Al, Julie and Nancy to arrive. Marie went back to the Chicago area so she would have some time to get ready for school. I knew she wanted to stay with Nancy, but that was never going to happen. Her family would never allow it. Summer was alright, but that was it.

Even with Linda and Marie gone, there were still plenty of girls to go around. Al arrived first, then the girls. Mark finally showed up and I could see he was immediately impressed with all the girls available. After we all had some refreshments and introductions were made, I gave Mark a quick tour of the house. Everyone was ready for a swim, so Mark and Al joined me in my bedroom to change into our swimsuits.

I knew that Mark would be a little uncomfortable with Al in the room as he changed, but this was an opportunity for us all to be naked in front of each other that I was not going to miss. It would set the stage for more fun that I had planned for later. Predictably, Al stared at Mark's package as he changed. I was happy to check out Mark's slightly freckled buttocks which I thought was the cutest I had ever seen on a boy or girl.

As we headed downstairs towards the pool I took Mark aside for a moment. I told him not to worry about Al and explained that I had a plan in mind that I hoped would straighten out the situation between them. My words were comforting to Mark and basically truthful. Yes, I did plan to straighten things out, but probably not in the way he hoped.

Ingrid, Bobbie, Diane and Laura were busy in my cousin's workroom. Although it was Saturday, Ingrid's continued success kept her and her off the books employees busy. That was fine by me. I also benefitted from their work and was making more money working for my cousin than I could possibly make doing anything else at that age and time in my life. Their Saturday schedule also gave me the opportunity to get try and get Mark together with Julie.

We played pool volleyball, had some splashing contests and swam around for a while. While I tended to hang with Nancy, I began pushing her towards Al. It was a sudden idea inspired by the fact that she kept looking at his muscular body. Since he had on a loose fitting bathing suit, she could not tell what he was packing and that was a good thing for the moment. It was not that I wanted to dump Nancy, it was just that something had to give when it came to all my girlfriends and I hoped this might be the start of the solution to my problem.

I could tell that Julie was interested in Mark, but I did not see him responding to the signals that she was sending his way. That was a disappointment. I really wanted them together. I was still thinking about how to get them together as we all got out of the pool for some refreshments and snacks. As we sat around taking a break and talking, Laura showed up. She was done working for the day and joined us. Ingrid, Bobbie and Diane took off to the store to pick up some supplies. Afterward, they planned to have dinner together. Laura preferred to stay with us which was my good fortune.

As we sat around, I was surprised to see that Mark took an interest in Laura. Although I never considered that possibility, it was good news. Julie was leaving anyway, so his involvement with Laura would mean one less girl for me to deal with. Throughout the rest of the afternoon I continued to encourage Al to get with Nancy and Mark to get with Laura. The two couples eventually sat together in separate areas of the house while I spent some time with Julie.

I knew this was a situation that had to be handled delicately, so while Mark used the restroom I took Laura aside and suggested she take him up to her room when he came out. She was surprised at my idea, but I explained that variety was the spice of life and that I thought that Mark would be a much better fit for her than I was for the long haul. Laura scolded me for my comments, but agreed to take Mark upstairs.

I knew that Mark was in good hands with Laura, so I concentrated on Al and Nancy. I invited them to join me and Julie in my bedroom. When we got upstairs, I said it was time for some fun and suggested we all undress. I explained that there was no need to worry about being interrupted. My cousin and the other older girls would be gone for the rest of the afternoon and part of the evening. Even if they came back, they knew better than to try to come into my room when the door was closed and locked.

I knew that Julie really wanted to have sex with me again, so getting her naked was easy and fast. Nancy was a bit more shy, but I encouraged her by having Julie help her undress. Al followed my example by getting naked. We all got into my bed and began making out. I paired with Julie, while Al got together with Nancy. Before long I started things off by having sex with Julie. Al and Nancy were still making out, so when we finished Julie and I went to work on them.

Julie got between Al and Nancy and began making out with him, while I took on Nancy. We worked it so that Nancy was eventually flat on her back with Al next to her. I pushed Al towards her and told him that Julie and I wanted to watch them have sex together. Nancy was quiet, but I knew she was nervous. I held her hand as Al got into position and eventually penetrated her. The two went at it pretty good. I encouraged then to try different positions until I felt comfortable enough to take Julie and leave the room.

With Al and Nancy busy in my room, Julie and I walked naked into Laura's room. Mark and Laura was surprised at our sudden appearance and appeared to be making out naked on the bed. I looked at Laura and she shook her head indicating that they had not had sex yet. Julie and I joined them on the bed. I explained to Mark that we played these kinds of games all the time. He was nervous and looked uncomfortable, but went along with the situation.

Julie and I made out next to Mark and Laura, then switched off the way we did with Al and Nancy. Eventually, we got Mark to do it with Laura. Once he got going, he really did a good job and went on for a long time before shooting his load. After he did, we all switched off and made out again. Julie got Mark into position for sex with her and he responded just as I hoped he would. Meanwhile, I penetrated Laura and could feel that she was still wet inside from Mark. I loved that feeling.

Mark had fun with Julie (Who wouldn't?), but I knew he liked Laura and that was great news for me. Julie and I eventually separated from Mark and Laura, left her room and showered together. After we got cleaned up, we saw that Al and Nancy had finished and grabbed our clothes from in my room. Mark must have had lots of fun because he and Laura did not show up downstairs to join the rest of us for another hour!

We all ate dinner, then watched TV for a while. At that point I decided to set the stage for my next game by explaining that the girls needed to sleep with the girls and the boys with the boys just in case anyone came by. After Ingrid and Bobbie came home I suggested they sleep in Ingrid's room. My cousin was all in with that! Nancy and Julie would sleep in Laura's room, while Al and Mark would sleep in mine. I explained that there would be plenty of time for more fun between the girls and boys on Sunday.

After we all played some pool and board games, everyone sat around listening to music and talking until we all got tired and headed to bed around the same time. As soon as Mark and Al got into my bedroom, I closed and locked the door. At that point I dropped the bomb. I told Al and Mark to get naked. Mark looked at me strangely and asked why? I explained to Mark that we needed to solve the problem between him and Al. I said that the best way to do that was to give Mark a chance to experience what it was like to fool around with a boy. Mark was stunned, but Al was already naked and laying on my bed.

I told Mark that it was not fair for him to judge how Al felt about him without even giving things between them a chance. I also admitted that I liked him as well and that there was no reason why we could not have fun as a threesome. Mark started freaking out and said he would have never

came over if he knew this was what I had in mind. I could see that Mark was about to bolt, so I thought quickly and came up with an idea.

I told Mark that he needed to stay and give my plan a chance. I said that if he tried to leave, I would tell his folks that he forced himself on Laura and Julie. I explained that all the girls were loyal to me and would say or do just about anything I told them to. Mark was shocked, but he knew as well as I did that his folks would not only be furious that their son could be facing a rape charge, but also that he had done it with a girl who was of mixed race. They were kind of old school bigots from what he had told me.

Mark stood in stunned silence, so I began undressing him. He eventually responded and got naked. Once we were in the bed, I got Al and Mark to jack each other off. I loved watching them together. Before either of them could shoot their load, I had Al suck Mark off until he ejaculated. Al loved it! While Mark laid flat and I jacked him off, I had Al lay right next to him and sucked him off.

After I sucked Al off, I took a turn on Mark and he ejaculated again. Then I went for the gold. I got Mark into position for anal sex. I sensed that he knew what was coming, but he kept quiet and reluctantly compliant in the face of my threat. I lubricated myself and went first, very slowly pushing my penis into his anus. Mark breathed heavily and gave off a few sounds as he moved around a bit and tried to deal with what was happening to him, but he let me have my way. I got my dick all the way in, then moved my penis in and out until I shot my load on to his buttocks.

Al took a turn after I cleaned up Mark. Because his penis was smaller and I had already trudged the road ahead, it was less painful for Mark. He again dealt with it until Al also shot his load on Mark's buttocks. At that point I lubricated Mark's penis and had him penetrate Al. Although Mark acted like he hated doing it to Al, he kept on and I could see he was getting into it. After he shot his load on Al's buttock's, I decided to pass on anal sex with Mark doing it to me. I did not want to push Mark over the edge.

I felt like Al had his fun, so we all laid down and I began making out with Mark. He resisted for the most part, but responded with his tongue after I began to play with his penis as we kissed. Mark's smooth face and skin really turned me on. His skin was the softest I had ever felt on a boy. I could see that Mark was worn out and needed sleep, so I left him alone and went for Al. I had anal sex with Al and sucked him off one more time before we went to sleep.

I knew there was a chance that Mark might bolt during the night, but I suspected that my threat would keep him in place. It did. I was the first to wake up in the morning and found both boys were still asleep in my bed. I went downstairs to breakfast and was joined shortly afterward by Ingrid. She looked happy and we shared the news of our triumphs over breakfast.

After I told my tale, yy cousin told me that she had Bobbie trained to the point where the two were now having sex in a comfortable manner. I knew that Bobbie would be the new Diane if she kept allowing my cousin to do her thing. That was fine by me because Ingrid was always willing to share. In fact, after we ate breakfast she brought me into her bedroom. Bobbie woke up to a surprise as the three of us had sex and made out together.

After we finished doing it, I showered with Bobbie upstairs and we eventually went to the kitchen where I made her some breakfast. Ingrid showered downstairs, then went into her workroom. I really liked Bobby and that threesome with my cousin was pure magic for me. As we sat in the kitchen Bobby told me that doing it with Ingrid still made her nervous, but when I was added to the equation it was fine. I knew that the only reasons that Bobbie was doing anything with my cousin at all was because the two worked together and because Bobbie did want to seem like a prude in those days of free love and sexual experimentation.

Bobbie left after breakfast. She had to study and type a paper for Monday. I watched TV in the living room and was eventually joined by Nancy. I asked Nancy if she liked Al. She did and I suspected that his smaller penis was probably less threatening to her than mine or those of other boys our age. I told her that I had no problem with her going out with him and suggested that we move our relationship to a friendship. She was a bit shocked, but understood my feelings about fooling around with so many girls and boys. We both knew that could not go on forever and would eventually get us all in trouble.

Nancy and I hugged each other for a while and I assured her that I would always be there if she needed anything. After Mark came down for breakfast, I encouraged Nancy to go and get into bed with Al in my bedroom. She did and I assumed the two had fun since that did not come down for another hour. Meanwhile, Mark was acting passive aggressive towards me. I could hardly blame him considering my threat and the fact that I had practically forced sex with Al and me on him.

I sat with him in the kitchen and apologized for what I did, but I also told him he was still on the hook with me. I said that Al would not be a problem any longer. I would lay the law down to him later that day now that he and Nancy were getting together. However, Mark had to know that he was mine and should be ready to give me what I wanted anytime I wanted it. I was not exactly being diplomatic, but I really liked Mark and knew that he would probably not give me the time of day as far as sex went unless I kept the pressure on. Anyway, Mark really liked Laura and ke knew that his access to her depended on me.

Later that afternoon while Nancy and the other girls were in the pool with Mark, Al and I went up to my room to change into our bathing suits. As we did I told Al that he got what he wanted from Mark and that was it. Mark was off limits. He was mine and Al had better not ever try to pressure him to do anything from that point on. Al was surprised and tried to protest, so I grabbed him by the testicles, threw him on the bed and squeezed his balls until he all but cried.

I had to let Al knew that I was the boss. Despite his muscular build, I could still easily take him. I slapped his face and said that if he ever tried to disobey me his time with Nancy would be over. I knew that he really liked her and that the two were a good fit for sex. Let's face it; considering his smaller dick girls would not exactly be lining up to screw with him and Al knew it. He reluctantly agreed to my terms and that was that.

By the time the sleep over ended I had Al with Nancy, Mark with Laura and with me. Julie was leaving in a few days, so I enjoyed a few final farewell intercourse sessions with her. Those

sessions reminded me how much I liked her. I did not really want Julie to leave, but fate had other plans. Meanwhile, I had a discussion with Laura that was almost the same as the one I had with Nancy. Laura and Mark were now an item just like Al and Nancy, so I was free of two girlfriends. Now it was just my cousin and Bobbie for the most part, with a side order of Mark.

Chapter Two: High School Starts and Darkness Falls

On Monday Julie came over to see me. Her grandfather had suddenly become ill. We guessed it was from all the stress of having to get ready to move so quickly. With the moving van coming, his grandmother very reluctantly agreed to go on ahead to the new place so it would be ready for their stuff. The moving company deposit was pre-paid, so there way to cancel or change the date without losing it.

Julie's grandmother spoke to my parents asking if she could stay with us until her grandfather's health improved. She was already registered for school because they had not yet had time to deal with withdrawing her from the junior high, so that was no problem. The idea was for Julie to be there for her grandfather's recovery and keep his spirits up. She was glad to stay having never wanted to leave Florida in the first place. I had mixed feelings on the matter.

I wanted Julie to stay, but that meant yet another complication and a potentially problematic one for me considering the fact that she was younger than I was. My folks had no problem with Julie staying and Ingrid loved the idea. She would officially bunk with Ingrid, but my bedroom door was always open to her when my folks were not around. Julie's grandmother offered some money to my parents for her room and board before she left for the new place, but they knew that Julie and I were good friends and refused to accept it. Instead, Julie would give me and Laura a hand with the household chores and also help us with Ingrid's ever growing home business.

School began on Wednesday. Julie biked off to the junior high, while I spent my first day in high school. I registered for all my classes and was really looking forward to Driver's Education. In just a few months I could have my driver's license if all went well! In the mean time Laura and I took the bus to school together. I worried about how she would be excepted by her classmates, but there were no problems. The other kids all figured she was either Hispanic or white with slightly tanned skin as some had. Besides, Mark and I watched out for her just to be on the safe side.

As things turned out, Al and Nancy ended up at another high school thanks to some courses they wanted to take which were not available at our school. That was fine by me and made things a lot easily for all of us. Mark and I were in the same P.E. class. That meant that in addition to whatever private fun I had with him from time to time at my house or the hotel, I got to see him naked just about every day. After a while I loosened up the leash I had on Mark so that he and Laura could work on their relationship some more. I cared deeply about both of them and they knew it.

Most days after school Laura, Julie and I worked for my cousin. My relationship with Bobbie grew and every time she attended any of my school dances or events as my date, everyone took

notice that I was dating a college girl. It made the high school guys think I was superman and the girls want to date me. I wanted to stay with just Bobbie, but I did occasionally give in to casual dates with some of the high school girls I found to be very cute. There was also Julie. I found it impossible to resist making out or having sex with her since we were living in the same house together.

I was good for a while as far as sticking to girls went, but my P.E. class was filled with cute boys. Fate was up to its old tricks when our P.E. teacher was suddenly struck down with an illness and replaced by my old P.E. teacher from the junior high school. The coach immediately put me in charge of towels and locker room clean up. I made Mark my helper. Once again I got an eyeful as I handed out towels to all the guys coming out of the shower. Several caught my interest, but two were really on my radar.

A kid named Wilson had bright red hair and some awesome freckles. Another boy named Adam had light brown hair and an equal number of well placed freckles. Both were shorter than me, had smaller penises, but nice of crops of pubic hair. Adam was in two other classes with me which made it sensible to hit on him first. Art class was informal, so I made sure that I sat next to him and stroke up a conversation whenever I had the chance.

Adam had his hands full. He lived in a trailer park with his dad. His mom had split on both of them when he was just a five years old to go into a treatment center where she eventually died. Like his mom, his dad was an alcoholic and drug user. He was always getting into fights and hassles. Sometimes Adam found himself in the middle of those situations and apart from my interest in his body, I felt genuinely sorry for him. As Adam and I got to know each other better, we became good friends. I liked Adam and kept my plans to fool around with him on hold.

As winter break neared, a fight broke out in the locker room after the coach and most of the class had already left. While Mark and I were picking up towels we saw that Wilson was getting beaten up by some guy that was bigger and had an attitude problem. He had been waiting for Wilson to come out of the shower, then jumped him.

The guy mistakenly believed that Wilson was trying to put the moves on the guy's girlfriend. As it turned out, Wilson did not even know the girl. The two just had a class together. She pulled his name out of the air after her boyfriend found out she was going out with another guy along with him. Not wanting to get her other guy in trouble, she chose to finger poor Wilson.

Once Mark and I saw what was going on, we got involved and kicked the bigger guy's butt. Wilson had just come out of the shower when the fight started, so he was still naked and had been kicked in the balls. I grabbed some towels, wet them with cold water and gently placed them around Wilson's penis and testicles. I loved his pale skin, freckles and bright red pubic hair. After I got him taken care of, Mark stayed with Wilson while I went to speak with the other boy.

Chris was my height with bright blond hair that was shoulder length. He was also naked having just come out of the shower, so I pulled him by his long hair back into the shower. He looked strong, but backed down to me. Once we were in the shower area, I grabbed his testicles and

squeezed them hard. He had a long penis and large testicles. As I slapped his face and warned him to leave Wilson alone, he tried pushing me off him. I came back with force and he backed down again.

At that point I grabbed his penis and jacked it. He look at me and was completely shocked, but I said he had better stand still and keep quiet. He penis got hard and really stiff. It was a work of art with a sharp and well defined tip. I said that from now on his dick was mine and that I would jack it anytime I liked. Chris just stood there stunned and let me do my thing. I was as shocked and surprised as he was, but kept going until I felt his penis jump and begin to pump out semen.

After he finished ejaculating, I told him to shower. I wanted to do more with him, but there was no time left. I would get back to Chris later. I went to check on Wilson and removed the towels from around his private parts. I told him to go to the school nurse's office if he still had pain down there after he got dressed, but he felt better and decided not to make a big deal out of the whole thing. Mark walked Wilson to his next class just to be sure he was alright. Well, business was picking up. In just one P.E. class I had felt two penises and testicles, jacked one off and set the stage for future fun with two cute boys.

My next class was art and I was shocked to see Adam with a black eye. I wondered why he had not been in P.E. class that day? Once again he had gotten into some fight that his dad started with some other adult in the trailer park. At that point I decided to try and give Adam a break from his misery. His dad was going to take Adam to a relative's house for Christmas. He told me that whenever they went there arguments broke out and fights sometimes followed.

I invited Adam to spend the Christmas break with me and my family. He was very surprised and really wanted to come, but was also afraid of what his dad might say or do if he asked. I called my dad during lunch and had him run interference with Adam's father. We all knew that if social services found out that Adam was in that situation, he would end up in foster care. His dad knew that too and agreed to let his son spend the holidays with us.

With the Adam and Wilson situation looking up, I concentrated on Driver's Education. I had just about completed the required semester and took my final test. I passed and was first in line that Saturday to take my Driver's Road Test. I passed and had my license in hand. Ingrid drove me there and allowed me to drive us home. Over that weekend my cousin and folks bought me a slightly used Chevy in great condition. I was shocked and could not have been happier. My dad covered the insurance and tags.

By Monday I was driving to school and got my first high school parking permit that very day. Now that I had wheels, I could run more errands for my cousin and get around on my own. I loved the freedom that car provided and made good use of it. Laura rode with me to school everyday. Mark was still to young for a regular Driver's License, but he did had a permit. I took Bobbie out on Monday night to show off my new car and we had a great time together. The next night it was Julie's turn. We went out to eat and then hit the drive in for a movie. That was the first time I had sex in a car.

It was the last day of school before Christmas vacation, so I made arrangements to have Adam bring his stuff to school and put it in my car. He would go home with me that day to start off our Christmas vacation time together. My folks did not want me anywhere near the trailer park or Adam's dad. As Laura, Adam and I headed to my house that afternoon we saw Wilson walking out of the parking lot loaded down with books and some other stuff. I offered him a ride and found that he lived just a quarter mile from my house.

Before I dropped him off, we exchanged phone numbers and I invited him over during the holiday vacation. He agreed to come over and I knew this would a very interesting Christmas. After we got home I showed Adam around the house and got him settled into my room. Ingrid, Julie and Laura welcomed him like family and we all got along really well that first day. Despite his troubled home life, Adam was a really nice guy who had good manners and was nothing like the rest of his family. I could see that he was smart and made an effort to be better than they were.

Bobbie threw a last minute surprise my way by telling me that she, her brother and her mom were going away for a week to visit some relatives. That was actually good news for me. It gave me a chance to spend some quality time with Adam, and Wilson if I could get him to come over. It also allowed me to continue my sexual adventures with Julie which I came to enjoy more and more in a more comfortable and un-obstructed way.

My parents spent a couple of days decorating the house in their spare time. Ingrid, Laura and Julie also pitched in and the place looked great. We had a real Christmas tree and lots of lights which stretched from the front of the house all the way back around the pool and patio. It was still a few days before Christmas, so I went shopping for presents. Now that I was mobile, I was also able to do my own store hopping and also help the girls with rides to the stores for their Christmas shopping expeditions.

During the first two days that Adam stayed with us, I kept things cool. During the day we played pool, went out to the arcade and did some other stuff. Adam was impressed by all the girls I had in the house, but he was too insecure to put the moves on any of them. At that point Julie was into me and very reluctant to even look at other guys, but I secretly hoped that she would take an interest in Adam just to take some of the pressure off of me.

Just when everything seemed right with the world, things began to change in ways I never thought they would. The changes began just before Christmas with Nancy dumping Al. He had kind of an attitude problem and I suspected she was tired of his little pecker. Regardless of the cause, she was now available and Adam was very interested. He told me that he liked her from Day One when he saw her at my house, but was reluctant to hit on her since she was already dating another guy. Now that she was available, he wanted my help in getting her attention.

I spoke to Nancy apart from Adam and found out that she thought he was cute. I set up a double date between her and Adam with Julie and I the day after Christmas. Adam was thrilled when I told him the news. On Christmas Eve we all sat together and opened our presents, along with my folks. Adam was surprised to find that we had gotten him gifts. He used the small amount of

money he had to get us gifts as well which showed that he had class and character. I really liked Adam and thought he would be perfect for Nancy.

Mark came over to spend some time with Laura after his own family celebration and we all had a wonderful Christmas Eve and Christmas Day together. Diane also stopped by briefly to exchange gifts, but had to leave. On Christmas night as Adam got into bed with me I reminded him about our double date the following night. I knew he did not have much money, so I said I would give him money for the date. He did not want to accept it, but agreed to my loan after I said he could work off by helping me, Laura and Julie work on my cousin's Spring Catalog and whatever else she wanted us to do for her business.

Ingrid left for a week just after Christmas to see her family back in New York and spend some time with them. Although I missed her, I was kind of relieved. I needed time to get my emotional act together. Now that Laura and Nancy were off my girlfriend list, I could concentrate on having some fun with the boys until Bobbie returned from her own excursion with her mom. Clarence decided not to go with them and instead was hanging out with Ballard for the holidays. That was an interesting development, but one that I did not mind. I already had enough on my plate and was getting weary of group sex affairs.

The next day Julie, Nancy, Adam and I all hung out together and finally went on our double date. I really enjoyed spending time with Julie and it seemed like Adam and Nancy were quickly becoming an item. I liked seeing them together. By the time we got home, Adam and Nancy were ready for some fun of their own. I told Nancy to take Adam into Ingrid's bedroom and have whatever fun with him she wanted. I planned on deep cleaning my cousin's room anyway and washing all her bedding while she was away.

Nancy had to go home later that night, so I drove her and then came back and headed up to my bedroom. Adam was getting ready for bed, so i asked him how things went with Nancy. he smiled and told me that they really liked each other and had sex. It was the first time he ever had sex with a girl. I did not have to as if he enjoyed it because I knew from personal experience that anyone who slept with that teen angel would be more than satisfied.

Speaking of being satisfied, I wanted Adam. I had waited and paid my dues by being nice to him, but the time had come to introduce him to my game. The funny thing was that I was not sure how to do that! Considering all the kids I had goaded into nudity and sex, I could not think of a single thing that might work on him. I was scared to death of taking the direct approach because he had shown me absolutely no sign that he leaned towards the kind of perversity of bisexuality that I did.

Thanks to my folks, I now had a small TV in my bedroom which we watched as we laid in bed. As we did, a rerun of that week's wrestling show came on. I asked Adam if he liked Professional Wrestling? As it turned out, he loved watching it as much as I did! At that point we were both in our underwear, so I told him to get up and try to take me down. I played the bad guy and we wrestled around for a few minutes until I had him on the bedroom carpet. At that point I stopped and said I would give him another chance. But I also said that I wanted to wrestle the way the Greeks originally did in the Olympics.

I asked Adam if he knew how they wrestled back in those days? To my surprise, he did. He knew they wrestled naked, so I asked him if he had any problem wrestling that way with me? At that point he had no reason to believe that I was putting the make on him, so Adam was not particularly surprised or upset at my question. Adam said that he did not mind if I didn't, so we both began to undress.

Adam took off his undershirt and underpants revealing a really nice and slightly freckled body with a penis about the same size as mine. He had a nice crop of light-brown pubic hair which turned me on even more. Before we began to wrestle, I suggested we make a bet. If I won Adam had to do anything I wanted him to do for the rest of the night. If he won, I had to do the same. Once again he did not appear to be threatened by the bet because I guessed that he saw no sign that I had hit on him before our match, so he agreed to my wager.

I found Adam to be a worthy opponent. I guessed that all those trailer park fights kept him in good shape. Despite his strength, I was a better Wrestler and got him pinned before long. After we got back up I saw that he had a bit of a boner. Trying to cover it up, he quickly grabbed his underwear and tried to get into them. I stopped him and said that I wanted him to stay naked and get back into the bed with me. He looked a little surprised, but complied with my order. I told Adam the tale of my neighborhood strip club and the games we all played at my house. He looked surprised at my revelations, but not as much as I thought he would be.

I explained to Adam that now that he was a part of our little group he needed to get with the program. That meant an introduction to some of the things we did and I said that I would give him that introduction right then and there. To smooth things over, I reminded him that I had already used my influence to get him laid. I told him that Nancy really liked him, but it was also true that she and the other girls would do whatever I said and that included screwing guys that I wanted them to. I promised to keep Nancy exclusive to him from then on and he liked that.

I explained to Adam that the last thing I wanted to do was bully him into anything after the way his father treated him. I said that what I wanted was to involve him in something he could really enjoy as much as I and the others did if he gave it a chance. At that point I told him to lay on his back. I asked if he jacked off and he said that he did once in a while. I said I was going to get things started by jacking him off. I took a towel and the Vaseline I had ready by the bed and began lubricating his penis. He laid still and seemed a little less nervous then I thought he would be as I jacked his penis. He must have liked it because his dick got very stiff very fast.

Before long I felt his penis jump and he began pumping out a ton of semen into the towel. Considering the smaller size of his penis and testicles, I figured that was quite a feat for Adam. I held on to his shaft while he shot his load. After I cleaned him up, I had him jack me off for a bit. By that time Adam was going with the flow and did not appear to be at all upset by what we were doing. I took that as a good sign and decided to take things a step further. I asked Adam if he knew what oral sex was? He said he did because he used to see guys getting blow jobs from girlfriends, wives or whores in the trailer park. Most of the guys left the shades or curtains open when they did it with girls as a badge of honor for all to see.

I said I was going to suck his penis off. Before he could react, I went at it. Adam did not protest and from the stiffness of his penis I guessed that he liked it. Im loved that his smaller penis fit all the way into my mouth. Before long he shot his load which I dutifully sucked down my throat. After I finished, I cleaned him up and asked if he knew what French kissing was? He said he did, but had never tried it. I said I would help him learn so that he was all ready to do make out with Nancy when she wanted to kiss him that way.

I was a little surprised that Adam and Nancy had not already tried French kissing with each other, but I also imagined that Nancy was probably nervous doing it with Adam for the first time. She had not had sex with any other guys except for her brother who raped her and myself. I guessed that she had kept herself emotionally distant as a defense of her own personal space when they had sex that first time. Making out on the level of French kissing probably would have been just too personal for her at that moment.

I began tongue kissing with Adam. He surprised me again by really getting into it and doing a pretty good job. I thought maybe he was kissing me good just so that I would stop. After I did, I gave him a full body massage and played with his package and buttocks for a while. Without any warning, I lubricated myself and got him into position for anal sex. I told him that I was going to have anal intercourse with him, spread his butt cheeks and aimed my penis at his anus.

Once again Adam surprised me. Although he moved around a little in kind of a mock protest, Adam did not say much except for quietly and insincerely asking me to stop just before I penetrated him. Once I got my penis into him, he remained pretty quiet only occasionally giving off a grunt or groan. He had a decent sized butt hole and I was a little surprised at how well he took what I was doing to him. In fact, his anus felt like it had already been penetrated several times before and even stretched out a little.

After I got into him all the way, I moved my penis in and out. It felt really good and Adam remained fully compliant. At some point I got ready to shoot my load and pulled my dick out just in time to ejaculate on to his buttocks. Apart from my experience with Mark, I don't think I ever enjoyed anal sex with anyone as much as I did with Adam up to that point. After I finished Adam let me clean him up and got comfortable on the bed. As much as I thought I had surprised him, he had a surprise in store for me.

Adam asked me if I wanted him to suck me off? I said that would be great and got into position for him. He gave me a world class blow job and sucked my semen down his throat like a pro as I ejaculated. After he finished and we cleaned up, I asked him if he had ever done that before. Adam reluctantly admitted that he had done everything we did that night (except for the French kissing) before. He said that his dad sometimes arranged for him to have sex with some of the guys in the trailer park for money or drugs.

I was shocked! I knew his dad was a low class freak, but I did not think he was that low. Who would pimp off his own son? Adam said that he had been having anal and oral sex with guys eighteen to around thirty years old since he was eleven years old. He explained that it did not happen all the time, only when his dad owed a lot of money or really needed drugs. He figured he had done it at least twenty times since he was eleven.

At that point I felt bad for what I put Adam through and told him so. He surprised me by saying not to worry about it. He said he normally hated doing those things, but he did not mind doing them with me. He said he thought of me as a brother and that no one had ever been as kind to him as I had been. I was equally floored by his revelations and remarks. I was also surprised that all his sexual encounters had been with guys. He told me that most of the girls and women in the trailer park did not have enough money or drugs to be of any use to his dad.

I told Adam to turn over and gave him a really nice back massage. I held him and said I wanted us to stay friends and brothers forever. Then we fell asleep naked and holding each other. The next morning I got up, showered and dressed. I was the first one up as usual, but was soon joined by the girls. With New Year's Eve just a few days away, Julie, Laura and I sat around the breakfast table planning a party. My folks were already headed to a big party at a ranch owned by one of his two bosses in another state. That left the place to us and that meant we could have some real fun while they were gone.

I guessed that I probably could not get Mark or just about anyone else I knew who was not staying with me over for the event because everyone probably had their own plans, but I hoped that we could still have a great time together. The girls felt the same. After Adam joined our breakfast brainstorming session, he was also invited to contribute ideas. Inspired by our previous night's Greek style wrestling session, he said we should dress in Greek robes and have a toga style party the way that college kids did. None of us had even thought of that and we all loved the idea.

Laura began designing some Greek style robes she could quickly throw together for all of us while Julie, Adam and I made up a party shopping list. I hoped that Nancy would be able to come to our party for Adam's sake. I suspected that she would since she usually did whatever she wanted to do regardless of what her parents wanted anyway. I called her after breakfast and told her about our party. She was immediately all in with it and could not wait to see Adam again.

Julie, Adam and I headed out and picked up everything we needed for the party. As a surprise for Adam, I picked up Nancy after we finished shopping and we all had lunch together at the ice cream restaurant in the mall. I knew that Laura wanted to see Mark again soon, so I called him while we were out to find out what he was up to and discovered that he had plans to spend New Year's Eve at home. His parents were going to a party at the home of some friends that he did not care for, so I invited him to our party. He was thrilled and accepted my invitation.

After we got home I gave Laura the good news. She smiled and blushed. Nancy came over to help Laura work on the robes we needed for the party and also spent time with Adam. Julie also got busy by helping me deep clean the house and get things ready for our party. After we finished cleaning, Julie started putting up some of the decorations we bought. Although the party was still a few days away, we wanted to have everything ready.

While the others were busy with their own tasks, I took a break and began to think about everything that was happening. As I did, Wilson was once again on my mind. I had tried calling

him a few times, but no one answered. I figured that I would give it another shot and this time he answered. I wished him a Merry Christmas and asked how his holiday went? He told me that his house had been filled with relatives who spent Christmas with his family, but now things were quieting down.

Just like Mark, Wilson's folks were going to a most adults-only New Year's Eve Party, so I invited him to ours. He seemed surprised at my invitation, but accepted after I told him that there would be no adults around and that most of the girls and guys coming were around his age and mine. I told him to plan on spending the night and he said that was fine with him. He was a responsible kid. His parents trusted him because he never got into trouble, so he already knew they would let him come to my party and stay overnight.

Thinking it might be a good idea to get him acclimated to my game, I asked if he wanted to come over a day early and stay an extra night? I explained that my folks were already out of town and that we had the house to ourselves. I said it would be a good way for us to get to know each other better and he agreed. I knew that Wilson had a large family, but not a lot of friends. His younger look, small statue and unwillingness to get involved with smoking, drinking or drugs kept him from most of the other kids at school. If he could get into what we did together, he would be a welcomed part of my extended family.

After I got off the phone with Wilson it dawned on me that I had just made my new friend a fifth wheel. With Adam and Nancy, Mark and Laura, and me and Julie paired up, he would be on his own. That would not do, so I had to act quickly. That afternoon as I drove Julie to the hospital to see her grandfather I asked her if she knew any girls well enough to invite one or more to our party? She said she would make a few calls after we got home. Julie did not have a lot of close friends, but she knew a lot of girls from school.

Two girls that Julie knew pretty well were sisters named Alison and Donna. Alison was Julie's age, while Donna was a year older. After we got home she called them. They wanted to come to our party and sleep over, but their mom was a really nice and somewhat religious woman who kept them on a short leash. Fortunately, Julie worked her magic and got their mom to let them come as long as a responsible adult was present.

Julie told their mom all about Ingrid and how she had her own business and was not into smoking, drinking or drugs. She explained that Ingrid looked after us while my folks were out of town. We both hoped that the mother would not insist on meeting Ingrid or coming to drop her daughters off at the party to be sure my cousin was there. As soon as Julie got off the phone I called my cousin in New York and had her call the two sister's mother and say that she would be at the party to be keep things in line. That turned out to be the truth.

Ingrid was already sick of visiting with her family, missed me and had been thinking about coming back to Florida early ever since she left. Her mom and dad were jealous of her business success and gave her lots of attitude. My cousin never really got along with her brothers, so getting away from them would be an additional holiday gift for her. After Ingrid called the two sister's mother and got her approval for them to come to our New Year's Even Party and sleep

over, she called back to tell me she would be back in Florida the next day. I told her that I would pick her up from the airport when she got in and everything was set.

With two extra girls present for the party and sleep over I was certain that I could get Wilson fixed up with at least one of them while he was over my house. Although I had no idea what they looked like or what type of personalities they had, I knew that Julie tended to hang with girls who were like her and that was good news. Just to be on the safe side and so that I would know what I had to work with, I had Julie call them and invite them to go to the mall with us later that evening for ice cream.

As we drove to pick up the two sisters Julie said they were nice girls that shunned smoking, drinking and drugs just as we did. When we arrived at their home, I met their mom. She was nice, but I could tell she was a no-nonsense kind of parent. Their dad was also vigilant, but too involved in a business he owned to constantly watch over his kids. That job was left up to mom. She already knew and liked Julie. After sizing me up and seeing that I was a clean cut looking guy who told her that I did not smoke, drink, do drugs or hang with anyone who did, their mom took an instant liking to me.

I hated deceiving parents, but in many ways I was not really lying to them. I did not smoke, drink or take drugs. People that did were not welcome in my house and I had no use for them. I knew that they would not be happy if they knew I was exposing their kids to the kind of sexual experimentation that we played around with, but better they do it with us in a nice and somewhat controlled environment then have their first sexual encounter in the backseat of a car with some drugged out freak or drunken idiot.

As soon as I set eyes on Alison and Donna I knew that Julie had really delivered the goods. Alison was beautiful, had shiny black hair, pale skin and a great body. Donna was also very pretty. She was a little taller than her younger sister, close to my height, and also had shiny dark hair and pale skin. Like all of us she had a few pimples here and there, but that went with being teens around our ages. The good news that none of us had severe acne problems. What she did have that I really liked was a face full of pin prick freckles unlike her sister who had none that I could notice.

As we drove to the mall we all talked and got to know each other better. After we arrived at the restaurant I asked the sisters if either of them were dating? They laughed saying that their parents thought they were too young to date. They didn't mind if the girls went out with friends like Julie or even brought a boy along like me to drive them all as long as they met me first and I told them exactly where we would be going, what we would be doing and had them home before ten at night, but no actual dating was allowed. I guess that was fair considering that Alison was fourteen like Julie, but Donna was my age and at almost sixteen that seemed a bit extreme.

I did not want to mislead or embarrass the girls, so while we ate our ice cream I told them up front that some of the things that were going to happen at our party would be a little naughty. My declaration brought more laughter from the sisters. Donna was more outspoken than Alison and told me that Julie had already told them about some of our nasty habits like skinny dipping and

the strip club. Donna said that she and Alison had even been thinking about asking Julie if they could come and try out the strip club sometime until I decided to discontinue it.

I was still thinking about Donna's revelations when she went on to assure me that she already knew what to expect during the party and had no problem with our shenanigans. If she and her sister did not want to take part in a particular activity for any reason, they would just sit that one out. I really liked the way that Donna spoke her mind and I was instantly sure that these girls would be a perfect fit for us. I wished that Julie had brought them to my attention sooner.

I knew that Julie spoke to the sisters on the phone on a regular basis, but I did not know she was sharing tales of our perverted adventures with them. I just figured they were girls she knew from school talking about whatever girls that age discuss. I joked that Julie was a tattle tale and promised a severe spanking for her when we got home. We all laughed and continued to get to know each better as we ate. After we finished our ice cream, I asked if the girls wanted to go to the arcade for a while? We still had well over an hour before their ten o'clock curfew. The girls looked at each other, smiled and said the arcade was a great idea.

Although Julie and the sisters brought their own money, I insisted on treating everyone to the arcade games and got a pile of change that we all shared. Julie and Alison played the bowling games, while Donna and I played pinball against each other. She was really competitive and eventually won the first two games. As we played I got that awful feeling in the pit of my stomach that I was once again falling for yet another girl. Even worse, she used body language to clearly indicate that she liked me.

By our third game Donna was playfully punching me every time I scored and leaning up against me when it was my turn to play. She was not over the top as far as physical contact went, but did just enough to let me know she liked me. I responded in kind by doing things like briefly putting my hand on her shoulder while she played. Despite my interest, I wanted to know more about Donna before I got involved and needed some serious input from Julie.

When it was time to leave, I congratulated Donna on beating me at pinball and said she would have to give me a rematch sometime. She said that would be fun and smiled. As we looked into each other's eyes, the fact that she liked me still had me caught off guard and made me wonder why? I felt she was extremely cute and just the kind of girl that any guy would hit on. I was not chopped liver sort of speak, but we both attended the same high school and there were lots of guys there that would probably be more attractive to her.

As we all walked towards the car I was tempted to hold her hand, but chickened out. I still was not sure if a relationship with Donna was a good idea? After all, I was dating Bobbie and was still kind of unofficially involved with Julie. Donna and I walked close to each other and I could hear Julie and Alison giggling as they walked behind us. I opened the car doors for the girls and expected Julie to climb into the passenger side front seat where she had been before, but she suggested that Donna sit up front with me. Julie said she wanted to gossip with Alison on the ride back to their house, but I knew better.

Julie was smart, cunning and had begun to play games of her own. She liked boys, but did not mind messing around with girls ever since being introduced to it. I suspected that she liked Alison and wanted to set the stage for some fun during the sleep over. Meanwhile, it was a bit chilly that evening. While the car heater was till trying to shoot out some warmth, Donna inched towards me on the car's front bench seat saying she was cold. I gave her my jacket and hugged her a bit to share my body warmth. She smiled and thanked me. Even after the heater was working fine, she remained next to me.

I got out, opened the car doors for the sisters and and walked them to the door. As they went inside, Donna reminded me about our pin ball rematch and invited me to call her. I said I would and left things at that. By the time I got back into the car Julie was already in the front seat and smiled at me. I smiled back and we both laughed. Things had went better than we hoped. We were both exhausted and went to bed as soon as we got home.

The next day Julie called the sisters. I asked her to get the scoop on how Donna really felt about me. A new relationship at that time could really complicate things, especially since I had planned to use the party and sleep over to make my moves on Wilson. If I was going to get involved with Donna, I would have just one day to get into Wilson's pants since he was coming over a day early and would be sleeping over that night as well as the next. While Julie spoke with her friends, I went to finish the wash

After Julie got off the phone she came and got me. We went outside for some privacy and talked about Donna. It seems that she first noticed me in Junior High. I had not noticed her at that time, but she thought I was good looking and liked how I got along with Julie. As Julie told her about some of our adventures, Donna began more interested. She was a good girl, but adventurous. Alison and Donna were a little shy about their bodies, but Donna liked seeing the other girls naked when they showered in P.E. class and she was the one most interested in the strip club.

After briefly speaking with Julie I put the whole Donna thing on the back burner and headed out to pick up my cousin from the airport in Tampa during the late morning. Ingrid was really happy to see me and visa versa. After she got into the car we shared some heart felt kisses and then we headed back to St Pete. On the drive back to the house I filled her in on everything that was going on. She liked the way that we were putting the New Year's Eve Party together and was fascinated by all the relationship developments including my interest in Donna.

After we got home Ingrid went to unpack and get settled in while I made lunch for everyone. After lunch Nancy came over and began helping Adam take care of some chores. Mark also came by and hung out with Laura as she got the toga style robes ready for the party. Now that the sisters were coming we needed some more. While Julie and I pulled the extra cots out of storage so that everyone would have a place to sleep, she continued to try and sell me on Donna.

According to what Julie got from Alison and Donna herself, Donna had never dated and most of the boys that showed interest in her got little or no reciprocity. She had very high standards and refused to even talk to guys or girls who smoked, used alcohol or did drugs. One thing that Donna told Alison she really liked about me was that I had manners. I opened doors for the girls,

helped to seat them, acted appropriately and did not come off as someone who was just out to get laid. That made me feel good.

Julie suggested that I call Donna later that day. I knew that her suggestion not only had my best interests at heart, but her own. She wanted to get closer to Alison. I understood and appreciated her situation, but I worried about getting too involved too quickly with yet another girl. I mean, having shed all my girlfriends except for Bobbie things were kind of normal in my life for the first time in a long time. I wasn't really sure if I wanted to disturb that tranquility.

With Wilson due over later that day, this was no time to start a new relationship with any girl. I called Donna and spoke to her for a while playing it cool. We both agreed that we had lots of fun the night before and I told her how much I was looking forward to seeing her the next day for the New Year's Even Party. I said that if I was not so busy getting things ready for the party and running errands for my cousin's business, I would liked to have taken her out that night to the arcade again.

Donna understood my situation and made it clear that she was definitely interested in being with me. I left me with the same assurance and instantly knew I was again involved with yet another girl whether I was ready for that relationship or not. She was just too cool and cute to pass on. However, with little time available I had to refocus my efforts on Wilson. His mom dropped him off around two that afternoon. After meeting Ingrid and being certain that he was in a safe place with some adult supervision, she left.

I had to temporarily shuffle everyone's sleeping arrangements around for the party. I placed cots in Laura's room, the recreation room and the living room downstairs. Adam and Nancy would sleep in the living room, while Mark and Laura would share a cot in a small room we normally used for storage downstairs near the kitchen. Wilson would sleep with me, but on New Year's Eve I had him in the recreation room in case things did not work out between us. Julie, Alison and Donna would sleep in bedroom that Laura normally used.

After I got Wilson settled into my bedroom, I took him around and introduced him to everyone he did not know. We then headed to the recreation room to play some pool. We both liked playing pool and had a good time together. Just staring at his bright red hair and much freckled face and body made me horny. However, once again I was faced with how I was going to approach him as far as my game went. What I needed was an ice breaker, but I decided to take things slow. I did not have a lot of time and just hoped there was enough to get things going with him.

Ingrid got into one of her baking modes and decided to bake a bunch of cookies and some small cakes for the party the next night. Julie joined her and helped. They were both really good at baking and enjoyed it. With Ingrid home and everyone busy, I decided to invite Wilson out to my dad's hotel during the late afternoon. My dad said that a indoor pool to compliment their outdoor one in chilly weather was finally open. It took them a long time to built it, but it was really nice and located just a floor below our suite. I knew that Wilson liked to swim from our P.E. class, so when I told him my idea he was all in with it.

We stopped by Wilson's house on the way to the hotel to pick up a bathing suit and let his parents know what we were doing. We also took along some extra clothes just in case we decided to stay the night in the suite. Now that Ingrid was back I had a little more freedom and did not have to worry about what was going on at the house. I knew that the others would probably be annoyed that I did not bring them to help me break in the new indoor pool at the hotel, but if I wanted to play around with Wilson I needed some privacy. I would bring them there another time.

After we arrived at the hotel I showed Wilson around, then we went up to the suite. We put our stuff in the bedroom I always used, then began changing into our swim suits. As I hoped, Wilson was not shy about changing in front of me and I loved seeing his cute penis and bright red pubic hair. The freckles that covered his face and body made me again feel very horny, but I managed not to show it keeping my dick in check.

We headed down to the pool and were just about the only ones in it. A few kids were around, but they left after a while. Most of the hotel guests were already at holiday parties, events, eating or in the lounge. Although the place was packed, it seemed empty to us and that was fine by me. We swam around for a while, had some swimming races which Wilson won and splashed each other. After a while we headed back up to the suite and changed into our clothes. I took Wilson to the cafe where we had some yummy junk food, then we played shuffleboard outside and later went and took on the air hockey table in the hotel's arcade and activity area.

Before we knew it, it was nine at night. I suggested we spend the night at the hotel and Wilson was fine with my idea. We got some soda and snacks from the cafe and went back up to the suite. I called Ingrid to let her know we were staying overnight, then I opened the curtains covering the long wide bay and sliding glass windows which overlooked the Gulf. It was a very romantic setting, but was probably not going to help me with Wilson. I would use it later for Donna if that opportunity presented itself.

Wilson and I got to know each other better that day, but I still had not told him what was to come during the sleep over or given him any indication about my personal perversions. Despite my doubts about how to break the ice and let him in on my secrets, I knew it was now or never. As we watched TV and enjoyed our snacks, we both began to get tired. I suggested we go to bed because the next day would be a long one with the New Year's Even Party beckoning. Wilson agreed and we headed off to the bedroom.

As Wilson fumbled around in his overnight bag for what I guessed were pajamas, I suggested that we just sleep in our underwear for comfort's sake. He was fine with that and after a quick trip to the bathroom, he climbed into bed with me. Earlier I had an idea about how to break the ice with Wilson, but it was a shot in the dark that could explode in my face. However, at that point I was out of time and had nothing better available to me.

After Adam's confession about having sex with guys in the trailer park, he later showed me a book and a couple of magazines he brought over to my house. He had them well hidden in his suitcase, but since the cat was out of the bag he decided to share his treasure with me. The book was about sex and had pictures of naked boys from around ten years old to eighteen. In those

days you could buy those kinds of books at most stationary or even book stores. They were not officially illegal pornography back then and did not cost much.

Adam's magazines also had photos of naked girls, teens and young women in them. Some were having sex, while others were just posing nude. His dad bought them for him so he would know what to do when he had sex. Adam admitted using them to jack off as well. I placed the book and magazines in the nightstand drawer next to the bed hoping I could use them to entice Wilson into having some fun with me.

I acted as if I was about to turn off the lamp on the nightstand, but opened the drawer and took out the book and magazines instead. Wilson was laying on his side and facing me. He saw that I had the publications and asked what they were? I said they were things I liked to look at sometimes. I handed them over to Wilson to look at. As he flipped through the pages, I explained that they came in handy for jacking off.

Wilson did not react to what I said, but kept looking at the pictures in the book and magazines. I asked him if he ever jacked off? He was surprised at my question, but said that he did once in a while. I asked if he ever did a circle jerk? He was not sure what they was, so I explained it to him and asked if he wanted to give it a try? He said, "You mean right now? Here? Isn't that kind of queer?"

Once he said the 'Q' word I knew I was in some trouble and had to think fast. I explained that there was nothing queer about sexually experimenting. At that point I told him that most of the people he met at my house already had already had sex with me and each other. Wilson tried not to look shocked, but I could tell that my revelation was a complete surprise to him.

I went on to explain about the original strip club and how that we all still went skinny dipping and had sex with each other whenever it pleased us. To take some of the edge off, I asked him if he every had sex with a girl? He said he did not and I told him that he could do it with some of the girls at the party if he wanted to. That really got his interest.

I knew that Wilson was not the type of guy who was probably as horny as I was most of the time, but with the same raging teenage hormones flowing through his body that were flowing through mine, he had to be thinking about sex at least part of the time. I suggested we try a circle jerk and that he let me show him some things that would help him to have fun when he finally got laid.

Wilson held on to the magazine he was looking at like a security blanket and asked what I had in mind? I recommended we start by getting naked and we did. I grabbed some lubricant out of the nightstand drawer, placed a clean towel on the bed and then positioned myself and Wilson in sitting positions so that we faced one another and with legs overlapping. I put some Vaseline on my hand and began to lubricate his penis.

Wilson sat still, but I could tell he was really nervous about me touching him. To help smooth things out, I recalled how I touched his penis once before to help him after Chris attacked him in our P.E. class. As his penis became stiff I joked that I was glad to see it was still working after being treated so brutally. That helped take some pressure off. After I got Wilson's dick fully

lubricated and hard, I took his hand and placed some Vaseline on it. Then I moved his hand towards my penis and had him lubricate me.

At this point I knew that Wilson was probably doubting his manhood and worried about what we were doing, but like most of my other game players he was still all in with what we were doing and lubricated my penis. At that point I began jacking his dick and told him to jack mine. I placed a couple of the magazines with pictures of naked young teen girls on the bed so that I could look at one while he looked at the other. I told Wilson not to think of himself or me while we jacked each other off, but of the naked girls he was looking at. That also helped to take the pressure off.

It was not easy to keep from shooting my load as I looked at Wilson's freckles, bright red pubic hair, stiff dick and good looking body. He really turned me on and jacking his cute little penis made the situation even more acute. Fortunately, Wilson shot his load first. As he did, he began jacking me more aggressively. I suspected he wanted me to shoot my load as well and just get everything over with at the same time.

I loved holding his penis and milking it like a cow's utter as the semen spurted out. His body shook a little as he ejaculated and I knew he was in ecstasy as I continued to jack him while he ejaculated on to the towel. Suddenly, my own penis jumped and began to pump out semen. Wilson let go of it, but I understood that since he was new to my games and probably though we were doing something queer despite my reassurances.

I got some damp towels and cleaned us both off. After I finished, I asked Wilson how he liked it? He said it was really weird, but felt good. I told Wilson that he did a good job, but added that he needed to get his penis a little harder if he wanted satisfy a girl. That really was not true since his penis was probably as stiff as it could get for his size, but I needed a hook to get him to do more with me.

I explained that I could help him to get and keep his penis harder by using oral sex as a kind of exercise tool. I asked him if he knew what oral sex was and he said he did not, so I showed Wilson some photos of two young teen boys having oral sex. The pictures were in Adam's book and showed each boy taking turns sucking one another off. Wilson was as shocked at the photos as he was at the idea of oral sex.

After taking a close look at the oral sex photos, he said, "I could never do that! It's just too weird!" I immediately explained that he did not have to actually suck me off, just allow me to suck him off. He responding by asking, "You would do that?" I said that I would and that until he tried it, he should not be so critical. I reminded him that girls liked to be licked and eaten down in their private parts. If he thought this was weird, how would he feel about doing that?

Wilson saw my point, but still insisted he had no interest in giving anyone a blow job. He was not even sure if he wanted to get one either. I told him to lay back and let me suck him off. He asked me, "Are you sure you want to do that?" I said I did and told my nervous new friend that once he found out how good it felt he would want it all the time. I explained that it was probably

the closest thing to experiencing what it was like to have intercourse with a girl as you could get without actually having it.

I knew that Wilson was still unsure about what we were doing, but unless he was a complete prude he would have to enjoy one of my world class blow jobs. After he got into position I jacked his penis a bit to get it hard, than slowly began sucking him off. Wilson laid quietly saying nothing, but his penis responded extremely well to my oral stimulation. Before long his dick was completely stiff and his body began to move slightly and in a way which told me he liked what I was doing.

Before long Wilson shot his load and was stunned that I kept sucking on his penis as it ejaculated. He lifted his body up enough to see what I was doing and stared in disbelief as I sucked and swallowed his semen as fast as I could. As he finished, he laid back and breathed heavily. I continued to suck on his penis and licked it until it was clean, then I gently massaged his dick along with his testicles.

I asked Wilson how it felt and he replied, "It felt great, but I still can't believe you did that!" I ignored his little observation about my willingness to suck him off and instead said that I was glad he enjoyed it. I also pointed to my dick which was really hard at that point. He looked at my penis, looked at me and then said, "You don't expect me to suck your dick, do you? I don't think I can do that."

I assured Wilson that he did not have to suck me off, but I also said that I needed a way to get the same kind of satisfaction that I gave to him. He asked if I wanted him to jack me off again. His was willing to do that, but not much more. I told Wilson that he was not really that good at the circle jerk thing or jacking me off because he let go just when I was starting to shoot my load. I pointed out that it would have been the same as if I took his penis out of my mouth when I was giving him oral sex just at the point that he began ejaculating. Wilson understood my little object lesson.

I told Wilson that I had something else in mind. I began by having him sit in the same position we were in before during the circle jerk. I pulled him closer to me and used one hand to rub our penises together, while I used the other to alternatively play with both of our testicles. Wilson looked puzzled about what I was doing, so I used my classic explanation that I was letting our dicks get to know each other. I loved the feeling of our penises making contact and before long both of them were very stiff.

I kept rubbing our penises together until I shot my load. When I did, I aimed for his bright red pubic hair and pumped out my semen into it. After I finished, I pulled Wilson up and we headed for the shower. As we showered together, he allowed me to soap him up. I apologized for shooting my load into his pubic patch, but I admitted that the bright red hair he had down there really turned me on.

As we showered we talked and Wilson told me that he hated having red hair and all the freckles he had on his body. He was very self conscious about those things feeling that it made people stare at him. I said that if they stared it was probably because most of them found his bright red

hair and freckles as fascinating and attractive as I did. I pointed out that they were not only attractive, but gave his body a uniqueness and character that he should be thankful for.

Wilson appreciated my comments, but he was also very insightful and after I said those things he said, "I guess that was why you wanted to do those things with me, right?" I said that was true, but only partly. I also liked his personality and thought we could be close friends if he gave it a chance. I also wanted to help him get ready for sex with one or more of the girls and to get into the groove of what our group often did together.

Wilson said he liked me and wanted to be my friend, but he admitted that what we did made him really uncomfortable. As we got out of the shower, dried off and got back into our underwear Wilson told me why he felt the way he did. Because of the cute way he looked several people including a relative and two neighbors had molested him over the past few years. It all started with a couple of neighbors when he was eleven.

Wilson started doing some small odd jobs like helping to clean up yards or garages for neighbors when he was ten. His parents did not mind him doing that and earning a few bucks as long as they always knew where he was and what he was doing. When he turned eleven an unmarried neighbor named Jack had him do some small clean up jobs in his house and yard. After he finished one day and was really dirty, Jack suggested he take a shower before going home.

While he showered, Jack put his clothes in the washer and gave Wilson a robe to wear when he came out of the shower. After the shower, Wilson sat on the couch with Jack watching TV. After he put Wilson's clothes in the dryer, Jack sat back down next to Wilson on the couch. He sat right next to Wilson that time and began joking about his freckles. Jack finally asked Wilson if he had freckles everywhere on his body?

Wilson did not know how to answer, so he asked Jack what he meant? Jack said, "Well, do you have freckles on your dick?" Wilson said that he was embarrassed and frightened by the question, but before he could say anything Jack said, "Let's see!" and opened the robe to look at Wilson's penis. When he did not see any freckles on his dick, Jack said, "Maybe they are hiding?" and began to touch and move his penis around acting like his was looking for the freckles.

At that point Jack began playing with Wilson's penis and testicles. Wilson got upset and jumped up off of the couch. He ran to the dryer, got his clothes and put them on as fast as he could. He then ran out the back door. Wilson did not tell his parents what happened because he knew it would lead to all sorts of problems, but he never went near Jack's house again. In fact, it was a while before he went back to doing any odd jobs. When he did, the same thing happened again.

While Wilson was cleaning out the garage of a widower named Bob, the guy invited him into the house for some lunch. He and his family knew Bob, his wife and two children for several years and were friendly with them. There had never been any problems with that family, so Wilson felt safe over there. Bob had to go out for a while, so Wilson ate lunch with Bob's son named Sean. Sean was nineteen years old and was home for that summer from college. His sister was two years older and also attending college, but lived off campus and out of state.

After the two ate lunch Sean invited Wilson into his room and began showing him some comics he had. Wilson like reading comics and Sean always passed the ones he had already read on to Wilson or other kids he knew around the neighborhood. As Wilson looked at Sean's latest comic books, the older boy went and got some magazines out from under his bed. He asked Wilson if he would like to look at photos of naked girls and boys?

Wilson did not know what to say as Sean showed him some of the photos in the magazines which featured naked young boys and girls posing and even having sex with each other. He was shocked at what he saw and began to worry. Sean told Wilson that he liked looking at young people naked and had even seen some of the kids in the neighborhood without their clothes on. He mentioned the names of two boys and a girl around Wilson's age. Wilson knew those kids and was shocked that they would even get naked for Sean.

Sean said that he would like to see Wilson naked, but Wilson said that he would not take off his clothes. Sean became annoyed and said that he was just a coward. He said to Wilson, "Come on. Being naked is not big deal. If you get naked I will too and you can see what an older boy looks like." Wilson again told Sean he was not interested in doing that and began to get up. As he did, Sean took hold of him and said, "At least let me see your dick."

Sean pulled at Wilson's pants and then his underwear until he had them down around his knees. Once his private parts were exposed, Sean grabbed Wilson's penis and began playing with it. As he did he pushed Wilson to the floor and took off his own pants and underwear. As the older boy leaned over him, the sight of Sean's large and erect penis scared the heck out of Wilson. Sean ignored Wilson's protests and began jacking himself and the young boy off.

Sean stopped jacking himself and Wilson long enough to get completely naked. Wilson thought about getting up and running, but with Sean blocking his way towards the door and his own pants and underpants still down around his knees that would get him nowhere. Sean kneeled back down over Wilson and pulled off the young boy's shoes, socks, pants, underpants and tee shirt until he also was naked. Just as he again started jacking himself and Wilson, they heard the front door open.

Bob was back and yelled for his son. Sean quickly got up, started dressing and told Wilson to get his clothes back on as fast as he could. Sean ran out to greet his dad while Wilson was still dressing. By the time Bob and Sean got to the bedroom, Wilson was dressed. Bob asked the boy if he was alright? Wilson was again afraid to say what happened, so he said that Sean had been showing him his latest comic books.

Wilson was sure that Bob knew what his son had done with him and some of the other kids in the neighborhood because he sternly asked Wilson to go outside and finish the garage. As Wilson walked past he could see Bob giving his son a look of utter disgust. Wilson finished the garage, got paid and did not go back to do anymore work for Bob until his son was back at college.

Several other incidents happened, including one with a relative. An older cousin who took Wilson fishing got him naked while they were on his uncle's boat together with no one else

present. He was only a few years older than Wilson and told him that he always wanted to see him nude. Wilson said he did not like taking off his clothes, but the cousin said he had better do it or he would pull them off. Afraid, Wilson undressed and allowed his cousin to play with his penis for a while. When he cousin tried to undress, Wilson told him that if he did he would tell his dad and the boy stopped. On the way back to shore the cousin said he was sorry and begged Wilson not to say anything. Wilson agreed for the sake of the family and kept quiet.

A couple of older neighborhood kids tried enticing Wilson into getting naked, but from what he said they did it in such a stupid and clumsy way that he knew what they were up to and never even allowed them to get alone with him. After his told me what happened, Wilson said that he felt relieved. He had never been able to tell anyone about those incidents. Considering what we did together, he felt comfortable confessing his bizarre experiences to me.

Wilson also scolded me a bit by saying that I kind of reminded him of those people that molested him, but the difference was that I gave him a choice and that made him feel comfortable enough to do what we did together. I understood his point, but I also knew that he really wanted to get it on with a girl and without my help that make take a long while to happen. A lot of girls were not into red hair and freckles, so that (along with his smaller penis) limited his choices as far as girls went.

The game had changed. Wilson was wise to me, but smart enough to give me what I wanted as far as he was willing to go. I knew at that point that I would have to be satisfied with what I got from him. I also felt bad after hearing the stories he told. I thought, "That could be me" a few years forward and I was determined that it would not be. I had played my game well and continued to so so, but I had to make sure I played it with kids my age. With the exception of Julie who I was already involved with, no more younger girls or boys. And no more forcing myself on anyone. I had to learn to take 'No' for an answer.

I knew that Wilson would never feel the same way about me that I felt about him, but it was probably more about lust than anything else anyway. As we fell asleep I looked at Wilson and hoped that things would work out for him at the party. I planned on trying to get him with Alison and saw the two as a good fit. The next morning we woke up, ate breakfast at the cafe and headed back to my house. After checking in with everyone and helping to put up the rest of the party decorations, I got ready for the arrival of our guests.

Alison and Donna arrived first. Their mom brought them over and met Ingrid. It was a good thing that she came back early! Ingrid and the sister's mom got into a conversation and started looking at some of my cousin's outfits. Like most people, the mom was impressed with her designs and actually ordered a couple while she was there. After she left, I got Alison and Donna situated and before long Julie took charge of Alison.

Donna hung out with me all afternoon. We enjoyed talking, listening to music and playing board games. By four Nancy and everyone else we expected to come to the party arrived. After everyone that was new got a chance to meet the others, people paired off too quickly including Julie and her friend. That annoyed me because it meant that Wilson would probably not get a fair shake with Alison. I took Julie aside and spoke to her about it.

I asked Julie to talk with Alison and find out if she had any interest in Wilson. I was not trying to pimp her or any of the girls off to him, I just wanted to give a guy who had been through a lot a chance to have some fun and find a nice girl to date. I knew that there was a limit on how involved I could get in that situation and wondered if I had already bitten off more than I could chew?

I spoke with Nancy for a while and was happy to see that she was getting along really well with Adam. Both of them had been through so much and were really kind of perfect for one another. Mark and Laura were also doing well as a couple. I wanted to be sure that bliss reigned in those relationships because the last thing I needed was to end up having to get back involved with Nancy or Laura. I liked them both very much, but I knew they would not be in it with me for the long haul.

Since we had all sorts of sandwiches and snacks available for the party, I decided to make a barbecue outside and cook up some nice hamburgers, sausages, hot dogs and ears of corn. Donna helped me to get dinner ready and before long we were all full. The more time I spent with Donna, the more I liked her. I was also happy to see that Wilson was making the rounds and began spending time with Julie and Alison.

After a couple of hours of playing music, games and watching TV, we all got into our toga robes and started the party. Laura had came up with a bunch of silly activities like nasty versions of bobbing for apples, musical chairs and pin the tale on the Toga. She was very creative and all her games helped make our party a hit. Since everyone decided to wear the toga robes with nothing underneath, that was also a great source of interest and overall fun.

As midnight approached I turned down the lights and lit some candles. Taking that as some sort of a signal, we all started taking off our robes. Even Ingrid and Diane joined in. Before long, we were all naked. It was not pre-planned, but just became a kind of happening. I saw Julie and Alison looking at Wilson's body and I knew that would help to get him laid. I could not imagine anyone being able to resist his cute face, freckles and bright red hair.

By the time we rang in the New Year, everyone was in good spirits. The party dragged on for about another hour, then people began to settle in for the night and pair off. Julie and Alison invited Wilson to pair off with them just as I hoped. My cousin had Diane in her room and the others slept wherever they pleased. By that time Donna and I had been making out, so I invited her to sleep in my room with me with no strings attached. I wanted her to be comfortable.

After I locked up the house for the night, I took Donna up to my room. We laid on my bed and made out with each other for a long while. Our kisses became more passionate and soon I found myself touching her breasts as we kissed. She was really beautiful and had a nice full crop of pubic hair that turned me on and made me want to go all the way with her. Despite my enthusiasm, there was no way I was going to jump the gun. I would wait for a signal or subtle invitation.

I told Donna that I really liked her and she said the same thing to me. Being as outspoken as she was, Donna asked me if I wanted to go all the way with her? I said I did and she laid flat waiting for me. She said that this was her first time and that she did not know what to do, so I took the reins and got into position. In just moments I found myself pushing my penis into her. She had a small opening, so it took some work to penetrate her all the way.

As my penis pushed through her hymen, Donna breathed heavily and said my name quickly a few times which I guessed meant she was in some discomfort. Once I got all the way in, she settled down and we did it for a long time. I was surprised at how long I lasted before I shot my load into her. I knew that was a bad idea, but it was her first time and felt too good for me to resist. Afterward, I made out with her and then we had sex again in various positions.

Once we finished having sex Donna feel asleep quickly. I began to dose off, but suddenly an idea popped into my head. I wanted to see what Wilson and the other girls were up to. I put on my toga robe and headed to the bedroom they were using. I could see the light on, so I went in and saw that Alison and Wilson were laying on the bed making out with their robes on. I asked where Julie was and found out that she was sleeping in a cot in the recreation room.

I asked Wilson and Alison why they still had their robes on? They acted embarrassed and said they felt funny making out naked. I asked if they had tried and they said they had not. I said that it was New Years and no time for shyness or restraint. I ordered both of them to take off their robes. Alison was already a looker, but she looked like a goddess naked. Her body was perfect and like her sister, she had a nice crop of pubic hair.

After they got naked, I sat on a chair next to the bed and said, "Now try making out!" Wilson asked me, "Are you going to sit there while we make out?" I said I was and that I would orchestrate the rest of their fun. Wilson knew better than to cross me at that point and probably figured out that me being in there was his best chance at getting laid.

I asked the couple if they knew how to French Kiss? They said they did not, so I borrowed Alison for a bit, took off my robe and made out with her naked on the bed. After I tutored Alison on how to properly French she went back to making out with Wilson and taught him. I was really turned on after my body touched Alison's while we kissed and watching them French made it hard to keep my penis soft.

After a while I asked the couple if they liked each other? They said they did, so I asked Alison if she wanted to do it with Wilson? She said, "Ah, I guess. I never did that before. Will it hurt?" I told her it might hurt a little for a second or two, but after that it would feel great. I positioned Alison at the edge of the bed with her legs spread. She was laying on her back with her feet hanging off the bed, so I had Wilson pick them up and lean them on his body.

Seeing his penis was not quite ready, I jacked it a bit until it got really hard and then pushed him towards Alison. It was his first time and he was clumsy to say the least, so I tried to move him into a better position to penetrate Alison. After a few tries, he still could not seem to get his penis into her. I was frustrated and horny, so I moved Wilson and said I would show him how to do it.

I suspected that Wilson's smaller dick was not up to the job of breaking in Alison. She had a hole that was even smaller than Donna's. As I got into position Alison looked shocked, but said nothing. Wilson stood to the side of me and watched intently as I began to push my penis into Alison's opening. It was so tight that I could barely get my dick into her. I wished I had some Vaseline at that point, but it was in the other room and there was no way I was going to stop and get it.

Fortunately, my penis was still a little bit lubricated from all the sex I had with Donna. Once I managed to get the head of my dick into Alison, I summoned all my stamina and began to push my shaft into her. It was like trying to push through a steel plate! Alison began to breath heavily and sighed as I slowly pushed my way into her. I gave it one last, quick push which caused her to take a few quick breaths and sigh loudly. Finally the deed was done.

Once I was all the way into her it was hard to just stop having intercourse. She was tight and my penis felt like it was being gently squeezed as I moved it in and out of her. I knew that Wilson was probably foaming at the mouth by that time, so I forced myself to stop having sex with Alison and got him back into position. This time Wilson's penis went into Alison without much of a problem. I sat down and watched as he did his thing.

Wilson did not last long and shot his load after what seemed like less than a minute. Alison looked disappointed, but I sensed an opportunity. I said, "Let's make this threesome official!" and began having sex with Alison again. I knew she was probably upset and maybe even in shock, but I tended to have that affect on people. After I shot my load I made Wilson take another turn. He again finished up quickly, so I told Alison I would show her how to give him a head job.

I laid Wilson on the bed and began to suck him off. He played along because I guessed he was too embarrassed not to. He was not able to ejaculate at that point, so I asked Alison if she wanted to give it a try? She said, "Yuck, NO!' Head jobs were obviously not her thing. I said it was Wilson's turn to get laid. Alison who was probably disgusted with herself for screwing two guys at once during her very first sexual experience said, "He already did." I replied, "Not like this!"

I pushed Wilson on to the other side of the bed until he was laying on his stomach and had his feet on the floor. With my penis still wet from Alison, I spread his butt cheeks with my hands and began pushing my penis into him. If she wasn't in shock before, Alison was in shock at that point while she watched one of her lovers screwing the other! Wilson loudly objected to what I was doing. He said, "Are you crazy? STOP! PLEASE! STOP!" I kept going until my penis was all the way into him, then I moved it in and out. So much for my self control.

As much as I disliked doing him that way, it felt really good and just looking at his freckled back really turned me on. I finally pulled my penis out, but it was still rock hard. I went over and pulled Alison towards me shoving my dick into her. She was probably too upset to make any noise or protest, so I quickly let loose into her. After I shot my load, I stopped and put my robe back on. I warned Alison and Wilson not to say anything about what we did and suggested they shower, then I left.

There was no blood on my penis so I guessed that Wilson's anus had been loose enough to accommodate my dick. I could not believe that I had broke in two sisters in one night and still managed to get the rest of what I wanted from Wilson. I showered in the downstairs bathroom and heard the water running upstairs as well. I guessed that Wilson and Alison had taken my advice.

After I finished cleaning up, I headed back upstairs and went to bed. Although I worried that Alison would tell her sister what happened, there was nothing I could do at that point. And as far as Wilson went, well, I did get him laid several times including once with me! What was done was done and I could not take it back. I fell asleep naked next to Donna under the covers and that was one of the best sleeps I ever had.

I woke up the next morning with Donna holding me and that was a great feeling. It was just around eight in the morning when I made a quick bathroom call, then came back into my bedroom and fumbled around for some clothes. I let Donna sleep and headed to the bedroom that Laura normally used to check in on Alison and Wilson. I opened the door quietly and saw that Wilson was sleeping right next to Alison. I hoped that was a good sign of things to come.

I went downstairs to eat breakfast and found Julie already in the kitchen. She cooked some bacon and sausages for all of us and was eating breakfast. As we sat together with everyone else asleep, she asked me how things went? I was not going to lie to her, so I quietly confessed to everything I did the night before. I thought she might be angry, but Julie just laughed and said she had a feeling I would take full advantage of Wilson and the sisters.

Julie joked that now we both had been with Alison! I knew that Julie was messing around with her friend and that was fine by me. I reminded her that from now on she and Alison could have even more fun because her friend was now fully open for business down there. Julie called me a pervert and laughed some more. I asked her if she was interested in Wilson? She told me that she would rather be with me. I said that she would always be in my heart and left it at that.

By the time we finished breakfast most of the others were up and moving around. From the looks on everyone's faces I guessed that our party was successful on many levels. Wilson and Alison were quiet, but they hung out with each other all the rest of that day. Donna joined us after a while and that reminded me that I might have a real problem with her. If she found out what I did with her sister, I was toast. Being as outspoken and unpredictable as she was, I had no idea what she would say or do?

As a nice finish to our New Year's get together, Ingrid and I took everyone to the hotel for a dip in the indoor pool during the late morning, then we all came back and hung out together until it was time for everyone to go home. Most of our guests had to be home for the New Year's Day dinner with their families. Donna and Alison had plenty of time to talk with one another during the day, so I guessed by her lack of outrage towards me that her sister had kept our secret. Julie later told me that the only thing that Alison told her sister was that she and Wilson had sex. Wilson said nothing to me all day, but appeared happy to be with Alison.

As everyone started to leave and Donna's mom came to pick up her and Alison. Donna and I stole a moment alone holding each other gently and kissing to say our goodbyes. Wilson also left, still without taking to me. With the guests that did not live or were not staying in our house gone, it was almost time for Ingrid, Julie, Laura, Adam and I to sit down to a nice New Year's Day meal. Ingrid and Laura did most of the cooking while Julie, Adam and I cleaned everything up from the party. My parents would return in two days so I wanted to be sure messes did not pile up. We kept everything clean and did the laundry every day.

The New Year started with a lot of changes. Wilson and the sisters were now a part of our group for better or worse, Diane was no longer with my Canadian friend who had moved on to greener pastures and I was now involved with Donna. Later that night another change occurred. It was one that I could hardly believe possible and one which had a profound affect on me.

The phone rang around eight that evening. Since my parents had been calling periodically to check on us, I assumed it was them. It was not. Clarence called to give me some horrible news. Bobbie and his mom had been in a bad car crash on New Year's Eve. Although he hesitated, he finally told me that Bobbie had died on the way to the hospital. I was instantly devastated and yelled for Ingrid.

Ingrid came running into the kitchen, but I could not say a word. I just sat at the kitchen table with the phone in my hand. Ingrid took the receiver from my hand and spoke to Clarence, then started crying. By that time Julie, Adam and Laura came into the kitchen to find out what was going on. Ingrid regained her composure enough to tell them about the tragedy.

For the rest of that night no one said very much. The TV was on, but no one was really watching it. My cousin called my folks to let them know about Bobbie. They knew that I really liked her and offered to buy me a plane ticket to go and attend her funeral the weekend before school started up again. I was too grief stricken to even move let alone get on a plane. I did not want to say goodbye to Bobbie; I wanted her back! My cousin went to represent our family and explain why I could not come.

Even after my folks got back and everyone in the house tried to comfort me, I was inconsolable. Clarence let us know that his mom was beginning to respond to treatment and recover. I was happy for him, but my Bobbie was gone and that was just about all I could think about. To make matters worse, Julie's grandfather suddenly and unexpectedly died a few days later. That was a funeral I had to attend and it took every ounce of energy I had to go.

Julie's grandmother got with my folks and agreed to allow her to stay and finish the school year with us. Now that her grandmother was busy trying to settle her late husband's affairs, the last thing she needed was to worry about Julie settling into a new school mid term and trying to adjust to a new area during such a difficult time. Julie was thrilled, but muted her joy in respect for my mourning over Bobbie. She loved living with us and liked being around me and Ingrid.

Adam was still in limbo and remained with us as his relatives tried to decide who, besides his dad, he could live with. That was fine by us. We loved having him around and he helped out every chance he got. I spoke to Donna a few times by phone during that difficult time and we

finally saw each other again at school. We talked for a long time. She understood how I had felt about Bobbie and how losing her affected me.

Clarence and his mom moved and I did not see them anymore. Any contact with her family reminded me of Bobbie. Donna and Julie saw me through my period of mourning for Bobbie. So did the others in our house, but they were especially patient and kind. After about a month I began to feel like my old self and started going out again with Julie, Alison, Donna and Wilson. With her parent's dating ban in place, going out as a group was really the only way we could all see each other.

Wilson started talking with me again, but nothing was ever mentioned about the night we had our threesome. That was fine by me since my new relationship with Donna, although stalled by Bobbie's death, was finally starting to move forward. Just as I thought I was finally getting some stability in my life complications arose in our little group. It began around Spring Break time.

We were all off from school for a week, but Wilson went away on a short vacation with his family. Adam was busy with Nancy, while Mark and Laura had there own plans. Ingrid was busy with her business and kept everyone in the house except for my parents busy with it as well. We did not mind and enjoyed the money we made helping her each morning and during part of the afternoon. With late afternoons and evenings free and my parents hanging around the house when they were not working, I needed a place to see Donna for some intimacy. That place was the hotel suite.

My parents never used the hotel suite during the week, so going there for privacy and fun was no problem. We also used the pool. On the first weekday of Spring Break Julie and I planned on picking up Alison and Donna for an evening of fun at the hotel. Even though Wilson was not available, I figured that Alison and Julie could find a way to stay busy while Donna and I did our thing after using the pool.

As far as the sister's parents knew we were going to my dad's hotel just to use the indoor pool and eat dinner at the cafe. They did not know about the suite and what they did not know was better for me and the girls. After Julie and I got to the sister's house, we found out that Donna was not feeling well. She had a bad sore throat and could not go with us. Alison felt fine so she did come with us.

After we got to the hotel we went to eat dinner. After we ate, we went up to the suite to change into out bathing suits and headed down to the pool. We had a lot of fun together and had began tight as a group. After the pool, we went back upstairs to change back into our clothes. The girls were going to use my bedroom while I changed in the bathroom. As I was headed towards the bathroom Julie and Alison yelled for me to come into my bedroom to see something. I walked in and found them both naked.

I figured that this was one of Julie's little pranks. She loved playing practical jokes on me. As I stood there Julie handed me a towel and asked me to dry her and Alison off. Julie reminded me not to be shy about drying every part of their body. I played along wondering what was up? As

finished drying them off, Julie sneaked around my back and pulled off my bathing suit. She and Alison then took the towel and dried me off.

After they finished their little chore, Julie pushed her body close to mine and kissed me. Julie told me that she and Alison wanted to fool around with me. Sensing my surprise, Julie said that she missed having sex with me. She also told me that ever since I broke in Alison that first night she had a secret crush on me. Alison was a little shy and no where near as outspoken as Donna or Julie, but she admitted that what Julie said was true.

I knew this was little triste was Julie's idea, but I could tell from the way Alison had been acting around me when Donna was not looking that she probably did have a crush on me and I also suspected that Wilson was not really giving her the kind of sexual experiences she hoped for. I was all into their game, but asked, "What about Donna and Wilson?" Julie and Alison told me they had no intention of telling them about our little game.

I was still in some emotional pain from the loss of Bobbie and sex was one way I used to help mute it. Donna and I had been doing it on a regular basis for some time. Always aware that any of the girls could get pregnant, I had some condoms that I bought from a head shop on the beach and used them or simply pulled my penis out before I ejaculated, depending on the occasion. On this occasion I had condoms and used them.

We got on the bed and before long I was making out with both girls alternatively, then having sex with them. Alison may have been shy most of the time, but she was really into what we were doing. I loved her tight pussy and youthful enthusiasm. Julie was less aggressive on that occasion, but sex with her was always an extremely sensual experience. Both girls were willing to suck me off, so I let them and returned the favor by licking their private parts.

After I finished having sex with the girls I said that I wanted them to kiss and make out with each other so that I could watch. Alison acted shy about it, but Julie quickly got her into a tight hug and the two were soon making out in a way which told me they had done that together many times before. I had them rub up against each other and eventually lick each other in all the right places as I had done to them. The way they did that told me it was a first for them. Julie later said that they had kissed and fingered each other, but that was all up to that point.

Although Alison did not seem to mind doing it with Julie, I knew she did not really lean very far in that direction. She was willing to mess around with her friend to get what she really wanted and that was me. I certainly did not mind having a threesome with the girls, but I wished it was a five-some which included Donna and Wilson. I doubted that would ever happen after what I did to Wilson during that first time with Alison. However, I hoped a foursome might happen if Donna was willing.

Once again I had sunk to the lowest depths of depravity. I did not mean for it to happen, but my games were now coming back to haunt me as my students were quickly becoming teachers. I knew that this latest development would not be a good thing in the long term and just hoped that everything would somehow work out. After we dropped Alison back off at her house, Julie and I went home and straight to our individual beds.

Spring Break was a mess. It turned out that Donna had somehow contracted pneumonia and ended up in the hospital. Fortunately, none of us caught it from her. I went to see her twice until she finally was released and in recovery at home the last day of Spring Break. After school started up some new opportunities came my way. The first began with Chris, the guy who had started a fight with Wilson in P.E. class during the previous semester.

Chris began talking to me before and after class. I was surprised because I did not think that we were not much alike. On top of that, I had all but made him a possible sex slave after the altercation with Wilson. I simply had not acted on my threat to do what I wanted with him because I was trying desperately to turn over a new leaf and busy with the girls. With a desire to avoid further problems I kept things cool in P.E. and decided to just be satisfied with looking at the variety of bodies that came to get towels from me.

Chris was well built, about my size, had shoulder length blond hair and very little body hair. I liked seeing him naked because he had a nice sized penis with a thick shaft which hung down handsomely from his ample crop of blond public hair. Although he was good looking, Chris was not really my type. He seemed like a kind of pseudo-hippie and that meant he might be a drug user. However, as we talked I was surprised to find out that he did not smoke, drink or use drugs. His parents were really strict about those things and brought him u with good values despite his otherwise rebel-like appearance.

Not wanting to be anti-social, I began walking with Chris to lunch after P.E. and invited him to sit with me whenever he wanted to. At that point none of my friends had the same lunch period that I did, so I usually sat alone or with some kids I knew casually from other classes. The more we talked and spent time together, the more I sensed that Chris liked me. What I had to try and figure out was in what way? I knew he had a girlfriend that cheated on him thanks to his mistaken fight over her with Wilson, but was he just into girls or like me and wanted something more?

I decided to invite Chris to the hotel suite for a weekend sleep over a few weeks into May. Julie, Alison and Donna were going away with the sister's parents to some event that weekend. It was the perfect time to see how Chris really felt about me. He gave me his address and I picked him up just before lunchtime. After we got to the hotel I took him up to the suite so that we could get settled in.

Chris and I changed in front of each other in my bedroom, than went out to the beach. I already knew not to read too much into that since we also saw each other naked all the time in P.E. class. The weather was warm and the Gulf was like bath water. We swam, rented some jet skis and had a great time. After we worked up an appetite, we threw our tee shirts on and ate some junk food in the cafe. We lounged in the sun for a while and talked, then used the outdoor pool which was filled with cute girls.

The girls at the pool liked Chris and a few hit on him almost immediately. I also received a few bites. We probably would have taken advantage of that situation, but we were still getting to know each other and decided not to complicate our weekend by inviting strange girls up for a

fling in the suite. Anyway, there was a bad outbreak of social diseases in Florida at that time and we were not ready to take a chance with girls we did not know.

We got tired of the pool and headed to the arcade and activity room. We played pinball and air hockey and then went and had another meal in the cafe. Finally, it was time to head up to the suite for the night. We both got changed into shorts and tee shorts. I enjoyed spending time with Chris more than I thought I would, but I still had no idea whether to just consider him a friend or something more.

We watched TV for a while until I saw the opportunity for a possible ice breaker. My old pal the TV Wrestling Show came on. As we sat near each other on the couch and watched, I started poking at Chris saying that I could beat him at wrestling. He got up, laughed and told me to try. I said I wanted to wrestle Greek style and told him to get naked just to see what he would do. Chris took off his tee shirt, shorts and underpants with no hassle, so I did the same.

The stage was set and we began wrestling. Chris was strong and pinned me twice. I came back and pinned him. As we wrestled I could see he had a woody. When he saw that I noticed his stiff dick he became red faced, stopped wrestling me and tried to cover it up with his hand. I laughed and said it was nothing to be ashamed of, then said I wanted to check and see how stiff it really was.

I pushed Chris on his back, took hold of his stiff penis and said, "Wow, that thing is really hard! I guess that is my fault, so I'll help you deal with it." I told Chris to stay where he was while I went and got some Vaseline and towels. He remained on the carpet and his penis was still hard when I returned. I lubricated his dick, then started jacking him off. Chris looked away from me as if he was disconnected from the situation.

I loved jacking his rock hard penis, but I wanted us to be more comfortable. I suggested we go into the bedroom and get on the bed. Chris followed me saying nothing and laid down on his back. Once again I began jacking him off until his penis throbbed, jumped and shot out a ton of semen. His dick remained rock hard even after he ejaculated, so after I cleaned him off with the towel I then moved him further down the bed and got into a position to suck him off.

Chris was silent and that kind of freaked me out. I went about my business and sucked him for a long time until he finally shot his load into my mouth. At that point I lubricated my own penis and laid next to Chris. I moved his hand to my dick to see what he would do and he began jacking me off. He kept going until I ejaculated and held on to my penis just as I had done with him. Afterward he looked at me and said, "I'm not queer, you know." I said, "Nether am I. I just like playing sex games with girls and boys."

I gave Chris the short version of some of my adventures while we laid naked next to one another. To my surprise, Chris had a similar story to tell. He grew up alone as the only child of strict parents. Originally from a small town in Ohio, his folks moved to Florida to retire just a few years before. Back in his hometown Chris admitted to fooling around with boys and girls in almost the same way I did. He stopped short of doing some of the things I did, but he could have basically been my perverted twin.

Chris tried to leave his previous life behind when he moved to Florida vowing to try and stick with girls his own age while avoiding boys altogether. I knew first hand that was not an easy thing to do and we both talked about how hard it was to resist temptation when you were served up an almost daily buffet of cute male bodies in P.E. class. Chris admitted that he had recently attempted to connect with a couple of the boys in P.E. class that he thought were cute, but was not able to find the common ground he needed to do it.

When I intervened in the fight between Chris and Mark by pulling him off my friend and taking him into the shower area, Chris said that he knew as soon as I started messing with him that I was like him. He wanted to wait until things calmed down between us to approach me. After we got past the mini-biographies, I asked Chris if he wanted to suck me off? He said he did and went to work. He gave great head and swallowed my semen just as I had done with him.

We both took a bathroom break, then when we got back into bed I asked Chris if he liked to French Kiss. He said he done it with girls his age and younger, but was always afraid to try it with the boys he played around with. They were always younger than him and he figured it would freak them out too much. I asked if he wanted to try it with me and he said he would. We got close to each other and nervously began kissing.

After a while our Frenching became passionate and we both enjoyed the kisses we shared, but in a kind of weird and slightly uncomfortable way. After we stopped I asked if Chris ever had anal sex with anyone? He said he always wanted to try it and told me that he had books at home that he bought at a truck stop in St Pete which showed how to do it. From what he said, the books were just like the ones that I had. There were photos in his books of young boys having anal sex together which really turned him on.

I asked if he wanted to try it with me? He blushed and looked away, but said he did. I lubricated my penis and got us into position. Chris was my body size and had a large enough buttocks with a decent sized anus that was perfect for my penis. I was certain I would not cause him much pain or any damage by having anal sex with him. As I penetrated Chris my penis slid in easily enough so that I knew I was right about not causing Chris too many pain or damage.

Chris made a few sounds and moved around slightly which told me he was experiencing some discomfort, but after I got all the way into him and began having intercourse he settled down and let me do my thing. He was quiet and breathing hard in a way which told me he was actually enjoying what I was doing. Looking at him and feeling my penis go in and out of his anus really turned me on. My dick became stiff and numb.

After a while I could feel Chris pushing his body towards me as if to get more out of my thrusts, so I pushed my penis into him harder and faster. I finally felt ready to shot my load, but I could not pull my penis out of him. It just felt too good and I ejaculated into him until my penis slid out of his anus on its own being wet and slick with Vaseline and semen. I apologized to Chris, but he said not to worry about it and headed into the bathroom.

After a while Chris came out of the bathroom and said that what we just did was the best thing he ever experienced. I was shocked! I thought he would be pissed, but instead he was pleased. I wanted to invite him take a turn in me but I was not sure if I could deal with his long and thick shaft. I was always more of a pitcher than a catcher. I explained my situation to Chris and he understood, but I also said I had an idea that I thought he would like. It would be a reward for his compliance.

I called Ingrid to ask her what she was doing? She said she was just hanging out with Diane, so I said that if she and Diane came over to the suite to spend the night I had a nice surprise for them. Ingrid knew I had some weird sex idea in mind and luckily for me she was in the mood for just that kind of thing. I told Chris what I had in mind as he and I dressed and waited for the girls to arrive.

After my cousin and her friend got to the suite their eyes instantly lit up when they saw Chris. I knew that he was just what they liked in a boy. After we spent some time talking so that the girls could get to know him better, I suggested we all go into my bedroom and play some games. The girls laughed and Ingid commented, "You are the Game Master, aren't you?" She was right.

We all got naked and soon I had Ingrid in my arms while Chris took on Diane. After making out we all started having intercourse. I could tell that Diane and Chris were having a really good time with each other. For my part, I loved having sex with Ingrid and each time we did it I felt like I was wrapped in a blanket of bliss. After a while we switched partners. It had been a while since I had sex with Diane and I really enjoyed it. I could not recall the last time Ingrid did it with a guy other than me, so I hoped she would be pleased.

Fortunately, Ingrid looked like she having a great time being laid by Chris. I could see that she was in ecstasy each time he thrust his thick shaft into her. We kept switching partners and positions doing everything and having everything done to us until we were all physically and emotionally spent. The girls took a shower together, then went into the other bedroom to sleep. I showered with Chris and as washed each other off he said how much he appreciated having the girls come over.

Like much people Chris was stunned that I had that kind of access to my first cousin, but I told him that Ingrid and I really cared for each other. I explained that we hated the kind of artifical barriers created by a society too afraid to act on the sex drive that came naturally to us all. He agreed and after we showered we also went to bed and to sleep.

The next morning I was the first to wake up as usual and gave a lot of thought to the situation with Chris. As much as I liked him and enjoyed what we did together, I also wondered how good we were for each other? We were both trying to move on from perversity and here we were doing some of the things that society labeled the most perverse of all. I went down to the cafe to get some breakfast sandwiches to go for everyone and by the time I got back to the suite the others were awake and moving around.

Diane and Chris were talking with each other and seemed to be hitting it off really well, so Ingrid and I went outside through the sliding glass doors and ate our sandwiches on the veranda. We sat

at the outdoor table covered with a large umbrella and talked quietly. As much as she liked his look and the way that Chris had sex with her, Ingrid was not looking at him for the long term. Last night was fun, but my cousin felt that Diane and Chris would be a better fit. I agreed and from that point on we encouraged their relationship.

By Sunday night Chris and Diane were an item. I knew that would be better for him and better for me. The last thing I needed was yet another partner in perversion. Diane kept Chris on the straight and narrow road and I already got more than what I expected out of Chris and could not complain. I remained friends with him, but left it at that. I made it clear that there would be no more games between us and that as long as he was with Diane I expected him to play the role of a boyfriend without being sidetracked by boys.

Chapter Three: More Complications and The New Kids On The Block

My relationship with Donna was getting more complicated by the day. Julie kept encouraging me to fool around with her and Alison. She managed to find ways to keep Donna busy with other things whenever she wanted me to take her and Alison to the hotel suite for sex games. Each time I tried to talk her out of it she started saying that I should tell Donna the truth and get her involved with us. She was right, but I had no idea how to do that.

Wilson and Alison were still seeing each other and going out with us as a group, but I could see that Alison was getting tired of him for whatever reason. Apart from having a smaller penis and not being very good at sex, he was kind of moody and sometimes difficult to deal with. I knew that Wilson had been through a lot, but so had Adam. In fact, he went through a lot more and still managed to act appropriately towards all his friends without flying off the handle.

As summer vacation neared I knew that I had to be honest with Donna and decided to take her out after school and spill my guts. After I dropped the others staying with me home from school, I took Donna to a small park near my house so that we could park and talk. She normally took the bus home from school, but called her mom to stay she was going to the library with me and Julie for a while and that I would give her a ride home after she got some books she needed for a school project.

I had no idea whether or not Donna's mother believed her flimsy excuse to see me, but either way this was my best shot tell her the truth about me, Julie and Alison. As I told her all that had happened between myself and the girls, she said she was not surprised. She knew I was that way from the stories that Julie told her even before we officially met. She also wondered why Alison talked so much about me and Julie when we were not around.

Donna said she understood how that I got stuck into that situation. She just wished I had been honest with her about it from the first. I agreed that she was right and apologized. After we talked for a while, Donna agreed that we should stay together. She was not into sharing me with Julie and Alison as I had hoped, so I told her I would try to get them hooked up with some nice guys their age.

We went to the library so that Donna could pick up a few books before I dropped her off home. After I got home I told Julie what happened and she still held out hope that Donna would eventually agree to a foursome. I told her not to push for that. If it happened it happened, but I did see any way that would come to fruition at that point. Although Donna was outspoken and even daring about some things, she was old fashioned about relationships in terms of being with one person at a time.

Although I knew that part of Donna's understanding attitude towards my confession had to do with the fact that she probably felt sorry for me having lost Bobbie, I also knew that we had been growing close to one another since the day we first met. Despite our bonding, the situation with Alison and Julie was yet another warning sign that my games were causing me more trouble than they might be worth.

Thinking that the situation between Alison and Wilson could be salvaged, I went to work on him. He might have been a little annoying at times and certainly could not help the physical cards that nature had dealt him as far as penis size went, but Alison was a tight fit even for me and I could not imagine her enjoying sex with some guy hung like a horse. They were actually a pretty good match if they would just give things a chance to work between them.

I spent time encouraging Wilson to curb his attitude and treat Alison in a manner that she deserved. As far as girls went they were not exactly growing on trees for a guy like him and he needed to understand that Alison was a real beauty and the perfect match for him. Wilson began following the advice that I gave him and things got better between him and Alison. Donna took notice of my efforts and appreciated what I was doing.

Julie was another situation. As summer vacation began I saw that she was beginning to resent my relationship with Donna. She had never done that before, but she was getting older and more possessive towards me. Julie's attitude made it really hard to keep things cool between her and Donna. It seemed like both girls were constantly in other's faces about anything and everything which made keeping the peace a real struggle for me.

The break I needed finally came when Julie's grandmother called and said it was time for her to come and live with her. Now that school was over and her grandmother had all of her husband's affair's settled, Julie needed to go back to her family. I knew it was breaking her heart to leave, but Julie knew the situation with us was not permanent. The day she left we all cried having become our own version of a close family.

Although I sometimes missed her, Donna and I breathed a sign of relief after Julie left. Our relationship was finally fully on the mend and moving forward. Wilson and Alison were also getting along really well and headed in the right direction. Mark was doing well with Laura and Adam was becoming ever closer to Nancy. Ingrid and I continued in the manner we had for years and Diane was happy with Chris. Despite the occasional sleep over party which featured nothing more bizarre than skinny dipping among the couples, the group sex games had ceased. Now that most everyone was paired off there was really no sense in playing them.

I guess I was always the kind of person that could never be happy when things were going well and somehow needed to upset the apple cart every chance I got. One of those chances came along during that summer after the Jensen Family moved into our neighborhood. Susan and Robin were sisters who lived with their mom, dad and adopted twin brothers John and Jerry. Susan was my age being fifteen, while Robin was thirteen. The twin boys were also thirteen years old.

The Jensen's bought the house where Julie once lived and moved in after she went back to live with her grandmother out of state. It did not take long to notice our new neighbors. The first time I saw the twins running through the sprinkler on their front lawn in their bathing suits I was instantly fascinated by them. They were short, thin with almost delicate looking body frames and appeared at least two years younger than their age. Both boys had short, thick and straight dark brown hair, big brown eyes and freckles scattered all over their faces and bodies.

As I watched the twins play from my front door their sisters Susan and Robin came out to check the mail and tell their adopted brothers to stop running all over the lawn and get inside for lunch. Susan was my height with a shapely body, medium sized breasts, a cute face and strawberry blond hair. Robin was adorable. She was short, had dark brown hair, an extremely cute face and a perfectly proportioned body with ample breasts.

The family was Norwegian as far as their ethnic heritage went, but the twins were likely of Irish or Scottish extraction. They lived with their parents next to the Jensen Family in New York until their parents were killed in a terrible car accident when they were eight years old. The Jensen family was not wealthy, but both parents had good jobs and could afford to offer the twins a good home. Since there were no relatives that could be located to adopt them, the twins ended up with the Jensens.

The Jensen Family moved to Florida to take over a business on the beach. The Jensens became controlling partners in a small hotel and restaurant that was owned by older relatives. After they were no longer able to run the place by themselves, they invited the Jensens to manage the property and take a lion's share of the profits. It was the kind of offer they could not refuse. Although it took a lot of work to manage and keep the property up to the proper standards, the place was a money maker. Still in their early forties, Mr and Mrs Jensen were up to the task.

Our two families met after my mom and dad and went over and welcomed the Jensens to the neighborhood. Before long Susan and Robin started coming over to hang out. They were followed by the twins. There were not many young people in our neighborhood, so we all tended to stay close to one another. With their parents at the hotel most of the time, the Jensen kids spent a lot of time at our house. That was fine with me and the others because the Jensen kids were fun to be around.

Robin looked like a pretty little forest Gnome, but she was more like a social butterfly who made friends easy and showed a lot of interest in me from the beginning. It was like having replaced one Julie with another. She would do things like ask me to give her horseback rides when we were in the pool and just come and sit right in my lap when I was watching TV. I didn't mind and as much as I enjoyed the attention, it was difficult to keep from acting on her hints and

signals. It was even harder to steer clear of the twins. They were amazingly cute and had different, but really nice personalities.

John was always polite and had the qualities of a leader always sticking to his opinions and decisions whether they were right or wrong. However, he could also be moody and sometimes felt ignored by his family. Jerry was friendly, easy going and more of a follower than a leader. Like most siblings the Jensen kids did not always get along with each other and when tempers flared between the sisters and their adopted brothers you did not want to be there! Apart from that, they were all fun to hang out with.

Things were finally settled for Adam. He moved in with a relative who lived about thirty minutes away from us. That kept him in the loop with us and allowed his relationship with Nancy to continue. Laura was another story. Her situation had become a big mess. The legal wrangling between her mom and dad got worse as time went on and it was finally decided that she had to had to go back and live with her mother. If she remained with us the lawyers told her mom she would end up in Georgia with one of her grandparents. Staying with us made it look like her mom could not handle her, even though that was not the case.

Laura did not live that far from us, so continuing to date Mark and visiting us from time to time was no problem. She remained in my high school taking the bus there. In those days bussing to schools outside of the area where you lived was a common practice. Laura was not happy with the situation, but I was. As much as I liked her and appreciated her company, I knew that if things ever went bad between her and Mark it was too much of a temptation to get back involved with her. I also welcomed the peace that came from not having a house full of so many people.

Laura continued to model for Ingrid on occasion, but could no longer help with sewing, designing and errands on a daily basis. Without Laura, Julie, Adam and Bobbie, my cousin was short of helpers. Diane and I tried our best to make up for the lost workers, but there was always so much to do. After having Ingrid speak with Donna's mom, my cousin managed to convince her to let her daughters come to our house three days a week and work for Ingrid during summer vacation from school.

Donna's parents had a great work ethic and liked the idea of Donna and Alison working with Ingrid. Both girls were smart and motivated. Donna was skilled at sewing thanks to her mom, while Alison had a gift for attention to detail which made her the perfect choice to help me run errands and handle various duties for Ingrid. With the sisters helping out, things eased up a bit for Diane and I. However, we were still short of help and I decided to see if at least one of my new neighbors might be able to join our labor force.

Susan was quiet until she got to know you. After she did, you were like family. She was smart and had an excellent work ethic. If she had any flaws they were low self esteem and occasional bouts with depression. She sometimes felt very alone and lacked direction. I spoke with Susan to see if she was interested in working with us. She was, so I said she could try it for a few days to see if she liked the work. If she did and Ingrid was satisfied with the job she was doing, the position was hers for the summer and after school the rest of the year.

I did not like running errands with Alison. She was still coming on to me and that was no longer an option as far as I was concerned. Wilson and her were getting along fine, but I knew she secretly preferred me. I liked Donna and with our relationship going so well I did not want to mess things up by having a fling with Alison during a weak moment. Susan was the answer to that problem.

With both of us being the same age and Susan learning to drive we were a much better fit to run errands for Ingrid than Alison and I. After I pointed this out to Ingrid and explained my concerns about Alison's unwanted advances towards me, Ingrid began training Alison to handle phone calls and paperwork, My cousin was so successful that she now had her own phone line and number. Alison turned out to be a real asset in her new role. I was just glad to have her at a distance from me.

I didn't worry about getting involved with Susan. We became good friends and she never sent any signals that she liked me in a romantic way. As much as Susan liked boys, she had not yet found a steady boyfriend. Like the other kids I hung out with she did not smoke, drink or do drugs. That limited her choices for dating which was a common problem for myself and just about everyone I knew. Her parents did not really want her dating at that point, but they were also realistic. Instead of having Susan go out with boys behind their back, they insisted on meeting them and allowed her to go out with some restrictions like a curfew and chastity.

The more time that Susan and I spent together, the more we got to know each other. Knowing I was involved with Donna, she did not come on to me. As close friends we shared a lot of things with each. The one thing I did not share with her were the lurid stories and secrets surrounding my sex games. I had no intention of playing them anymore, so I did not feel the need to confess my previous indiscretions with my new friend.

Robin and the twins hung out around at our house a lot. With their folks always working at the hotel and Susan helping Ingrid and I, their parents and mine felt better with the Jensen kids at our house then alone in theirs even though it was just across the street. Robin was all over the place and had girl friends coming and going. If she went out she had to let one of us know where she was going. She never wondered far, but she was a bit of a wild child and we all worried that she would eventually end up in trouble if we did not keep her on a short leash.

The twins had a few friends, but there were not many kids around our neighborhood and until school started up again their social interactions were limited. Most of the kids that did live near us spent their time at an elementary school playground a few blocks from our house. The friends the twins did have were kids they met at that playground. Most were younger because boys their own age did not believe the twins were thirteen.

During some late afternoons and early evenings Susan, Robin and the twins joined me in the pool until their parents got home. With the Jensens around it was no more nudity or skinny dipping and hands off the neighbors. Even when it was just Adam, Donna and Alison and me, we behaved ourselves. It was just too tempting to fool around as a group if we started getting naked with each other again. My self imposed exile from nudity and the sex games came at a cost. I

was so used to playing around with other kids that I began frustrated and easily annoyed. Even though Donna and I were having sex, I missed my perverse lifestyle.

Susan finally got her license and that meant that we could get a lot more done. After allowing her to drive my car for a week and seeing that she was a careful driver, Ingrid and I decided to let her use my car and run some of the errands that had been exclusive to me when I was busy with other things. Everything was going really well until late one afternoon in mid-July when Mrs Jensen called and asked me to get one of her kids to go over to their house to check and make sure she had locked the back door. She thought that she might have left it unlocked.

With Susan running errands and doing some shopping for Ingrid, Robin shopping with friends and the twins up at the playground, I got the duty. We had spare keys to the Jensen house in case there was an emergency or one of their kids lost their keys and got locked out while their parents were working at their hotel. I was just finishing up some odd jobs for Ingrid anyway, so I grabbed the spare keys and headed across the street.

The front door was locked. I opened it, entered the house and went to check on the back door. It was locked, but I heard some noise in the twin's bedroom. John was in there covered in mud spots and packing a small suitcase. I asked him what the heck he was doing? He told me he was running away. He was sick of Florida, missed his friends in New York and planned to hitchhike back there.

Wow! This was not a good situation, but rather than just call his parents I decided to talk with John and find out what was going on. He told me that some boys had pushed him down on to a muddy area of the school playground created by rain the night before. Whenever they came by the playground the same boys always picked on him and Jerry because of their size. The boys were a little older than the twins and bigger. Knowing there was more to this situation then just John being bullied, I continued to question him.

It turned out that Jerry was having more success making friends than John was and he felt left out of everything. Susan was working for us, Jerry was always hanging with his new friends and Robin was off somewhere shopping with her girl friends. John wanted to go to the hotel and help his parents by doing odd jobs, but his folks said he was too young and worried about him being around so many strangers.

Having traveled extensively around New York City when I was much younger and often by myself, I explained the hazards of doing so for someone as young and inexperienced as John. Despite my words of wisdom, John was still set on leaving to return to New York and an uncertain future. Thinking that I needed time to get him out of his running away mode, I tried another tactic. I told John that no matter what he was planning, there was no way he could go anywhere looking the way he did.

I walked John into the bathroom and told him to take off his tee shirt which was covered in mud spots. His shoes and socks were next. After he took off his shoes, his socks were so muddy that they were stuck to his pants. John said to me, "I'll have to take off my pants to take off my socks." I replied, "Well then I guess you better do that." It was obvious that John was shy when

John was extremely cute and just what the doctor ordered as far as my game went. Instead of moving forward at that moment, I ran the bath water for him. He still had mud on him from the clothes he had been wearing and needed to take a really good bath. I said I would come back after I checked on the washer and talk with him some more. I left John to himself for a few minutes, than came back and found him sitting in the bath water washing himself off.

I pulled up the wooden chair and sat down in front of the tub. I told John that before he even thought about hitchhiking anywhere, there were some things he needed to know about life. One was the story of the birds and the bees. He looked at me oddly as I asked what he knew about sex? I admitted that he did not know much, so I told him that his penis was for more than just urinating. John told me he knew that, but not much more.

I told him to stand up in the bathtub so that I could show him what I meant. After he was on his feet and facing me I said that I needed to touch his penis to explain. He looked uncomfortable, but did make a protest about my statement. I told John that if he played with his dick, it would get hard and proceeded to jack him a little. His small penis responded immediately by becoming stiff. I explained about how it needed to hard to enter a girl.

Seeing some Vaseline on the bathroom shelf, I took a small amount and began to spread it lightly on John's penis. I jacked him with a tight grasp on his shaft and said that was how it felt when a guy's dick was inside a girl's vagina and they were having sex. I also explained that his testicles were there to produce semen so that he could ejaculate into a girl and that was how babies were made. I also pointed out that sex was not always about trying to make babies, but also about having fun.

As we talked I kept jacking John's penis to see if anything would happen. He became a bit impatient and I guessed he did not really like me touching it, so John brushed my hand away and began jacking it himself. His penis remained nice and hard, but nothing was happening so I suspected he needed more or better stimulation. I wiped the Vaseline off his penis, told him to finish his bath and then meet me in the bedroom that he shared with Jerry. After a short while John walked into the bedroom with a towel wrapped around him. I removed the towel and had him lay naked on his back on the bed.

I said that I could show him what it looked like when a guy ejaculated and began to open up my pants. As I did, John said, "If you take your clothes off I am going to put mine back on." He was smarter than I thought, so I said that I might be able to get him to ejaculate by oral stimulation and explained what a head job was. He might have been shocked or upset by what I was suggesting, but he did not show it.

Although John did not want me to take off my clothes, he was willing to let me try and suck him off. He knew that I had him alone in the house, at a disadvantage and that if he told his folks what we did it would ruin things for everyone. He even told me so! I agreed and said that as long as he did what I said and promised not to run away, I would keep my clothes on. I also promised to keep his misguided idea about hitchhiking back to New York a secret between us.

I got John into position and kneeled down at the the foot of his bed. As I began to suck him off, I loved the feeling and fit of John's small penis in my mouth. Even when it was stiff it still looked and felt small. Despite its size, John's dick still had lots of potential. I knew his dick would get bigger as he got older, but the twins were short and I doubted they would ever be very tall or end up well hung.

I was impressed by how stiff his penis was in my mouth and I suspected that sex would be a big part of John's passion once he got into it. Before long his penis jumped a bit and some liquid came out. It was not much and shot out instead of pumping, so I was not sure if it was semen or just the lubricant that always shot out first. Once I rolled the tiny amount of fluid around on my tongue and tasted it, I realized it was probably lubricant with a few drops of semen mixed in.

At that point I worried about the time and cut our session short. I did tell John that from that point on his body belonged to me and that anytime I wanted to see him naked and play around with him, he had better be available and ready for action. He didn't say anything, so I told him to get dressed in clean clothes and brought him back to my house. There was no way I was going to allow him be by himself just in case he tried to run away even after our agreement.

A few days slipped by and I felt confident that John was keeping our little secret. If he told his parents or sisters, they would be right up in my face. I doubted he would tell his twin because at that point they were barely even on speaking terms. Just to be sure things remained cool, I kept a close eye on John. He hung out at my house more often avoiding the playground and the bullies that ruled it. John and his siblings loved to use our pool and play games in our recreation room, so keeping him close was easy.

One evening as I watched the Jensen kids swim in our pool I felt particularly drawn to them. After what happened with John, I wanted a price of each one of them and it suddenly dawned on me that I was being too easily controlled and manipulated by Donna. I wanted a relationship with her, but we were not married for goodness sake! The games I liked to play were a big part of my life and without them I felt empty and more out of control then when I played them.

Ingrid and I still had sex with each other once in a while and I sensed that Donna knew about it. If she did, she let it slide knowing that we were inseparable. However, even my sessions with Ingrid did not fulfill the perverse need I had to play the sex games. What happened with John taught me that whether I liked it or not, those games where a big part of my life. When I refused to play them I felt lost and impotent. It was once again time to make some big changes and they had to begin with an adjustment to my relationship with Donna.

I took Donna aside one evening shortly after my adventure with John and told her that it was time for some changes. I said that I cared a great deal about her, but that I needed sex games to be happy. She thought I was being selfish. If I was it was needful. I had always been the Puppet Master, not a puppet. I was tired of pretending to be someone I was not. Donna did like my ultimatum, but surprised me by saying she would go along with the changes I had in mind as long as I kept my relationship with her a priority.

It was easy to read between the lines regarding what Donna said. She knew there would be others as I played my games. She just wanted to be first in my life and as long as that was the case Donna would tolerate my defects. Before I went after the other Jensen kids there was some unfinished business I had with John. I was really annoyed that I allowed a kid his age to dictate the terms of my game to me. That would change very soon as I planned our next session.

After finishing up my work late one afternoon, I found John playing in the recreation room. Susan and Robin were at the store doing the weekly grocery shopping for their folks, while Jerry was at a friend's house. With Ingrid and Diane out buying some supplies, it seemed like the perfect time to continue my session with John. I called him into my room, then shut and locked the door.

At the end of our last session I asked John to practice jacking himself off and let me know if he was able to ejaculate or shoot out any lubricant out without my help. I had him stand in front of me as I sat on the side of my bed and began to ask if he had any luck jacking off? He said he tried, but had no luck. I suspected he was lying and had not even tried, but that didn't really matter. It was time for me to have more fun and for him to learn to obey me.

I told John not to worry and that I would help him again. I ordered him to take off his clothes, beginning with his pants and underwear. John replied, "I don't really even want to." He said it in a meek and almost begging manner which I guessed was his attempt to avoid angering me. I stared at him without saying anything, then decided to act on a nasty thought that popped into my head while thinking of a Three Stooges episode I saw on TV the day before.

Acting in a typically and sarcastically "Moe" manner, I said, "That's alright kid. You don't have to take off your clothes. I mean, if you don't want to you should not have to, right?" Just as John shook his head in agreement with me, I suddenly grabbed his pants, pulled him towards me and snarled, "Come here, you!" I quickly pulled down his pants and underpants exposing his small and soft penis.

John knew he had made a huge mistake by not doing what I told him to do, so he played along saying, "See. It's not even hard, and when I make it get hard nothing really happens." I answered his observation by saying, "I'll take care of that, but first I have to get some punishment out of the way!" I told John that not obeying me was a big thing and that he still owed me for what he did the other day. I pulled the rest of his clothes off, then had him stand back in front of me.

I explained that I was going to punish him for what he did just then and for trying to tell me what to do the other day. I said he made a big mistake by not obeying me, but an even bigger one by threatening to put his clothes back on if I took mine off when we were in his house. I said that after his punishment, I was going to get naked and do whatever I liked with him.

I grabbed John, placed him over my knees and began spanking him hard enough to leave some red marks on his buttocks, but not hard enough to actually hurt him. After some really hard whacks to his butt, I said that punishment was for not obeying me right away. I then stood him up in front of me again. I got some Vaseline and put some on one of my fingers. I was determined to act out a fantasy I thought of one night as I jacked off in bed.

I had him stand sideways to me and began squeezing his testicles with one hand as I moved my other towards his anus. I pushed my lubricated finger slowly into his anus until just the tip penetrated him. John tried to move, but I had him from both ends and he could not. After he began begging me to stop, I ceased my torture and hugged him. I apologized and told John that I would never do that to him again as long as he did was I said from then on.

I got naked and made John jack me off as I jacked him. Before long my penis pumped out semen. John said, "That's gross!" I told him it was not gross. It was what would happen to him after he got a little older and more mature. Getting nothing out of his penis from the jack off session, I sucked him off and had better luck. His penis shot out the lubricant and semen mix again. I could taste the drops as they clung to the inside of my mouth.

I told John that he did a good job, then began lubricating my penis. He asked me what I was doing and looked very nervous (and rightfully so). I did not answer his question and sat up on the bed. I told him to sit in front of me the way he had while we jacked each other off. I sat with my back firmly supported against the bed's head board. Looking at John naked made my penis get instantly hard. He was really adorable and I especially liked the freckles he had scattered all over his face and chest.

I began by rubbing our penises together as I often liked to do, then I pushed John down flat on his back and pulled his legs and buttocks up towards me. I leaned his legs up against my chest, then pulled his buttocks up towards my penis until it began to slide into his butt crack. With full control of John's body, I began rubbing my penis between his butt cheeks just inside the crack. I knew there was no way that I could fully penetrate him with my dick because his opening was just too small, so I satisfied myself by pushing just the tip of my dick into his anus.

I was tempted to do more, but John was already in pain. He moaned and begged me to stop as his eyes teared up while I moved the tip of my penis in and out of his opening. Seeing his anguish, I took pity on my new friend and stopped. Instead of pushing my penis into him, I just rubbed it in his butt crack until I ejaculated. I figured that having at least pushed the tip of my dick into his anus counted as anal intercourse and I could cross that item off my game list.

After I cleaned myself and John's buttocks up, I had him get on his knees and suck me off. He knew better then to protest, so I gave him a break. When I finally ejaculated again I shot my load into a towel. I hoped there would be future sessions where he would suck me off and swallow my load, but even if that was possible it was still along way off. He needed more training and that would take some time.

After I finished my session with John I told him to keep his mouth shut about it. I knew that he would never tell anyone for any number of reasons including the fact that he did not lean towards playing around with boys. Even if I did not get much more from him, I had the fun I wanted and that got me back into the game. Now that I was active again I mentally put his twin Jerry and sisters on the 'to do' list for my games.

Things were getting dicey between me, Alison and Donna. Donna ignored my perversions for the most part and was willing to remain my girl friend with the understanding that anything else I did with anyone was just about my sex games. What she was not willing to do was allow me to fool around with her sister. That was just too close and personal. With that in mind I continued to encourage the relationship between Alison and Wilson. They were getting along well, but that was not enough for Alison.

Alison was not an easy person to ignore. I could see that she was obsessed with me. Given my own nature I completely understood how she felt. Once I set my eyes on a target, that was it! It was not about love, sex or even attraction. It was just about obsession. I knew that giving in to Alison and sneaking around behind Donna's back was not the answer. I suspected that part of Alison's obsession with me was having her sister know that we were fooling around together. Having no doubt she would tattle on me to Donna, I to handle her in another way.

After giving it a lot of thought, I visited the head shop on the beach where I bought condoms. It was just the kind of off the grid store that sold all sorts of stuff including some sex toys. I knew that Alison had a small opening. If I could make sex between us really hurt, maybe she would back off? I purchased a huge dildo and hoped it would help do the trick.

One afternoon after I finished running errands for my cousin, Ingrid took Donna and Susan to the store with her for supplies. Afterward, they planned to have an early dinner together at a nice restaurant across town. It would be a kind of reward or perk for a job well done. Alison was also invited, but I convinced her to stay behind promising a nice surprise.

After the others left I brought Alison up to my bedroom. I told her that I was willing to fool around with her once in a while, but that she could not tell Donna and would have to play my game the way I wanted her to play it. She smiled and was all in with my idea. Before long we were naked and making out in my bed. At some point I began having intercourse with her. Needless to say, I wore a condom.

After we did it for a while and I shot my load into her, I got Alison into the position for anal sex. Like most girls she hated it, but I was the Puppet Master and was going to do whatever I wanted with her. After lubricating myself up really good, I went all out and really gave it to her with passion. Alison was in tears by the time I finished, but the worst was yet to come.

I turned her back over and acted like I was going to have regular intercourse with her again, but instead I took the dildo out of a drawer and began lubricating it. Alison asked me what I was going to do with it? I said I was going to use it to help stretch her hole and make it bigger. I said that as much as I liked the tightness of her opening, after a while it began to hurt my penis.

I could see that Alison was scared of the dildo and as I began sticking it into her she grimaced in pain. The dildo was supple enough to go into her and simulate a real penis, but hard enough to penetrate any sized opening including one as small as hers. I really went at it until Alison started crying and begged me to take it out. I did, but said we were not done yet.

I turned Alison over and began trying to push the dildo into her anus. She immediately jumped up and off the bed screaming that there was no way I was going to shove that huge thing into her ass! I told her that if she wanted to have sex with me, the dildo was a part of my game that she would have to deal with. Alison called me a freak, got dressed and said she was done with me.

I knew that Alison would never tell her sister about what happened. She probably figured that I was doing the same thing with Donna. If her sister could handle it and she could not, that would be a major embarrassment for Alison and one that in her mind was not worth outing me for. After she calmed down we both talked. We agreed not to tell Donna about our fling and to avoid future sexual encounters with each other. My problem with Alison was solved.

With Donna and Alison working for Ingrid at our house from Monday to Thursday that left the rest of the week as an opportunity for me to have some fun with the Jensen kids. As much as I wanted to fool around with Susan and Robin, I knew that Jerry should be next on my list. The idea of playing my game with identical twins was just too enticing to ignore. I waited until he was at my house by himself and no one else was around to get things started.

John was attending the birthday party of the one real friend he had who lived a few blocks away. He liked John, but did not get along with Jerry. Susan and Robin were out shopping with their mom. Ingrid was over Diane's house and not expected home until late. Jerry was in our pool when I came outside in my swimsuit and joined him. He was friendly as usual, but I sensed that my lone presence made him feel a little uncomfortable. I figured that John had said something. I knew he would never tell his twin or anyone else what really happened between us, but he might have told Jerry to avoid being alone with me.

I tried to smooth things over by talking to Jerry and playing pool volleyball with him. He began to respond better to me and we got along pretty well from that point on. After we got out of the pool I made Jerry a snack and got us some cold drinks. While we sat on the patio and dried off I asked Jerry if he was shy? He said he wasn't, so I told him that I needed some help with something. I said I was developing a new game for kids between his age and mine.

Jerry looked at me nervously, but unlike his brother he was a lot more agreeable with people. Jerry asked me what the game was? I said that I could not really explain it and needed to show him. After we were dry I brought Jerry upstairs. I told him that first I needed him to take a shower and wash the pool chemicals off his body. We almost always did that after a swim anyway, so my request was not unusual.

To test his shyness I followed him into the bathroom and told Jerry to take off his swimsuit. I said I would throw it in the dryer and get his clothes for him from the spare bedroom where he always changed when he used our pool. Jerry was not thrilled about getting naked in front of me, but I guessed he also did not want to look like a prude. He counted 1...2...3, dropped his swimsuit to the floor and quickly got into the shower hoping that I would not see much.

By the time I came back with Jerry's clothes he was finished showering and wrapped in a towel. Instead of handing him all his clothes, I only gave him his underpants explaining that for the purposes of my game I needed him to leave the other things off for now. Jerry reluctantly

dropped the towel, got into his underpants and followed me into my bedroom. Once inside I closed the door, locked it and began explaining what I needed for him to do.

I took out my trusty dirty book and showed Jerry some naked photos of boys and girls his age. I asked if he liked looking at them? He said he did, but I had no idea if that was the truth or if he was just playing along with me to look cool. Either way, I told him that when he started Junior High that fall he would have to take showers in P.E. class. That meant that he would have to show his body to other kids and he would get to see theirs. I knew that Jerry was not as modest as his brother, but he was still kind of shy and I was sure he would not like getting naked in the shower with other boys.

I explained that in the past I had strip clubs and such which allowed boys to see each other naked. That made it easier for them to deal with showering naked in front of each other when they started Junior High. It also gave them a chance to learn about sex and play around with each other. Jerry listened to me carefully, still glancing at the photos in the book occasionally as I spoke. I asked Jerry if he knew about sex? He said he knew that boys and girls did it with each other, but he was not sure how.

I said that I was going to help him learn about sex while practicing my new game idea on him just in case I decided to start up a new strip club. Although it was a lame excuse, I expected it sounded credible enough to pass muster and provide me with the opportunity to have some fun with him. I reached over and began to take off Jerry's underpants explaining that he needed to be naked for my lesson. He allowed me to pull his underpants down and take them off, then sat up on the bed as I instructed with the book still in his hand.

I gave Jerry the basics explaining how guys and girls had sex, then told him that his penis needed to get hard to penetrate a girl. I began touching his dick and jacking it until it was stiff. As I jacked him I explained more about sex, including how he would eventually ejaculate if his body was ready for that. Jerry looked surprised at my revelations, so I doubted that he had ever played with himself. He looked at a photo of a naked young girl in the book while I jacked him off.

After a while Jerry did the same thing his brother did and pushed my hand away from his penis. He said he would jack himself. He was doing a pretty good job, but nothing was happening. Sensing it was a good time to introduce him to French kissing and oral sex, I explained that sometimes boys fooled around with each other for fun and practice so that they would be ready when a girl was available.

After some finessing, Jerry allowed me to show him how to French kiss. We laid on the bed facing each other and went at it. I loved kissing him and kept going until he finally began pushing his tongue into my mouth the way I pushed mine into his. I occasionally played with his penis and hugged him while we Frenched, then decided to move on. At that point I told Jerry about circle jerks and oral sex. I said that I thought I should try oral sex on him explaining that it might help him ejaculate for the first time.

I got Jerry into position while I kneeled down at the edge of the bed and began sucking his dick. Before long his penis began to throb. I grabbed his hands and held them as I sucked. Every once

but I liked holding his penis and directing his stream into the toilet. Rather than ask him to hold mine, I had him stand to the side of me and jacked his dick with one hand while holding my own penis with the other to direct its urine stream.

After our weird bathroom adventure, I cleaned off our penises with a wash rag and we went back into my bedroom. I had Jerry stand at the foot of my bed and bend over until he was laying on his stomach with his feet on the floor. After lubricating my penis, I began rubbing it in his butt crack. Jerry asked me what I was doing? I told it I was going to have sex with him and gently pushed the tip of my penis into his anus.

As I moved my crown in and out of his anus, Jerry kept quiet. I guessed that it did not really hurt him much because I had barely penetrated his opening. After I while I started pushing my dick just a little deeper into him. Jerry loudly proclaimed, "Oh, that hurts!" I pulled back and just satisfied myself with moving the tip of my penis in and out of his opening. I liked Jerry too much to hurt him, so I stopped messing around with his butt and cleaned off my penis before I had a chance to shoot my load.

I ordered Jerry to kneel on the floor and suck me off just as his brother had. In a moment of evil weakness, I said he had better swallow my load or I would stick my dick all the way into his ass as soon as it got hard again. Before long I ejaculated and to my surprise Jerry kept my stiff penis in his mouth as it pumped away. He grimaced and almost choked during a few forced swallows, but my new sex partner got the job done and did it well.

Jerry got up and ran into the bathroom to rinse his mouth out. After he returned, I told him to go shower and dress. We went downstairs together and watched TV until it was time for him to go home. As I thought about what we did together I guessed that Jerry had at least a slight leaning towards boys. He was much more into my sex games than his brother and actually seemed to enjoy them a bit when he allowed himself to do so.

I did not want to push things much further with either of the twins right then and there, so I decided to lay off them until I had a chance to score with their sisters. I liked both the girls, but I had a particular attraction to Robin. She would also be the easier of the two sisters to score with, so I set out to conquer her first. I loved her cute face, well rounded breasts and short statue.

Robin was already kind of wild and had sent me signals that she liked me. She did things like jump on my lap as I sat around watching TV and hung on to me so that her breasts rubbed up against my chest when we were in the pool together. Even with her swimsuit top on I could feel the tips rub against me. Of course it was always possible that I was misreading the situation, but she did those things in front of her sister and anyone else present. I suspected she might be marking her territory in a weird sort of way.

Robin was almost always with her family or friends, so it was difficult to get her alone. My first opportunity to play around with her came on a Saturday afternoon a few days after I played my game with Jerry. Since that time he and John were trying to avoid me by staying at their house instead of coming to mine whenever possible. Little did they know that they were actually doing me a favor on that particular day.

Robin and Susan came over to hang out at my house and go into the pool while my parents were away for the weekend and theirs were working at the hotel. Ingrid was out with Diane and their friends, so that just left Susan as an obstacle to my fun with Robin. While I tried to think of a way to get her out of the picture for a while, my old friend Fate intervened on my behalf. We were all playing a board game out on the patio when Susan's parents called and asked if she could come and help out at the hotel for a few hours?

After Mrs. Jensen came and picked Susan up, Robin and I decided it was time for a dip in the pool. She had her bathing suit with her and headed upstairs to use the spare bedroom to get changed. I followed her and said, "Hey, why don't you just get changed in my room with me?" Robin smiled and said, "You're a bad boy!" I replied, "The worst!"

I suspected that Robin wanted to see me naked as bad as I wanted to see her and I was right. She followed me into my room and slowly began taking off her clothes. I stood watching her for a few moments to see what she would say. Once she was down to her bra and panties, Robin looked over at me said, "Well, what about you?" I took off everything except my tee shirt and underpants.

We reached a stalemate. Robin and I stood looking at each other in our underwear. We laughed nervously and she said, "It's your turn!" I walked towards her, picked her up and placed her on my bed. As I did, I took off my tee shirt and laid next to her while she asked me in an excited voice what I was doing? I said I was taking my turn, then I began kissing her. She responded to my kisses and before long we were Frenching.

As we kissed I began touching her ample breasts which were still caged in her bra. Robin sighed and said, "I want to, but I am afraid." I pulled her on top of me, reached around her back and began fumbling with the bra catch until it was undone. I laid her back on her side while slowly removing her bra until it was completely off. She had nice large nipples that begged to go into my mouth.

As I sucked on her breasts gently, Robin moaned and quietly said, "I can't. I can't." Despite her protests she did not try and stop me from pulling her panties off after I finished sucking on her breasts. I threw her panties on the floor and stared at the nice patch of dark brown pubic hair that Robin had. It sat above her opening, but did not circle it as with some girls. Robin had very little body hair which made her look even younger than she was.

I pulled down my underpants, threw them off the bed and went back to making out with Robin. After we stopped kissing, I lead her hand to my penis. She grasped it and began pulling on it in a way which told me she wanted it to get as hard as possible. My penis obliged and became stiff in short order. Robin sat playing with it while I was laying flat on the bed, so I said, "Why don't you try putting it in your mouth and sucking on it like a lollypop?"

Robin looked at me like I was an alien, laughed and asked, "Are you kidding?" I assured her I was not. She played along by asking me what it would taste like? I said she would never know

until she tried tasting it. After shrugging her shoulders and smiling, she surprised me by taking me up on my offer. Robin laid down, pushed herself up on her hands and tried sucking my dick.

She put it in her mouth, then took it right out when some public hair got into her mouth. She said, "Yuck!" and tried again. Robin slowly sucked my penis until she got the hang of it. After a short while I could see that she really liked sucking my dick and went at it with typical youthful enthusiasm. I asked her to stop so that I would not ejaculate, then said, "My turn."

I had Robin lay down and dove for her vagina. I licked her down there and stuck my tongue into her hole as far as it would go. Her opening was medium sized, had well defined lips and I easily slid several fingers in until they hit her hymen. Robin acted surprised as I licked and fingered her. I doubt she even knew exactly what it was I was doing, but from the look on her face she appeared to like it.

Just as I was about to get into position to have intercourse with her, Robin must have figured out what I was up to and grabbed me. She pulled me back down next to her and began making out with me again. Between kisses she said, "I want to...but I can't. I'll get in trouble and so will you." I told Robin not to worry, bounced back up and before she could stop me I was pushing my penis into her opening. No lubricant, no condom, just brute force and will power!

Robin took a quick breath and shuttered a little as I pushed my penis through her hymen. I loved the way my dick fit perfectly inside of her. It slid in and out easily and before long Robin was wet inside. She was into what I was doing and hardly uttered a word as I jammed myself into her as hard as I could. It might have been the best sex I ever had with a girl. There was just something about her that really turned me on.

I led Robin through several different positions as we had intercourse. We did it doggie style and she liked that one the best. I even got her to get on top of me and go up and down on my stiff penis. My dick was numb by the time we finished and I finally ejaculated into Robin. She knew that I shot my load because I held her down tightly on my penis as I ejaculated into her. After I finished she laid down next to me, we began making out again and melted in each other's arms.

Things had not gone exactly as I planned. I wanted to have sex with Robin, but ended up making love to her. As soon as we finished and Robin went in to clean herself up in the bathroom I knew I had made a mistake. She was too young and acted too wild for a real relationship. What we did certainly meant something to her, but it was even more meaningful to me and that was not a good thing. I did not need to fall for a young girl like her and end up having my heart ripped out of my chest from an emotional standpoint.

After we both cleaned up and got into our bathing suits, we didn't say much to each other for a while. We just went swimming in the pool and every once in a while looked at each other, smiled and laughed. She said, "I can't believe we did that!" I told Robin that I really liked her and enjoyed what we did. I knew better than to ask her if she liked it. Guys always ask girls those kinds of questions after sex and girls hate being asked them. Sex is a more much private thing to them and one they normally hate to talk about.

Although I ignorantly did not use a condom on that occasion, I was not really prepared for the feelings I experienced or the way we just started doing it. I thought it would have taken me a long time to get into her pants, but that was not the case. Once we got going I really wanted to feel myself inside Robin and to have her absorb my semen into her body. I wanted to become a part of her and for her to become a part of me.

As we swam around Robin again surprised me. She began holding me and making out with me in the pool. I did not figure her for the romantic type. I had her pegged as a young wild child that was going to have sex with somebody very soon, so it might just as well have been with me. Now she was acting like we were boyfriend and girlfriend. The way she kissed me told me she liked me and that it was not just about physical contact.

The Robin situation was a major complication for me. I had started something that I did not regret, but was also not completely ready to deal with. As much as I liked Robin I also had to deal with Donna who was now embedded in my family thanks to her work with Ingrid. Rather than over think the situation, I just let things be for the moment and hoped that things would eventually work themselves out in my favor.

After Robin's parents came home she went back to her house. I was alone on a Saturday night. It was the first time in a long time that happened and I welcomed the quiet solitude. Donna called and we made plans to go out together during the coming week, but I needed the weekend to recharge my physical and emotional batteries. Susan was next on my list and having already befriended her, she would be a challenge.

Sunday started out as a lazy day. I watched TV until mid-morning when Ingrid came home and we had brunch together. I always enjoyed spending time with her. After a shower and a change of clothes she was off again to spend some time at the mall with her friends. Before I could decide what I was going to do for the rest of the day my doorbell rang. It was Robin with some friends. I invited them in wondering what was up?

Robin amassed a small following of close friends which included girls and boys. Kathleen had dark hair, a cute face and tons of freckles everywhere. She looked younger than she was and had a very sports-like physique with small breasts. Patty had blond hair, pale skin and was almost as tall as I was with a very thin body and nice breasts. Jenny had dirty blond hair, a shapely thin body with nice breasts, fair skin and a perfect face. She could have easily been a teen model.

Robin also had some friends that were boys. Rob was from England having come here as a young child. He no longer had the accent. His dad was a naturalized American citizen originally from Ireland who married a British girl while he was working for an American company in the U.K. After his wife developed a serious illness and eventually past away, Rob's dad brought him and his younger sister Rosemary back to the USA and took a job Stateside.

Rob had very short blond hair, a well built body and was a little shorter than me. He had a great personality. His sister Rosemary had long blond hair and was about Robin's height. She was adorable with a very cute freckled face and a great body with ample breasts. Unlike her brother she could be moody sometimes, but she got along with everyone and tended to hang out with

Robin and the rest of her friends most of the time. Colin was a boy Robin's age with a slim build and medium length dark hair. He was a very good looking boy that some of the girls liked to chase after.

All of Robin's friends hung out as a group. Most of them were thirteen years old, the same as her. Rob and Rosemary were the exceptions. Rob was fourteen and his sister Rosemary was twelve. As soon as I met Robin's friends I began to size them up. The girls were mostly into what most thirteen year old girls were into in those days which was make up, music and mayhem. Not that they were bad kids, just wild like Robin.

Susan disapproved of Robin's friends, but I was more open minded. I welcomed Robin and her friends into my house beginning that Sunday. I knew they needed a place to hang out and I did not mind if that place was my place as long as they behaved and were not there all the time. I actually enjoyed having them around and quickly became good friends with Rob. He was barely a year younger than I was and we had a lot in common as far as our personalities went.

I saw some potential in that group as far as my games were concerned, but I was no longer willing to take a chance on group activities with younger kids involved. If I was going to have fun it would have to be with one of them at a time. My first opportunity came with Rob. His father's name was Eddie. He was still a single dad and reliable babysitters were as hard to come by back then as they are today.

After Eddie met my cousin and parents when he stopped over to pick up Rob a couple of times, he was impressed with our values and the fact that my adult cousin was around most of the time when my parents were out to provide adult supervision. Eddie was a strict parent who believed in keeping his kids on a short leash.

Whenever he was unable to find a babysitter or had to go out of town on business for a few days, Eddie asked my parents and cousin if Rob and his sister could stay with us. That was never a problem for my folks and I loved having them around. My only problem was that each time they stayed over there were too many other people around for me to try and score with them.

During the middle of summer Eddie came over to our house one evening to ask my parents a favor. He was being sent out of the country for a month and would not be able to bring Rob and Rosemary with him. He wondered if they could stay with us? My parents asked me what I thought about it and I said it would be great! I got along really well with both of them and especially enjoyed having Rob around. My parents gave their approval and it was a done deal.

Although they said no monetary assistance was asked for or needed, Eddie was the kind of guy that never wanted a free ride and left a stack of cash on the coffee table to cover his kid's housing and food expenses. He also left Rob and Rosemary with some spending money. A few days later the siblings arrived with some luggage. I got them settled into the spare bedroom upstairs and began to make some plans of my own for the month to come.

As much as I liked Rob as a friend, the nasty side of me was again attracted to the idea of playing my game with yet another set of siblings. The only obstacle was Susan. She was still a name on

my list which I could not yet check off. I had gotten sidetracked by Robin, the frequent presence of her friends at the house, my work for Ingrid, my relationship with Donna and the new development of Rob and Rosemary staying at our house. However, it was time to get back on track.

Fate again threw me a bone in the form of a development with Donna and Alison. Their parents decided to send them to a month long camp during the middle of summer vacation. Their church would pay for the entire thing and sent the invitation to the sisters, so it would be hard to turn it down. With Donna out of the picture for a month, I had a much better chance of having my way with Susan and anyone else I wanted. The bad news for Susan was that she had to do a lot more work for my cousin to replace Donna and Alison.

Things between Robin and I cooled off a bit as I expected. We continued to have sex when there was no one else around, but our physical relationship did not transfer into a dating one. Thankfully, I did not feel as bad about that as I thought I might. The presence of so many new prospects kept me happy and hopeful. The only downside of the whole thing was that with so many people around it was difficult to get the alone time I needed with Susan to set things in motion with her.

After trying my best to secure some alone time with Susan at the house, I gave up and moved on to Plan B. With Ingrid busy at home and available to keep an eye on Rob and Rosemary, I decided to treat Susan to a visit to the hotel. The timing was perfect because Ingrid bought a present for Susan to thank her for all the extra help she provided after Donna and Alison went away to camp. One afternoon after work I asked her if she would like to come to the hotel where my dad worked for a cruise on the charter boat, dinner and a show.

A couple of times a week during the busy season the charter fishing boat anchored on the bay side of the hotel complex took guests out for an evening cruise. It was romantic and fun. I figured that after the cruise we could eat dinner in the restaurant, then head for the lounge where a popular local show band was playing that night. Susan shared a passion for live music with me and I was certain all those activities would help set the stage for some fun in the suite afterward. Of course I did not mention anything to her about my plans to take her up to the suite or the present that Ingrid had there waiting for her.

Susan accepted my invitation and got permission from her parents to go to the hotel with me. We both dressed up and headed out to the hotel around five to make sure we got there to make the evening boat cruise which started at six. The cruise was all I hoped it would be and more. Susan was normally shy compared to Robin, but the time we spent working together for Ingrid had already been an ice breaker for us and the cruise was just icing on the cake.

As we stood at the rail of the boat looking at the calm water and beautiful tropical scenery that passed by, we talked about our lives and enjoyed our time together. I was surprised at how close we had become by that time. After the cruise we had a wonderful dinner, then went into the lounge and had a great time watching and listening to the local band. After the show ended, I told Susan that I had a surprise for her.

As we headed to the suite I explained that one of the perks my dad enjoyed as the manager of the hotel property was a free suite that was exclusive to us. I told her how we could use it anytime and that her surprise was waiting there for her. Susan didn't mind going to the suite. She knew I was involved with Donna and having been at my house many times tended to trust me.

As I opened the door to the suite Susan was suddenly surprised and excited to see a brand new expensive bicycle sitting in the middle of the floor. Susan had wanted a nice bicycle for some time. Even though she had her drivers license and was an excellent driver, she liked biking around town for fun and exercise.

I told Susan that the bicycle was from Ingrid, while the cruise, dinner and the show were from me. As Susan checked out her new bike, I opened the suite curtains to reveal the beautiful Gulf view. As soon as she finished looking at the bike, I took her on a quick tour of the suite which ended in my bedroom.

Susan admired the nice bed I had in there and flopped down on it on her back with her legs hanging over the front edge. She said, "Wow, it's been an amazing day!" I agreed and flopped down next to her. Before she could do anything else, I turned over so that I was on top of her and kissed her on the cheek. I then rolled off her and laid on my back again.

Susan looked shocked and said, "Wow, you waited a long time to do that! I was about to give up on you." Susan confided that she had a crush on me and wanted us to date for a long time. She did not want to break up Donna and me, but she noticed we had not been seeing much of each other and hoped I would go after her. This was yet another major complication I had not counted on.

I did not to over think the situation about her liking me and just decided to see how far I could go with Susan. I told her to get up off the bed, then I stood right in front of her. I took off my shirt and tee shirt, then began lifting up her blouse. She rolled her eyes, but did not stop me from taking off her top. I stopped there and made out with her. Before long we were French kissing, so I reached around and unhooked her bra.

Susan tried to cover her small breasts as I pulled off her bra, but I held her hands at her sides and hugged her so that our chests met. I pulled her back into bed and we made out for a long time. I really enjoyed kissing her and she was good at it. At some point I unsnapped her jeans and tried pulling them down. Susan grabbed my hands and said she was not ready for that. I said that it was too late to tell me she was not ready and I managed to pull off her jeans.

Susan was annoyed with me, but not enough to try and get away from me. I got up and pulled off my own pants, then laid back down next to her. We made out some more until she said that she had to use the bathroom. After Susan came back from the bathroom she tried grabbing her top, bra and jeans from off the floor to get dressed. I jumped off the bed and stopped her, then pushed her down on the bed and got on top of her.

I had no idea what set off Susan's attempt to flee, but I was now in a very precarious situation. Rather than do anything more, I asked, "What's the matter?" Susan told me she was worried

about having sex. She did not mind making out in her underwear and was even willing to get naked, but sex was something she feared. She had a friend back in New York who got pregnant while she was in junior high and that destroyed her life.

I rolled off Susan and as we laid next to each other in the bed we talked for a while. I told her that if she wanted to stop what we were doing right then and there it was fine by me. I understood her fear of getting pregnant, but promised that I would not shoot my load into her if we did go all the way. As we talked, Susan became more relaxed and told me she wanted to make out with me some more and try it naked.

Susan slid out of her panties. She had a plentiful crop of strawberry blond pubic hair which hid her opening well. That surprised me because like her sister she did not have hardly any body hair. After I took off my underwear we began kissing again and touching each other. I gently fondled her small breasts and then began to kiss them. I moved down to Susan's opening and started licking her.

Susan asked, "What are you doing?" I replied, "Something you will like." Her opening was about the same size as Robin's even though she was taller. I loved licking her well defined lips amidst her soft strawberry blond pubic hair and pushed my tongue in as far as it would go. Susan began to move around in a way which told me she liked what I was doing. After her body shuttered a few times, she asked me to stop and pulled me back up towards her.

Susan began touching my penis and playing with it. As she did I kissed her and gently touched her breasts again. She got me so turned on that I could no longer help myself. I jumped up and pulled her towards the edge of the bed, then spread her legs apart and shoved my penis into her. With her opening already wet from my licking, it slid right in and pushed through her hymen right away. As it did, Susan took a quick breath and swallowed hard.

I pulled Susan even closer to me and kept thrusting my penis into her as hard as I could. She made a few sounds and acted as though she was out of breath, but said nothing. After a while my penis was numb, so I stopped for an instant to reposition my new lover. I turned Susan over and pulled her down until her legs were on the floor. I spread them apart and had intercourse with her doggie style. She made sounds which told me that she really liked what I was doing.

I finally felt ready to shoot my load, so I pulled my penis out of her and ejaculated on to her buttocks. Afterward I helped Susan up and lead her to the bathroom. While she showered I got a huge beach towel for her to dry off and cover herself with afterward. After a few minutes Susan came out of the bathroom wrapped in the towel and smiled at me. That was good news because I knew that I had kind of forced myself on her.

I unwrapped her out of the towel, laid her back on the bed and laid down next to Susan. I began making out with her, then worked my way back down to her opening. I began to lick her again until she practically begged me to stop. Deciding that I wanted more, I turned her over and got Susan into the position for anal sex. I'm sure she thought that I was just preparing to do it doggie style with her again, so this would be a big and perhaps unwelcome surprise!

I lubricated my penis and then began rubbing it between her butt cheeks as if I was going to slide it down and into her vagina, but that was not the plan. I took hold of Susan's shapely buttocks and began gently pushing my penis into her anus. Susan yelled, "Hey, you got the wrong hole!" I assumed that she thought I missed my mark, but I quickly corrected her by saying, "I got the one I wanted!"

Susan tried to get up, but I pushed her down and told her to lie still and give what I was doing a try. I promised to stop if she did not like it after my penis was all the way in and I moved it in and out a few times. She still struggled, but it looked to me like her anus was large enough to accommodate my dick without doing any damage or causing much pain. I penetrated her all the way, then began moving my penis in and out. Even though Susan surprisingly settled down and just let me do my thing for a couple of minutes, she began crying after that so I stopped and pulled my dick out of her anus.

I turned Susan back over, went up to her face and kissed her. She was not angry, just surprised and a little disappointed at what I did to her. I promised to never do that again, made out with her and soon her tears stopped flowing. The more we made out, the more passionate our kisses became. I stopped briefly, cleaned off my penis and laid flat on my back. I was really horny and my dick was again very stiff.

I positioned Susan on top of me and told her to let my penis slide into her. She shifted her position several times until it did, then Susan followed my instructions by moving up and down on my dick. She really got into it after a while and before long my penis was again numb. At some point I felt an ejaculation coming on, so I told Susan to stop and climb off me so that I could ejaculate into a towel.

Susan got off me, but had a surprise of her own ready. She quickly wiped my penis with a towel and began sucking me off before I shot my load. When I finally ejaculated, Susan swallowed my entire load. While she was wiping off my penis I asked her, "Wow! Where did you learn how to do that?" She admitted that although she had never had intercourse or even got naked with a guy before, she did give a guy she knew blow jobs every once in a while.

When her family still lived in New York a guy that was dating a friend of hers who lived next store used to come by looking for her friend so that they could go out. The first time he did not find his girlfriend home one afternoon, he knocked on Susan's door to ask where she was? When she said she did not know, he asked to use her phone. She let him in and he called around, but was unable to find out where she was.

Susan was home by herself and not supposed to let anyone in, so she asked him to leave. He said that his girlfriend should have been home when he came by and that he needed a favor from her. He told her he wanted a blow job and Susan told him to leave. He was much bigger and stronger than her. He took down his pants and underpants, then forced Susan's mouth towards his penis until she began sucking on his dick.

He did not ask or force her to take off her clothes or do anything else, but he punched her in the chest when she took his penis out of her mouth while he was shooting his load. After he left

Susan said she cried and wondered what to do? His family was close with her friend and telling on him could cause all sorts of trouble in the neighborhood. She decided to keep quiet hoping that what happened was a one time thing, but the guy came back a few days later. After she answered the door he pushed his way into the house and got her on the couch.

Once again the guy forced Susan to suck him off, but this time she followed his instructions and swallowed his semen to avoid getting punched again. This went on two more times over a couple of weeks until Susan could not take it anymore and told her friend what was happening. As big as he was, her friend's brother was bigger and went after the guy. Based on what her friend told her later, he got beat to within an inch of his life and never troubled Susan again.

Susan said that she hated giving that guy a blow job, but at least she learned something from the experience. I felt honored that after the horrible way she was introduced to oral sex Susan would perform it on me. Once again we cleaned up, then made out some more. After we showered and dressed, we took Susan's new bike and put it into my car. I was time for her to go home. As I drove back to our neighborhood Susan hinted that she wanted us to date if I was no longer seeing Donna. I said that we could date regardless of Donna and left things at that.

Susan was a surprise in so many ways. I really liked her, but I also knew that because I was having sex with her sister and brothers this was not something that could last. After I dropped Susan home and went into my own house I began to think that I had a terrible mistake by getting involved sexually with her. I figured that I could probably keep my experiences with John and Jerry a secret since they had no desire for anyone to find out about what we did, but Robin was another story. She was the ultimate wildcard.

Robin and I were still having sex and I knew that if Susan found out she would probably go ballistic, even if Robin did not. While Robin did not mind just screwing with me without all the romantic entanglements, Susan had a high sense of moral values. She and I were the same age and liked each other so sex was appropriate enough even if she got kind of forced into it by me, but in her mind there would just be no excuse for me to be having any sort of a physical relationship with her younger sister.

As if things were not crazy enough, Robin began using me as a kind of problem solver for her friends. I guess I had a natural gift for troubleshooting situations because I had been through so much and was always forced to find my own solutions to almost every problem which came along. Rob had a problem and it was a big one. At fourteen he was dating a girl almost a year younger than him and one that enjoyed having sex.

I cannot say that Rob was a sex fiend, but his girlfriend was. She lost her virginity at just twelve years of age and had been having sex ever since. Rob was the third guy she had intercourse with (on multiple occasions) and once they started having sex they did not stop. Even though Rob was living with us and we got along really well, I guessed that he was not quite ready to share the intimate details of his life with me. He did share them with Robin, but that was all he shared with her.

Rob was a great boyfriend in terms of loyalty. Robin told me that a lot of girls liked him, but he stuck with his girlfriend and did not fool around on her. The problem was that she did not believe that. She was not just sex crazy, but I think she was also mental. Even with them doing it two or three times a day at her house when no one was home, she was still certain he was seeing someone else. I just wondered when she thought he would have the time to do that?

After he told her she was crazy and that he wanted to get away from her, his now ex-girlfriend got back at him for her wacky belief that he was cheating on her by telling her friends that he was actually gay and cheating on her with a guy named Mitchell. The rumor spread quickly and made trouble for everyone involved. Mitchell was Rob's age, big boned, well built and taller. He could easily beat Rob to a pulp if he wanted to and that was exactly what it looked like would happen unless I intervened.

Robin knew Mitchell, so I asked him to come over to talk with me before he kicked Rob's butt. Robin told me that Mitchell was very sensitive to any rumors about him being gay because of an incident that occurred about a year before. He had gone on an overnight trip to a nearby lake with a couple of his friends. One of their parents dropped them off and picked them up the next day. The boys camped in a tent overnight, went swimming and did some fishing during the day.

Mitchell was a nice kid, but he was a follower. When his two friends began drinking the wine that one of them got from an older brother, they invited Mitchell to join them. He did not drink, so after he and his friends ended up finishing off a couple of bottles of strong wine he was barely conscious. All three boys still had their bathing suits on from going swimming during the day, so one of the two other boys said they should change into dry clothes before going to sleep.

As they all took off their bathing suits and were naked in front of each other, the two other boys noticed that Mitchell had a huge woody. They automatically figured that Mitchell's penis was hard because he liked seeing them naked and that started a nasty rumor which had never gone away. Anyone that knew Mitchell knew that he had never actually made any advances towards any boys, but once the rumor was started the damage was done. Mitchell told his other friends that he probably had a woody from the wine.

Rob's ex-girlfriend knew exactly how to do the most damage to him. Mitchell was furious and blamed Rob for the problem. Robin brought him over to talk with me to see if I could make peace between the two victims of a nutty and very over-sexed girl. Mitchell was as tall as I was with a large framed body, black hair and fair skin. He was not overly handsome, but not bad looking either.

As Robin, Rob and Mitchell sat with me in my house I explained the situation to Mitchell. Rob apologized for what his girlfriend said, but everyone already knew she was kind of nutty. Robin promised to help quell the rumor and make Rob's ex an outcast among the local girls. Mitchell knew that with Robin on the case the problem would probably go away and was not worth beating Rob up over. Mitchell also liked the fact that I would vouch for where Rob was whenever his ex claimed he was fooling around with him.

Things were straightened out and Mitchell became a part of Robin's group and yet another kid who often visited my house. I grew to like him and admired the huge bulge he had in his pants. The first time he came over to go swimming I could see that nature had been generous to Mitchell in terms of penis and testicle size. Even with a loose fitting bathing suit on his family jewels shined through.

Despite the unexpected addition of Mitchell to our little group, I could not let my interest in him side track me from Rob. He and his sister were next on my list because they would only be staying with me for a month and it was time to take full advantage of that. Rob and his sister respected each other, but were not really close. After a few nighttime disagreements, she refused to sleep in the spare bedroom with him.

Even though he slept on a cot while she used the bed, Rosemary knew that he liked to whack off at night and could sometimes hear him doing it. She did not want to be in the same bedroom when he did, so I moved Rob in with me. That was just the break I had been looking for and I took full advantage of it. The first time he got changed and naked in front of me fate gave me another break. I noticed that his testicles were really swollen and said that he needed to do something about it.

While I was having sex with a lot of girls at the same time I had the same problem after I reduced my pool of sex partners. My brilliant friend Clarence did some book work and found out that my testicles might have been were swollen because I was used to having a lot of sex, then cut way back as my list of girl friends dropped off. With Rob having constant sex with his ex-girlfriend and stopping cold turkey after they split up, the explanation made sense.

With Rob's sister on him about whacking off while they slept in the same bedroom, he was not even able to relieve himself by jacking off and ejaculating a couple of times each day. It all fit and gave me the perfect and very legitimate excuse to get Rob into my game. I told Rob about my theory and said that he needed to jack himself off at least twice a day until the swelling went down. If that did not help, he would have to see a doctor.

Rob did not want to go to the doctor. If he did he would have to admit having with his nutty ex-girlfriend and that would get them both in trouble. I told Rob a little about my own exploits and offered to help him with his problem. I said that monitoring how much semen if ejaculated each time he jacks off is important. I also told him that the way he jacks off could also affect how fast the swelling of his testicles goes down. I made up those last two things, but I figured Rob would not know the difference and let me do whatever I wanted to him as long as it got the swelling down and kept him out of trouble.

That night as we got ready for bed I told Rob to get naked and lay on the bed. After he was in position I asked him to show me how he would normally jack off. Rob had already told me he was shy and that even getting naked in front of me was a challenge for him. I reassured Rob that what we were doing was necessary. I also pointed out that it was an excellent way to help him get past being so shy.

Rob took hold of his penis and showed me how he whacked off. I stopped him and said that his first mistake was not using lubricant. I took out my trusty jar of Vaseline and told Rob that I was going to show him how to properly lubricate his penis. As I began spreading the Vaseline on his dick Rob laid quietly and made no protest. Because he was so shy I figured it was easier for him to watch me touch his penis than for him to touch it while I watched. That gave me another idea.

While I lubricated my newest player I suggested he allow me to jack him off so that he could learn the best way to do it. I placed a towel on his abdomen to collect any semen that he ejaculated and then went to work. Rob was not overly handsome, but he was good looking. He had a muscular body, very little body hair, extremely white skin, dirty blond pubic hair and a large penis. It was easy to enjoy jacking him off.

Rob was understandably nervous about what I was doing and considering his shyness it was no surprise that he still had not managed an ejaculation after nearly fifteen minutes. I decided to take things to the next step since what we were doing was getting us nowhere. I asked Rob if he knew what oral sex was? He did, so I suggested we try that. Before I even tried to get my mouth near his penis I explained my situation. I gave Rob the short version about my strip clubs, games and explained how much I liked sexually experimenting with both girls and boys.

He did not seem all that surprised or upset by my revelation, so I guessed we were good to go even if he was just being compliant because we allowed him and his sister to stay with us while his dad was away. Rob was smart enough to appreciate our hospitality and my efforts to help him with both the Mitchell mess and his present dilemma. I got Rob into position for oral sex and began sucking his dick. I sometimes enjoyed large penises like his, but I also liked small ones like those the twins had because I could fit them all the way into my mouth.

Oral sex made the difference and Rob shot his load into my mouth after just a few minutes. I told him that he did pretty well, but that the swelling of his testicles probably caused less semen than I would have expected to ejaculate. I said that we had better do this again for a few more nights. After that he could jack off on his own and keep track of how much liquid came out. After reminding him that he needed to jack off again in the morning, I hinted that I might be able to provide a female sex partner for him and one that was not as crazy as his ex-girlfriend.

I knew that my experiences with Rob would be limited because of his shyness. I also knew that I might be able to get past that by providing him with a girl to have sex with as often as she pleased. The next day I went to work on that project after finishing my work with Ingrid. As soon as Robin stopped by I took her aside and asked her if she liked Rob? She said she did, but more as a friend. I also asked her if she had sex with anyone else besides me since we first did it together? She said she did not and I believed her because she kept coming back to me for more sex. Even if she wanted to have sex with the boys she knew, Robin did not trust them to keep their mouths shut about it.

Robin was perfect for Rob. She was cute, just about his age and liked having sex as much as he and I did. If I could make an arrangement between the three of us everyone involved would benefit, so I told Robin about Rob's problem and explained how that helping him with it could be some fun! Robin was wild, but not so much when it came to sex. She thought it might be

strange to have sex with a guy who was more a friend than anything else. I reminded her that her statement just about summed up our own situation and that we were having great sex together.

Seeing this would not be an easy rendezvous to arrange, I asked Robin to meet me back at the house around eight the next night using a night swim in our pool as an excuse. Susan told me that she would be busy with something her parents needed help with at the hotel during that time. With her out of the way, I just had to make sure that Rosemary did not find out what we were up to. Thinking it might be time to start in with her, I had an idea that would help me with that problem as well.

A huge carnival set up shop in nearby Pinellas Park for the week. Rosemary mentioned how much she enjoyed carnivals, so I asked her if she wanted to go that night. She was thrilled with my idea. Just to keep up appearances I invited Rob and Susan to go along with us. The carnival was terrific! There were lots of rides and attractions that kept us out late. I planned it that way so that by the time we got back Susan would have to go right home instead of hanging out at my house.

Everyone had a great time at the carnival. After we got home Rosemary went into the living room to watch TV. Rob headed for my bedroom and laid in bed ready for me to service him. I made quick work of the blow job, then got cleaned up and went downstairs to visit with Rosemary. I asked her if she wanted to go for a night swim to wind down from all the fun we had at the carnival? Our adrenaline was still flowing and neither of us were anywhere near ready to go to sleep.

Rosemary met me down at the pool and before long we were splashing around and having all sorts of fun. I liked Rosemary. She could be moody, but when she was not she was great fun to be around. At some point I pretended to be a sea monster going underwater towards her until I had her up against the side of the pool. I jumped up out of the water, snarled at her and began pretend biting on her shoulders and neck.

As Rosemary laughed I worked my way to her face and began gently kissing her on the cheek. She smiled, blushed and asked, "What are you doing?" I told her I was kissing her on the cheek, but that I would rather kiss her on the mouth. Rosemary replied, "I dare you to do that!" and tried pushing me away in a playful manner. I responded by pushing right up against her, taking hold of her shoulders and kissing her on the mouth.

I gently manipulated my tongue into her mouth until she responded in kind. She was clumsy at first, but soon began French kissing like a pro. She was shorter than me so I had to bend down a bit to make our mouths fit together, but it was more than worth it. Everyone else in the house was finally asleep, so I began to carefully remove her bathing suit top. Rosemary put her hands up to stop me and said she did not want me to do that in the pool, so I suggested we go up to her room.

We grabbed our towels and headed up to the spare bedroom that Rosemary was using. I followed her in, closed and locked the door. Before she could say or do anything I went over to Rosemary and took off her bathing suit top. As she tried covering up her shapely breasts, I used that

opportunity to pull down and take off her bathing suit bottom. I said, "You can't cover everything up and you are so pretty that you should not even try."

Rosemary blushed and finally let her arms drop to her sides. I took a towel and dried off her beautiful nude body. She had a nice crop of very blond pubic hair that really turned me on. As I took off my bathing suit, Rosemary blushed again and looked away while I dried off. I was tired of bending over to kiss her, so I laid down on her bed and pulled Rosemary next to me. I began making out with her again and it felt like magic. Our mouths fitted each other perfectly.

I could hardly believe how easy it was to get Rosemary naked and into bed with me. The next challenge was to try and have intercourse with her. I alternated between kissing her mouth and her breasts, then asked Rosemary how she felt about me kissing her down there? Before she could answer I was already muff diving. I loved the blond pubic hair she had down there. It was still growing but already began to surround her opening.

I licked her small opening and stuck my tongue into her as best I could. I tried to get it as wet as possible in preparation for the insertion of my penis. With Rosemary in a cooperative mood, I anticipated no problems. Licking her down there really made me horny, so I decided to just go for the gold. I lubricated my penis and got into position for intercourse. Rosemary knew what was coming and put her hands over her face as I penetrated her opening.

Even with lubrication it was not easy to push my penis into her. Her opening was not just small, it was also very tight. Rosemary took quick breaths as I pushed my dick into her and quietly said, "Please...it hurts!" After summoning all the strength I had, I finally managed to get my penis all the way into her. When I finally began moving my dick in and out of Rosemary, we both breathed a sigh of relief and enjoyed the intercourse. I loved the tight fit of my penis in her vagina and the way it slid in and out thanks to the Vaseline.

At some point I felt a sudden jitter. My penis felt like it was exploding into Rosemary. I did not have many ejaculations like that one and the feeling almost reminded me of getting a blow job by a girl who really knew how to suck and swallow. After we finished, Rosemary threw on a bathrobe and went into the upstairs bathroom to take a bath. I put my bathing suit back on, got some clothes from my room and headed to the one downstairs for a shower. After we both finished cleaning up, we met back in her room.

Although she acted shy, I sensed that Rosemary was anything but that. She enjoyed the sex as much as I did and I knew this would not be our last encounter. We made out for a while, then it was time to go to bed. Rob was fast asleep by the time I walked into my bedroom. That was good news overall considering the fact that I just taken his sister's virginity from her and was too exhausted to make an explanation if he had heard me go coming and going from his sister's bedroom. After we woke up the next morning I guessed that my secret was safe since Rob didn't ask me any questions about what I did the night before with his sister.

The day flew by and soon it was time for Robin to come over. Rob spent most of the day helping my cousin with some unexpected mailing volume that I could not handle by myself. After Susan finished working for Ingrid, she went to her folk's hotel to help them out. Rosemary had been

quiet all day, but attentive when I was around. She made lunch, cleaned up the house and helped with the laundry. After Robin arrived she joined Rob, Rosemary and myself in the pool. Ingrid was invited to join us, but she was busy with some paperwork in her room.

Rosemary acted overly friendly towards me and I was sure that Rob noticed. I just hoped he would chalk up her behavior to innocent flirting and not give it a second thought. I guessed he did because he sis not ask me about it. After a while Rosemary left us for a TV show she wanted to watch with my folks. Her timing could not have been better. By the time we finished up playing around in the pool, everyone in the house was in bed. I invited Robin and Rob up to my bedroom and told them that we could all change into our clothes in there.

Rob was his usual shy self taking his time about sliding his bathing suit off, but Robin and I got right out of our swim suits. As we all finally stood naked looking at each other, we started laughing. I dried Robin off, Rob dried me off and then I had Robin dry him off. Instead of getting dressed, Robin jumped into my bed. I followed and invited Rob to join us. As we all laid in the bed together I told my two friends that I loved playing games like these and were glad to have both of them involved. I said that I would call the shots and if they listened to me, we could all have fun.

I began by telling Rob to make out with Robin. He did a pretty good job and before long was touching and kissing her breasts. I went muff diving while they made out and licked Robin's opening until she could not take it anymore. At that point I got the Vaseline and lubricated Rob's penis. He was red faced as I did, but I needed to let both of them know that this was my game and I was in control. I could tell that Robin liked watching me lube up Rob, especially after it caused his large dick to become fully erect.

I had Robin lay flat on her back on the bed and spread her legs. As she did, Rob looked at me like he wanted me to leave before they began having sex. There was no way I was going to miss out on the fun, so I told Rob to get in position and carefully penetrate Robin. He was gentle, but his large stiff penis was a lot for Robin to take. Once she settled down and was able to deal with his size, they both went at it like rabbits. I loved watching them have intercourse, but it made me really horny. At some point I threw on a bathrobe, slipped out and headed for Rosemary's room.

Rob's sister was asleep, but I eased into her bed and laid next to her. I began rubbing her shoulders and kissing her neck. Before long she woke up and responded to my gentle prodding. We got naked began making out. I loved her passionate kisses. After kissing and sucking on her breasts, I got into position and began having intercourse with Rosemary. After I shot my load into her, we went back to making out until she was too tired to continue.

I quietly left Rosemary's room and took a quick shower before rejoining Rob and Robin. Robin was on top of Rob and they were still having sex. After he shot his load, he went to the bathroom to take off his condom and clean up. While Rob was gone I surprised Robin by making out with her. By the time Rob came back into the room we were having sex. It did not appear to bother him, so I told him to lay on the bed with us. This was my chance to get to the next level.

Rather then shoot my load into Robin, I pulled my dick out of her and cleaned myself off with a towel. I asked Robin if she wanted to see me and Rob have sex? She laughed and said she did. I guessed that Rob thought I was going to give him a blow job. Instead, I lubricated my penis and had Rob get into position for anal sex at the edge of the bed. I had him laying on the bed on his stomach with his legs on the floor. At that point he was nervous and asked me what I was going to do? Rather then answer his question, I told him to just stay still.

I forced his legs apart, then pushed open his butt cheeks and began shoving my penis into his anus. Rob tried getting up, but I pushed him down and slowly penetrated his anus. As I pushed my dick into him, Rob asked, "Are you crazy?" I replied, "No, just really horny!" Once I got all the way into him and started moving my dick in and out he settled down a bit. I guessed he did not want to make a scene in front of Robin.

Sensing I had take as many liberties with Rob as I could for one night, I pulled my dick out of him and shot my load on his buttocks. As soon as I wiped him off and got out of the way he ran into the bathroom. If Robin was freaked out by my actions, she did not show it. It was time for her to get home so as soon as Rob got out of the bathroom, she used it to shower and then got dressed in my room.

Rob put on his underwear and got into bed without saying anything to me or Robin. After she got dressed, Robin left and I got into bed with Rob. I said I was sorry for what I did, but explained that I really liked his body and could not control myself. He remained quiet and we both went to sleep. The next morning after we woke up and before we went down to breakfast Rob finally spoke. He said he really liked having sex with Robin, but made me promise never to have anal intercourse with him again.

The next day after we all finished work I took Susan out to talk to her. It was time for a dose of truth. I knew that I could no longer hide everything I was doing with her sister and brothers. We went to a quiet area of the beach at Fort DeSoto Park where most people never park and I began confessing me sins to her. I told her about my past, my games and admitted to having sex with Robin and her brothers.

Susan got out of my car, walked up the beach a ways and stared at the water. I gave her a few minutes, then went to join her. She began by saying that she could not believe what I had done. She was less angry and more freaked out. I told Susan that Donna already knew about my perverse ways and accepted them. She was surprised about that, but still unsure how to react to my confession.

Susan knew that telling her parents about what I did was a non-starter. It would not only ruin things for her and everyone else, but it would cause more chaos than it would help solve anything. Instead, I suggested we just go on as we had been doing. I said that just because I did it with her sister and brothers, did not mean that I did not did not care deeply about her. Doing the things I did was just me being me and she had to accept it. I knew that Susan was not comfortable with keeping my secret, but she had little choice in the matter.

My parents would be out of town for the July 4th weekend. It was the perfect time to get some of the kids together for fun. Two days before my folks left I begin getting everyone in line. Now that Susan knew everything, Robin was next. She already knew about me and Susan, so I took her aside and told her what I did with her brothers. She could have cared less. Robin liked me and loved that I had included her in my fun with Rob. Her and Rob had already had a couple of good sex sessions together without me so that paring was a successful one.

Rob and Rosemary were the only ones that did not know everything I was doing. I needed to get with them and tell them the truth. After I told Rob everything, he was not as surprised as I thought he would be. He knew that his sister was cute, a little wild and actually blamed her for coming on to me. Either way, he understood that I wanted to have sex with Rosemary and did not hold it against me. Nothing I said really offended or upset him, so I left it at that.

I took Rosemary out for a ride and told her everything. She was a little freaked out, but also did not really seem to care. She liked having sex with me and loved the way I treated her. I not only took her to the carnival, but we went out to eat, to the mall and to the movies. Rosemary was big on things like that and as long as I kept spending time with her, I knew I could do anything that I wanted to do to other kids with her blessing.

With everyone now in line, I planned some more fun with the twins. They began coming over again and were no longer afraid to be around me. What I really wanted was to fool around with both the twins at the same time. After my parents left early for their July 4th Holiday out of town thing, I got my chance that very evening. The twins were already at my house with their sisters. Rob and Rosemary were also there. We were hanging out in the pool, so I figured it was a good time for some real fun.

I had everyone get out of the pool, then announced that this was the start of my long weekend of July 4th weirdness and bizarre fun. I told everyone that it was time for one of my games and this one was skinny dipping. I suggested we all get naked and then go back into the pool. Everyone laughed, but I told them I was serious. I took off my bathing suit, then grabbed Rob and pulled his off. Next I went for the twins and got theirs off. The girls were laughing until I got behind Robin and pulled down her swimsuit bottom.

Robin chased me around the patio trying to get her swimsuit bottom back, but I kept a tight hold on it and she finally gave up. I took off her top and told the others they were next. Rob playfully chased Susan around until he had her swimsuit off, while I took care of his sister and got her naked. Once we were all nude and back in the pool, I said, "That's better and more fun, isn't it?" My guests enjoyed looking at each other naked even if they would not admit it.

As we played pool volleyball Robin and Rosemary kept trying to keep their ample breasts from bouncing up and down by holding or covering them, but they finally gave up and got into the swing of things. Susan's were too small to bounce around very much. We all had fun, but I new we needed more boys to help pair everyone off before the next time we went skinny dipping. I was already planning a big July 4th Weekend party and that would be a great chance to let everyone have as much fun as I planned to.

session by trying to have anal sex with Colin. I went and got some Vaseline and towels from the bathroom, then came back and turned him over on to his stomach. I pulled Colin to the edge of the pull out bed until his feet were on the floor.

By this time Colin was really out of it and it looked like he was half asleep. After I finished lubricating myself, I carefully spread apart his butt cheeks. My penis was stiff from just looking at his cute body and nice shapely ass. I started pushing my penis into Colin slowly until I felt my crown penetrate his anus. He began to move around a little and muttered something as I pushed in further, but he remained compliant.

Colin had a nice sized butt which was not large or small, but fit his slim build really well. It did stick out a little like a girl's butt and that made it a very desirable target for me. I moved my penis in and out of Colin until I felt ready to ejaculate. I pulled my dick out of him and shot my load on to his buttocks. I did not see any blood, so I guessed that I had not harmed him. After cleaning Colin up, I had him laying on on his back again. He was fast asleep by then and just looking at him laying there got my juices going all over again. I began playing with his penis until it was nice and hard. I hoped for another ejaculation.

As I played around with Colin I had a surprise visitor. Rosemary came down stairs to get a drink, saw the lights on in the living room and came in to see what was happening. She laughed quietly at what I was doing, but I could tell just by the fact that she was staring at Colin's naked and still form that she found him as attractive as I did. I dared her to join in the fun with me. Looking at Colin, Rosemary asked, "Is he dead?" I replied, "Sure, I just invited you to join me in having sex with a dead guy!"

I explained about what happened to Colin's friend and how he arrived at the house already high on something. I told her that I did not know what he was on, but whatever it was it made him very cooperative and was probably the reason he was in such a deep sleep. Instead of talking with her further, I got up and began undressing Rosemary. She acted annoyed, but let me undress her. Both of us climbed back on to the pull out couch as naked as Colin.

I made out with Rosemary for a little while, then lead her hand to Colin's penis. She jacked it so roughly that I was afraid she would hurt him, so I lubricated his dick before allowing her to continue. She went at it again as he continued to sleep soundly. Rather then let her go on until he ejaculated, I told her to get on top of him and have intercourse with my cute new friend. She blushed and said she was not a whore. I said that I never thought she was. Nothing we did was about judging anyone, it was about having fun and she knew that.

It was easy to see that Rosemary wanted a piece of Colin. She just did not want to appear too eager. After some mental finessing, I finally got her to mount him. She guided his penis into her small opening with her hand, then began having intercourse with Colin. She loved doing it with him because his penis remained stiff as a board. Rosemary got tired of doing all the work and called it quits after about ten minutes.

I don't know if Colin ejaculated into her or not. What I did know was that watching them do it made me horny all over again. I lubricated my penis, got Rosemary into the doggie style position

and began having intercourse with her. My lubricated penis slid in and out of her easily and she let me do my thing until I finally shot my load into her. She was a beautiful young girl and having sex with her was like eating your favorite food for the first time.

After Rosemary headed back up to the spare bedroom I realized how really exhausted I was and went to bed. I was too tired to try and get his clothes back on, so I left Colin sleeping on the pull out bed covered with a comforter. If anyone walked by they probably would not even notice that he was naked. At least that was what I hoped.

When I woke up in the morning I headed downstairs to the kitchen and found Ingrid already having breakfast. She jokingly asked why there was a naked kid sleeping on the pull out bed in the living room? I explained all the events of the previous night and she just laughed. I knew better than to ask if Ingrid had already checked him out. I was sure she had and after we finished breakfast I decided to have some fun with my cousin.

I told Ingrid to come with me to check on Colin before she began working. I said that I was worried about him sleeping so long. I pulled the comforter off and he appeared to be breathing normally, so I decided to have some fun. I told Ingrid that I wanted to test a theory and needed some help. I was certain he was still in such a deep sleep that even having sex with her would not wake him up.

Knowing that only Ingrid, Rob, Rosemary and I were in the house, I dared my cousin to get naked and mount Colin. She laughed, took off her clothes and got ready to get on top of him. After I lubricated Colin's penis and jacked it until it was stiff, my cousin climbed on top of him and worked his penis into her. She really went at it with him until she got tired and then quit. I was amazed and amused that I had gotten Colin laid twice since he came over to my house and he probably did not even know it.

After my cousin got dressed and went into her workroom, I lingered over Colin. I loved the scent of Ingrid on him and how the juices from her vagina were still all over Colin's penis. That made me really horny, so I began sucking him off until he shot a small amount of liquid into my mouth. After I cleaned him up a bit, I left him naked on the couch to sleep off whatever demon pill he had swallowed the night before. By late afternoon Colin finally woke up. Rather then ask me why he was naked, he just got dressed and left after thanking me for allowing him to spend the night.

With the July 4th Holiday just a day away I wanted to begin tying up loose ends. One of those was Mitchell. He was not exactly what I normally liked in terms of my usual male game players. He was as tall as I was and had a large body frame. Mitchell was about a year younger than me and had black hair. He was not hairy and had no chest hair or anything like that, just more hair on his arms, legs and under his arms than I was used to.

There were two things about Mitchell that I did like: His penis size and the fact that I sensed he liked boys as much as girls. Having seen the huge bulge in his bathing suit for myself and heard the story about him getting a woody when he saw two of his other male friends naked placed him

on my radar screen. The problem I faced was how to go after Mitchell? I did not want to piss him off or scare him away.

Susan was again helping her folks out at the hotel that day, so I called Robin. She was coming over that afternoon with the twins, as well as her friends Kathleen and Patty to hang out and go swimming. I asked her to get hold of Mitchell and bring him with her as well. She knew better than to ask me why. I also needed Rob and the twins to help me. I told Rob about my plan to bring Mitchell into my game. I left it up to him to brief the twins on their part. He was not thrilled with the idea, but had grown accustomed to my perversity and knew better than to turn me down. He was quickly becoming my sidekick and I think he was enjoying that position more than he admitted.

Mitchell arrived with Robin, the twins and her girl friends in the early afternoon. The twins changed into their bathing suits in the upstairs bathroom. The girls used Rosemary's room because she was out. I allowed Mitchell to change into his bathing suit alone and unmolested in my room. There would be time enough to get an eyeful of him later. Rob and I were already in our swimsuits and hanging out by the patio. Now that everything was cool between Mitchell and Rob they got alone pretty well. Mitchell seemed to like me and appreciated the way I helped with the problem involving Rob's ex-girlfriend.

As we hung out and swam around in the pool I watched Mitchell carefully. Robin, Kathleen and Patty were all pretty girls and it was hard not to look at them in their two piece swimsuits, but Mitchell was more interested in eyeing Rob and the twins. He was careful about it and if I had not been watching him regularly, I might have missed it. Since Mitchell acted too straight to be gay, so there was no doubt in my mind that he leaned in both directions when it came to sex.

I played around with Robin and her friends in the pool. I liked them, but it was more than that. I was laying the ground work to have some fun with Kathleen and Patty in the near future. However, that day belonged to Mitchell and I was certain that I would be able to use Rob and the twins to lure him into my web of sexual experimentation and fun.

By late afternoon Ingrid left and headed out to meet Diane and some of her friends at the mall. Rosemary came home and joined everyone else in the pool while I made sandwiches for my guests. After we all dried off, ate and had some cold drinks, Robin and all the girls dressed and went over to her house as I had pre-planned with Robin. Mitchell, Rob and the twins stayed with me. It was time to begin working on Mitchell.

As we hung out on the patio talking, I asked the guys if they wanted to stay around and watch the Pro Wrestling TV show that evening? Rob and the twins said they did, so Mitchell went along with them and said he would also stay. We talked about wrestling for a while, then I asked the twins which one of them was the better wrestler? They got into a mock argument about it until I said that they should settle the matter right then and there.

After once again announcing that no one could see us in the backyard to make sure that Mitchell knew that, I told the twins I wanted to see them wrestle Greek style. Even though Rob and the twins already knew what that style was from my previous encounters with them, I explained how

that ancient Greek athletes wrestled naked. I said that I thought it would be fun to watch them wrestle each other without any clothes on. Rob agreed with me while Mitchell remained quiet as I expected. After the gay rumors that plagued him he was not going to admit that he liked seeing boys naked.

On my orders the twins slipped off their bathing suits and began wrestling each other. Mitchell watched them closely and keenly just as I knew he would. After a while Jerry finally pinned John and the matter of who was the better wrestler was settled. Jerry had a woody after he finished wrestling his brother. I noticed it and I'm sure that Mitchell did as well, but I did not say anything at that time. Just to keep the flow going I told the twins to stay naked and skinny dip in the pool to cool off. They did as I said and that brought me to the next part of my plan.

I began joking with Rob that I was a better wrestler than he was and we went back and forth on that argument just as the twins had done. Finally I said that we should wrestle to settle the matter and Rob agreed. Before we began Rob asked me, "Greek style?" I said, "Yep!" and we both slipped out of our bathing suits. Mitchell watched us carefully as we wrestled and in the end I pinned Rob after a few minutes. Rob had a woody when we finished the match, but again I said nothing.

Rob and I jumped into the pool naked just as the twins had after their match. I suggested that Mitchell take off his bathing suit and join us. I explained that we skinny dipped all the time, even with the girls. He took the bait. I guessed that he probably did not want to look like a prude in front of all of us. Anyway, I had given him no signal that I was interested in anything more than having fun with my friends that afternoon. Little did he know!

After a while we got back on the subject of wrestling and Rob said that although I was a good wrestler, he was sure that Mitchell could beat me because he was very strong. I said there was only one way to find out and I challenged Mitchell to a match. Once again he took my bait and accepted. As we got out of the pool and dried off, Mitchell tried putting his bathing suit back on. Before he could do that, I told him that we should to wrestle Greek style.

Although I was sure that Mitchell was not entirely comfortable with wrestling me in the nude, he went along with that as well and we began our match on the grass. He was very strong, but I had a lot of wrestling experience. As we went at it I wondered if letting him win might give me an advantage later? Then it occurred to me that if I wanted to be in control of him I had to always have the upper hand.

Before long I managed to pin Mitchell and win the match. He was not angry about it because I had more wrestling experience then he did and it was all in good fun. After the match Mitchell had a woody. He saw that I noticed and apologized for it, but I said that it always happens to me or one of the other boys when we wrestle. I pointed out that both Jerry and Rob had stiff penises after their matches. It was just a normal and natural reaction to nudity and close body contact; nothing to worry about or be ashamed of.

Mitchell and I jumped into the pool naked and joined the others. His penis was large and thick for a guy his age. He had a patch of shiny black hair above it and I could not wait to play around

with him. To set the stage for my fun I told Mitchell that Rob, the twins and I were going to play a game in my bedroom before the wrestling show. I said that he could watch and even join in if he liked. The only thing was that everyone had to be naked and no one could tell anyone else what they saw us doing. Mitchell looked at me strangely, but said he would come and check it out.

We got out of the pool and dried off, then grabbed our bathing suits and headed up to my room still naked. I closed and locked the bedroom door, then told the twins to lay on the bed. I explained to Mitchell that we were going to play sex games. I made it clear to him that we were not gay, had sex with girls and loved it. It was just that we did not let gender stand in the way of having fun. I told him that most teens were a little sexually confused whether they admitted it or not and would experiment with their same sex if they had the chance just to see what it was like.

Mitchell listened to what I said, but remained quiet. I knew it would take more to get him into the game than just words. I had Mitchell sit on a chair next to the bed while Rob and I got into position to suck off the twins. He watched us intently and eventually began touching himself when he thought none of us were looking at him. After Jerry shot his small load into my mouth I went and got some lubricant. I told Mitchell he did not have to hide what he was doing. Jacking off while watching what we were doing was fine and I offered to help.

I began lubricating his large penis. He did not protest so I continued until his dick was well lubricated and stiff. I handed Mitchell a towel just in case he needed it, then Rob and I switched twins and continued jacking their dicks and sucking them off. By this time Mitchell was getting into what we were doing, so I asked him if he would like to take a turn with Rob just to see what it was like? Mitchell blushed and said he wasn't sure if it was for him. I suggested he try it at least once and reminded him that everything we did in my house stayed in my house. We never talked about our activities with anyone outside of our circle of game players.

Mitchell must have been worried about the rumor mill, but after I reassured him that no one would talk about what we did outside of my bedroom he decided to give it a try. Rob got into position and after a brief tutorial by me, Mitchell began sucking Rob off. As he did I had the twins lay on top of each other on the other side of the bed and suck each other off. I loved watching them do that!

While Rob shot his load Mitchell kept his dick in his mouth and did the best he could to swallow it. He did a good job for his first time and I told him so. After he went to the bathroom and rinsed out his mouth, he came back and I had him lay on the bed. While Rob fooled around with the twins I told Mitchell that I was going to suck him off. He did not protest, so I went ahead and did it. His penis was so large that I could not fit the whole thing in my mouth. It felt great to suck his huge dick and when he shot his load it seemed like the flow of liquid would never stop.

I cleaned up a bit and then took Mitchell aside to where Rob could not hear us. I told him that I wanted him to have anal intercourse with Rob. Even though Mitchell remained quiet I knew he was into it. He had already watched intently as Rob and I carefully stuck the tips of our penises into the twins and got the idea about what to do. I explained to Mitchell that there was no way

their small holes could take full blown anal sex even after the sessions we had with them up to that time. Rob was a different story. I felt he might be able to handle a big dick.

Rob was more than a little surprised and not very happy when I had him get into position to have anal sex with Mitchell. I promised that Mitchell would only put his crown in and if it hurt too much he would stop. Rob was unconvinced, but obeyed me and got into position. I helped Mitchell get properly positioned and showed him what to do. Before long his stiff penis was entering Rob's anus. Mitchell pushed his dick further in than I expected. Rob winced in pain, yelled into the covers and tried moving away. I held him down as Mitchell did his thing.

Mitchell only got his penis about half way into Rob's anus before he stopped pushing forward. His dick must have been at least six to seven inches long when it was hard and even half of his thick shaft was more than most guys could handle in their butts. Seeing the pain he was causing, Mitchell moved his dick halfway in and out of Rob a few times until he shot his load on Rob's buttocks. Rob was pissed. He grabbed some clothes and stormed out of the bedroom and into the bathroom.

To keep Mitchell in the game I had him suck off each of the twins. He liked doing that. After he finished with the twins, I told them to get dressed and go back downstairs. I did not want to make Mitchell feel self-conscious about what I was going to do to him by having them watch. With Rob and the twins out of the room I tested my control over Mitchell by having him get into the position for anal sex. He was surprisingly compliant and let me push my lubricated penis into him. He had a large buttocks and good sized anus, so I was able to push my dick all the way into him without causing him any damage or too much pain.

Mitchell let me really go at it with him and I was certain he liked it. The harder I pushed my penis into him the more he seemed to enjoy what I was doing. It felt great to me and was probably the best anal sex I ever had with any boy. After I got done I moved him up by the pillows and asked if he ever tried French kissing? He said he did not, so I offered to teach him how.

I thought for sure that Mitchell would back off, but he let me kiss him and was soon responding in kind with his tongue. I liked Frenching with him and let him play with my dick as we kissed. I reciprocated by playing with his. After a while we stopped kissing and got into good jerking positions. We jacked each other off until his penis exploded into my hand and shot liquid all over me. He was apologetic and upset, but I told him I loved it. I took my turn by shooting my load at him.

We cleaned ourselves up with wet towels and got dressed. There was not much that needed to be said about what happened, so we both headed back downstairs and hung out by the patio for a while. Although Rob was annoyed with me for a while, that did not last long and soon we were once again as right as rain with each other. The twins became used to being caught up in my games and resigned themselves to it. They were not as bothered as they had been by what we did with them or if they were they kept it to themselves.

Mitchell had to leave, but I invited over for our July 4th Party the next day. He agreed to come as long as he could be home by eight so that he could join his parents in watching a municipal fireworks display nearby. With Mitchell crossed off my list and available for future fun, I moved on to some of Robin's other friends. Kathleen was first because I loved her dark shiny hair and freckle covered body. On top of her good looks, she had a great personality and was probably closer to Robin than any of the other girls or even her own sister.

With Susan busy working with her folks at their hotel during the July 4th weekend, I had free rein and I knew just how to make the most of it. As I planned my upcoming holiday activities Fate again had a surprise in store for me. Just around eight that night Robin and Kathleen came over. Robin said she needed me to do her a favor for her friend. I was all ears and could not wait to hear what she had in mind.

Kathleen had busy parents. They gave her a lot of leeway as far as hanging with Robin and her other friends went, but there were limits. They knew all of her female and male friends. If any of them did not meet their approval, it meant she was banned from seeing them. One of those banned friends was a guy named Matt. He had a generally good reputation when it came to school work and not doing drugs, but a bad reputation with girls. He was known as a guy who liked to pop cherries and move on to greener pastures shortly afterward.

Matt was my age and one of Robin's friends. Although he came over once in a blue moon, he tended to focus in on girls he could date instead of just hanging around with girls he knew as friends. He was cute from a girl's standpoint. He had medium length dirty blond hair and a muscular build. I had no interest in him because he was not my type and I knew I could never get anywhere with him.

Kathleen had a crush on Matt. She had been seeing him away from her parent's prying eyes at local parks and other places while they thought she was with Robin. Kathleen told me that up to that point all they did together was hold hands, hug and kiss. Not surprisingly he wanted more. Her problem was that as much as she wanted to give him what he wanted, Kathleen knew that if her dad ever found out he would probably kill Matt.

Kathleen's dad was a union official with alleged Mob ties. That did not bother me because I knew how to keep things low key with my game players. However, Kathleen's crush on Matt was not low key and I knew it would cause lots of problems that neither of them would be able to deal with. Considering this information update, I considered crossing Kathleen's name off my list. The only thing that kept her on it was an opportunity that was just too good to pass up.

Robin wanted me to allow Matt to meet Kathleen at my house once in a while when my folks were not around. It was not hard to figure out what they wanted to do during those meet ups. Despite the danger, I said I would think about it but needed to speak with Kathleen alone. Robin probably knew what I was up to, but as long as she scored points with her friend by getting me to let Kathleen meet and screw with her crush at my house that was enough for her.

As a courtesy I told Kathleen that as much as she liked Matt, he had a reputation as a guy who did it with a lot of girls and she was probably just one of many. I knew my warning would fall on

deaf ears, but I had to try. Typically of a girl with a serious crush, Kathleen told me that her relationship with Matt was different. She just knew it was something special and wanted to do everything she could to keep from losing him.

Although I felt sorry for Kathleen, my desire to have sex with her outweighed my compassion or common sense. I decided to give up on talking her out of doing it with Matt and went into my predatory mode. I told Kathleen that I had no problem with her and Matt occasionally coming over together and meeting at my house. I said that I knew what she wanted to do with him and also had no problem with that, but there were some ground rules she needed to know and strictly follow.

The last thing I needed was a connected guy coming to my house looking for Matt or anyone who had helped him get into Kathleen's pants. She needed to plan her visits with Matt very carefully and make sure that Robin could be used as an alibi. With Robin living just across the street from me, it would take just minutes to get Kathleen on the phone if either of her parents called looking for her. Robin could always say she was in the bathroom, then come over to my house and get her so that she could talk to her folks when or if they called.

If her parents showed up Robin could say that she and Kathleen were over my house planning to go in the pool and that she had just come back to her house to get their bathing suits. Matt would just hide out in one of the rooms until they checked on Kathleen and left. It was a good plan that presented some excellent opportunities for everyone involved. The way I had it figured, once Matt got what he wanted out of Kathleen a few times the relationship would fizzle. After she realized that he was only after a piece of her or he moved on, that would be that and eliminate the risk once and for all.

Matt was the wildcard in my scheme and I did not like wildcards that I could not fully control. My next rule would allow me to control him. I told Kathleen that she could not see Matt outside of my house. If they got caught and he blabbed about meeting her at my house to save his own skin, I would catch more hell than he would. I also told her that when they were at my house and did their thing, she would have to let me watch to be sure he used protection. I knew she would hate that rule, but it was a great way for me to get to watch them do it and still make sure that I would not have to deal with the consequences of a pregnant Kathleen.

As we talked I began to make it clear to Kathleen that I was sure Matt liked girls with some experience. I said that as a guy I would rather do it with a girl who had sex with other guys before me. That way I knew that the girl had already tasted some more of what life offers and would be less likely to cheat on me. Choosing me over her other lovers meant that it was not just about wanting to have sex with a guy, but more about the fact that she really liked me and that I meant something special to her.

Most of what I told Kathleen was crap that would only make sense to a girl with a serious crush and she was that girl. Apart from being incredibly attracted to her body and personality, I genuinely did not want a guy like Matt to be her first. He was only about how many chicks he could screw and I knew it. Not that I was any better in the bigger moral scheme of things, but I

cared enough about Kathleen to show her some respect and make sure that her first time was not just a 'wham, bam, thank you ma'am' moment.

It was no surprise that Kathleen bought my argument. I told her that I thought she was very pretty and had a great personality. I said it would be an honor if she allowed me to be her first and teach her what she needed to know to please Matt. Kathleen was not surprised at my offer, but she was also not suspicious about it. She knew that I already had sex with Robin and Susan. Robin sung my praises to her and that gave me a lot of credibility.

Too much talk was never good, so I told Kathleen to get up, took her hand and lead her to my parent's room. With Rob sleeping in my room, Rosemary in the spare bedroom and Ingrid in her room there was not a lot of choice in the matter. Since my folks were away it was no big deal. I closed and locked the bedroom door so we would not be disturbed, then had Kathleen lay next to me on the bed. She was a bit shy, so I did not have her take off her clothes just yet. Instead, we began to make out. I said it would help break the ice using that as an excuse to kiss her.

Kathleen was a great French Kisser and I felt envious of the spell that Matt had cast over her as our mouths met and I stared into her beautiful green eyes. I knew that she was probably more obsessed with him than anything else, but no amount of talk or explanations would derail her desire to be with him. Like the other girls Matt had been with, she would have to learn her lesson the hard way. I wished that was not the case, but I knew it was.

After a short while I suggested we strip to our underwear. Kathleen and I got up off the bed and began undressing. I took off everything but my underpants, while she stripped down to her bra and panties. I was amazed that one girl could have all the freckles she had on her body and I loved it. Once again we laid down and made out for a bit until I carefully unhooked her bra and slowly removed it.

Kathleen had small breasts, but they matched her thin and athletic body type. Her nipples were light red and well defined. I massaged, then kissed and sucked on her breasts as we made out. I lead her hand down to my crotch and had her feel my penis through my underwear. I showed her how to jack me, then had her pull off my underpants after my dick was nice and hard. I told her to get the Vaseline I had brought into the room with me and showed her how to lubricate my penis. I explained that lubricating it would make her first time more comfortable.

After she finished lubricating my dick, I gently pulled off her panties revealing a nice patch of shiny black hair above her opening. Before taking the plunge I made out with her a little while longer and fingered her opening. I finally got Kathleen into a comfortable position for sex and slowly pushed my penis into her. Although her hole was small, my penis slid right in. I think it was because all the making out we did got her a little wet in there.

My stiff penis cut right threw her hymen causing her to shutter a bit and and take a deep breath. I loved the tight fit of my penis inside her and knew it was time for a condom. I had not put one on because I really wanted to experience natural sex with Kathleen. She was so cute and I did not want to spoil the feeling with plastic. I pulled my penis out, showed Kathleen how to slide a

love. I was glad I had been her first and sometimes regretted having her lay down with other guys, but I figured that she would probably play the field anyway and felt better that I could supervise to make sure she did not end up injured or pregnant.

After Robin and I finished we talked for a while, then she went back across the street to her house. As I watched her go into her front door from mine I thought how cool it would be to get her with Kathleen. I sensed the two girls would hit it off as far as sexually experimenting with each other if I encouraged them in that direction. It was not something they would ever try by themselves, but with me urging them on I felt it could happen.

I was amazed at how quickly I had already burned through most of the list I had of Robin's friends. Patty was next and I was sure she would not be much of a challenge. Robin told me that she already lost her virginity to a guy named Ed who was a year older than her and lived nearby. They did it together several more times since that first encounter, so Patty was definitely not a prude. With Ed it was all about sex. He had no real interest in Patty or a real relationship with any girl. I guess she was alright with that because she told Robin he had a big penis and she liked getting laid by him.

Robin came over the next day with Patty, Kathleen, Mitchell and two new boys. Jenny was a 'no show' because she was away with her folks for the holiday weekend. Robin arrived early with the others to help me get things ready for our July 4th Weekend party. The new boys that I had not met before were Jimmy and Tommy. They were both a year younger than me and known as the local Irish Mafia. Their grandparents on both sides came from Ireland and both sets of their parents were rumored to support organizations that helped to fund the IRA. All I cared about was that they were cute.

Jimmy had half moon eyes, a cute face, pale skin and light freckles all over his body. He had an outgoing personality, was about my height, skinny and showed a lot of interest in the girls. According to Robin he had not scored with any yet. Tommy had wide eyes, dark brown hair, a few freckles scattered about and a normal body frame for his size. He was a little shorter than Jimmy, not as outgoing and sometimes had a quick temper. They were not related, but as friends both boys stuck together like glue.

As soon as I met Jimmy and Tommy I saw some potential for my games. The only problem was that during their first visit to my house I found that field had already been plowed, planted and harvested. When it came time to get ready for swimming both boys wanted to change into their bathing suits in the bathroom instead of with Rob, Mitchell and I. They later explained their reasons for doing it that way while we were all in the pool together. Those reasons were valid, compelling and disturbing.

When Jimmy and Tommy were thirteen they were hanging out in the playground at the nearby elementary school. They were with a bunch of other kids so when a guy asked if he could take some pictures of them they did not think it was a big thing. This went on for a few days until he finally offered the boys twenty dollars each to allow him to photograph them in their bathing suits. He said that he might be able to get some catalog interested in making them young male bathing suit models for big bucks.

Even at thirteen both boys liked having money in their pockets. Both sets of their parents made good money, but they were not particularly generous with it when it came to giving their kids spending cash. The boys were already attending prestigious private religious schools and their parents probably figured that was generous enough. As a result, Jimmy and Tommy were always looking for odd jobs that could earn them some spending money. The man's offer looked like an easy gig for them, seemed legitimate and just as a show of good faith he offered to give them the money in advance.

Jimmy and Tommy made arrangements to meet the man at nearby motel room. He said he was in from out of town scouting for prospective young models and taking the photos there would give them more privacy. He also asked them not to mention the gig to their parents because they might not like having their kids photographs even though it was a great opportunity. The man said that he would take their phone numbers down and call their parents if he could get some interest from model agencies or retailers that independently hired models for their catalogs.

Once again Jimmy and Tommy were not particularly concerned about the situation because the motel was located on Central Avenue just a few blocks from where they lived. Both boys figured that it was worth twenty bucks to let the guy take a few photos of them in their bathing suits. If things worked out further and they became models their parents would probably be proud that they had the initiative to give the opportunity a try.

Jimmy and Tommy met the man at the hotel on a Saturday afternoon during summer vacation. They came with their bathing suits on under their clothes. Both boys were modest and disliked undressing in front of strangers. The man paid them both up front as he had promised, then they stripped down to their bathing suits and the man took them to the hotel pool area. After he took some photos of them there, they all went back to the room where he said he wanted to take a few more photos.

After taking a couple of more shots of the boys in their bathing suits, he told them about another opportunity. He asked them if they would like to earn another twenty dollars each right then and there? He explained that sometimes companies which published medical or instructional books also hired young people as models. The man said they liked boys with bodies like Jimmy and Tommy had and would block out their faces if they decided to use them as models. The only catch was that they would have to pose nude in various positions.

Since the man had been as good as his word thus far, the boys were not really suspicious about the new opportunity he offered to them. Besides, they liked the idea of walking away from the session with forty dollars instead of just twenty. They asked the photographer what they would have to do? He said that the medical book publishers just needed front, side and back photos of them naked together and separately. The instructional book publishers wanted naked photos of them which highlighted their sex organs.

At that point Tommy was a little worried, but Jimmy said that as long as the man paid them up front and their faces were blocked out on the photos he thought it was alright. The man gave them both another twenty dollars and they slipped off their bathing suits. The first photos he took

I decided to place Jimmy and Tommy on my list, but they were a project that would take a lot of planning and that weekend was not the right time to even try to get anywhere with them. After hearing what they had to say, I asked Robin if she thought they might blow the whistle on anything the other kids and I did while they were over my house? She said that they kept quiet when it came to things that others did and would only blab to their parents if it involved them. Knowing they had to leave to join their own families for July 4th celebrations, I kept things cool until after they left just to be on the safe side.

Susan was again a no show because when she was not busy working for my cousin, she was at her parent's motel helping them cope with a particularly busy and profitable tourist season. That was fine by me and opened the door for more un-obstructed fun. In fact, the crowd at my house was changing fast. Robin and her friends had replaced people like Nancy, Mark and Wilson to name a few. Rob and Rosemary were there because they were staying with us and were now more like family then house guests. I trusted them and they trusted me which made it alright to do most anything I wanted to do with the other kids. Besides, I was still having sex with both of them and they were not about to rat me out to anyone.

With Donna and Alison still away at camp, Robin and her friends were fair game and Patty was my next target. She was definitely different from what I was used to in a girl. As pretty as Patty was, she had more body hair than I liked. Like most American Girls her age she shaved her legs so that was not an issue, but she she had a lot of hair on her arms. In some ways it kind of made her look exotic because it was not like the hair that most guys had on their arms, but it still bothered me a little. Looking back from today, she reminds me a lot of Sarah Michelle Gellar and had the same type of forearm hair.

After Robin's revelations about Patty and her first and only lover Ed, I knew I could get into her pants without too many hassles. That did not mean I thought that she was a slut or anything like that. I had to make sure that anytime I went after any of Robin's friends I did so with class. Robin was very protective of her friends and Patty was definitely a part of her inner circle. Robin, Kathleen and Patty were always together and that made me want to have a group encounter with them somewhere down the road. But first things first; I had to make it with Patty before I could do anything else.

The best laid plans of mice and men often go awry and my guess that Patty would be an easy mark turned out to be partially wrong. I spent most of the afternoon trying to break her away from Robin and Kathleen. That proved unsuccessful, so I told Robin that I wanted come personal time with Patty. She already knew that Patty was on my list and did not mind at all. She hated Ed and would do anything to get her friend away from him.

In the early evening Robin, Kathleen and I were in the pool. Mitchell, Rob and Rosemary were hanging out in the recreation room playing pool or listening to records. Robin asked Kathleen to go to the store with her while Patty was changing into her bathing suit. By the time she came down to the pool area, Robin and Kathleen were gone. I explained that they were on a store run and would be back in short while. That did not seem to bother her, so I began playing around with Patty in the pool.

She was a fun loving person, so it was easy to get things started with her using some splashing and a challenge to a game of two person pool volleyball which I won. She playfully claimed I cheated, so I said we would play again and this time the loser would have to take off their bathing suit and skinny dip in the pool. Patty smiled and agreed to my terms. As I suspected, she was not shy when it came to her body as evidenced by the skimpy two piece swimsuit she was wearing.

Once I again I won the game, but I told Patty that since Robin and the others often skinny dipped in the pool with me I would join her naked. She rolled her eyes as she took off her swimsuit and tried to ignore me as I took off mine. Once we were naked in the pool I started splashing Patty and playing around with her. I did my famous sea monster act and came up on her from underwater until I had her pinned on the side of the pool.

Patty asked, "What are you doing?" and acted disinterested in me as I held her arms and growled at her in a monster sort of way. Seeing that was not working, I began tickling her. I noticed that Robin and the girls would occasionally begin tickling her just under the arms around the abdomen where she was apparently very ticklish. Patty began laughing and begged me to stop.

I moved my hands from her abdomen to her breasts to see what she would do. As I started gently stroking and handling her small breasts Patty stopped laughing and said nothing. I will admit that I had placed her in a no-win situation. She knew that Robin and her other friends liked me and Patty probably did not want to start trouble by rejecting my advances. On top of that we were at my house, in my pool and no one held a gun to her head to get naked. If she refused me she might be labeled a cock tease.

Realizing that I was being more than a little unfair to Patty I decided to back off a little. I let go of her breasts and apologized saying that I got carried away by the moment. She offered a slight smile and said she understood. It did not seem like she was into me at all, so I moved on to Plan B and told Patty that I would make up for my bad behavior to her by giving her a pool massage.

Patty had never been around during the times when Robin and the others skinny dipped in the pool with me, but she had been there on occasions when we were all in the pool together with our swimsuits on. She saw me give Robin and the others what I called a 'pool massage' without being naked and as far as Patty could tell, there was nothing all that sexual about it beyond simple petting. She told me to go ahead and give it a try.

I turned Patty around so that she was facing the side of the pool and began massaging her shoulders. I worked my way down her back and pushed myself up against her buttocks every so often in a teasing sort of way. I massaged her buttocks and went partially underwater to massage her thighs and legs. She had smooth soft skin having taken the time to shave her legs. Her crotch was not shaved and sported a large amount of light blond hair.

I could hear and feel Patty breathing heavily, so either she liked what I was doing or it made her nervous. I really could not tell at that point and decided to kick things up a notch. I slowly reached around her and gently took her breasts in my hand and began to massage them. She slyly said, "I guess we're back to that again!" I asked her if she preferred that I stop touching her

breasts? She laughed a little and said, "I guess if I want the whole massage you get to squeeze my small melons!"

I was beginning to appreciate Patty's sense of humor and frequent use of sarcasm. In that way she was a lot like me. I eventually turned her towards me and stopped massaging her to ask if she wanted to make out? I knew that Patty was again backed into a corner. She would have been fearful of insulting me by saying she did not want to make out knowing that would piss off Robin. If she did want to make out with me she risked having to take things further until we were actually having sex.

As much as I felt sorry for Patty she was not a virgin and if her body was good enough for a sleezy jerk like Ed, it was good enough for a pervert like me. We began kissing and I got the impression that she was enjoying it. The more we made out, the hornier I got. She had a very pretty face which along with her athletic body began to really turn me on. I liked her smaller breasts which were very soft to the touch with nicely shaped and well defined nipples. Her soft blond pubic hair was making me stiff.

I took Patty's hand and led her out of the pool. I used a towel to dry her off, dried myself and then took our bathing suits and placed them on a pool chair to air dry. We wrapped ourselves in large beach towels and went inside to get a cold drink. After the refreshments, I led patty up to my room. Mitchell, Rob and Rosemary had gone over to Robin's house to hang with the others for a while so we had the house and my room to ourselves.

I unwrapped Patty from out of her towel, allowed my own to drop to the floor and laid her on my bed. She did not say anything, but offered a slight smile which told me she was alright with what I was doing regardless of her real motivation. I slid on to the bed next to her and we started making out again. She was an excellent kisser and we both Frenched together like pros. I do not know if she felt the passion I did, but it seemed that way.

Before long I mounted Patty and began having intercourse with her. Her opening was average sized with well defined lips that were surrounded by her soft blond pubic hair, but she was a machine when it came to having sex and really got into it. My penis was numb after just a few minutes and we went at it for what seemed like forever before I finally shot my load. After I did my penis remained stiff, so I turned her over and we did it doggie style.

Patty was very wet inside and my penis was drenched with her fluid. We tried different positions until I decided to eat her out. I loved the feel of her soft pubic hair on my tongue as I made the rounds down there and shoved my tongue into her. I got so excited that I turned her over and licked her buttocks and anus which was also surrounded by her soft blond hair. At some point I got into position and gently pushed my penis into her anus.

Patty was surprised by my action, but did not protest. I pushed my penis slowly and gently into her anus. I don't know if she ever had anal sex before, but knowing Ed I suspect she had. After a while I slipped my penis out of her butt and back into her vagina. I was amazed at how wet she was and enjoyed doing it with her. My only regret was that I had become the thing I hated the

most: A person who had sex for sex sake. Of course in my case it had more to do with fulfilling a conquest list, but I still disliked the fact of what I had become.

I shot my load into Patty and felt her own body shutter from what I guessed might have been a teenage version of orgasm, then we fell back on to the bed exhausted. Patty went to get cleaned up and dressed in the upstairs bathroom. After she finished I did the same and went back downstairs to meet her back out on the patio. By that time Robin and the others were back from her house. They joined my cousin and Diane who had arrived a short time ago and were hanging out on the patio.

We all had pizza and instead of heading out to nearby fireworks displays, we decided to watch the ones visible from my back yard. Those included a couple put on by the neighbors and a municipal show at a nearby park that was easily visible from our vantage point. Ingrid and Diane went back out after the fireworks ended to meet up with some friends at a party with more people there age. Thinking it would be fun to mess with my guests, I suggested that we all skinny dip in the pool. Robin instantly played along with me. She had become a willing ally in my quest for perverse fun.

Once we were all naked, I could see that Mitchell showed an interest in Patty. he kept looking at her naked body. That confirmed my suspicion that he leaned both ways when it came to sex. When he eventually took a bathroom break I took Patty aside and spoke to her privately. Now that I was closer to her I felt comfortable talking about things like sexual link ups. I told her that Mitchell was checking her out. She was not particularly interested in him until I mentioned his big dick.

I told Patty that he was in desperate need of her body and invited her to take a shot at him if she so desired. I thought I might anger her with my indecent proposition, but in those days of free love it was merely an invitation she could accept or refuse. She decided to accept providing me with more evidence that my sex with Patty had been more fruitful than I first thought. It had opened to the door to her involvement with my games.

After our skinny dipping session we dried off wrapped in beach towels and had some snacks. Kathleen went inside to get dressed and then headed home to make her curfew. With my cousin out, that left me with Robin, Patty, Mitchell, Rob and Rosemary for the sleep over. Robin was sleeping over since her Susan and her folks were staying at their motel for the night. Patty and Robin were supposed to be sleeping in Rosemary's room while Rob bunked with me as usual and Mitchell slept with us on a cot I had set up for him in my bedroom.

Still wrapped in beach towels, I invited everyone up to my room. Rosemary opted out saying she was tired and went to her own bedroom to go to sleep. Sensing what I was up to and in no mood for group sex after his last painful run in with Mitchell, Rob opted out saying he was going to sleep on the pull out couch downstairs in the living room. That left Robin, Patty, Mitchell and I. We headed up to my bedroom. Once inside I closed the door and told everyone to drop their towels. Robin and Patty giggled as we were again naked in front of one another.

I picked up Robin and gently placed her on one side of the bed while inviting Patty to lay on the other side. I began making out with Robin and asked Mitchell, "What are you waiting for?" He nervously laid down with Patty and they started kissing. Before long I mounted Robin as she giggled and said that this was the best sleep over she had ever experienced. Mitchell was slow out of the starting gate, but Patty eventually got him to mount her.

I loved having intercourse with Robin while watching Patty and Mitchell do it. Patty loved his huge dick and got on top of him. She rode Mitchell like a pro and had him in a state of complete ecstasy. I whispered to Robin asking her if she wanted a turn with Mitchell? She hesitated, but then said she did. After Mitchell shot his load into Patty, I suggested we switch partners. Once again I found my penis deep inside Patty's vagina surrounded by her soft golden pubic hair and I loved it. Robin struggled to deal with Mitchell's big shaft, but she managed to enjoy it after a while.

After Mitchell and I again shot our loads, the girls wrapped themselves in their towels and went into the upstairs bathroom to shower while we did the same and took turns using the downstairs one. We all met back together in my room and got naked again. At that point I told the girls that I wanted to see them kiss each other. They laughed loudly and Robin said, "No way!" with a sly smile on her face. I laid Robin on the bed and ordered Patty to lay next to her saying, "Hey, if you try it we will too!"

The girls giggled at the thought of Mitchell and I kissing, but I had him lay on the bed. I knew that kissing me in front of the girls was probably the last thing Mitchell wanted to do. To get him into the game I whispered that I had some cute young boys and maybe some more girls for him if he did what I told him to do. He got the message and knowing that I held the key to his sexual fun for the time being, he began Frenching with me.

The girls just stared at us, giggled some more and made faces like they were all freaked out by what we were doing. I got them going by having Robin lay on top of Patty and kiss her. They continued to giggle every so often, then settled down and actually began Frenching each other like they meant it. I knew this was my best shot to take things all the way with these kids and I was not going to miss out.

I shocked the girls by getting into position and sucking Mitchell's dick. They tried laughing it off, but I stopped and got Robin into position to lick Patty. I showed her what to do, then made her take a few licks just to be sure she tried it. She did, but was more into pushing her fingers into Patty after I showed her that move. I guessed that Robin was a little put off by all the pubic hair Patty had down there. Robin really got into fingering Patty and at one point it looked like she was able to fit most of her fingers into her friend.

While Robin fingered Patty I sucked off Mitchell until he finally shot his load into my mouth. After washing my mouth out I had Robin and Patty switch places. Patty licked Robin and was more into that than Robin had been. She licked all around Robin's opening and even did her friend's anus after I showed her how. Robin was red faced with embarrassment, but endured the situation for her friend's sake and mine.

Instead of having Mitchell suck me off I further shocked the girls by getting Mitchell into position for anal sex. I lubricated and then shoved my penis into him. Robin and Patty looked stunned, but I told them that was how guys had intercourse with each other. They watched intently as I pulled my penis out of Mitchell and ejaculated on to his buttocks. It was a wild night from then on. We had sex with the girls again, made them give up blow jobs and switched places with Robin and Patty twice. Finally exhausted, we all fell asleep on my bed.

The next morning we all ate breakfast together acting like nothing happened the night before, except for the smiles on everyone's faces. By mid-morning my overnight guests was gone and I looked forward to a quiet afternoon. Rob and Rosemary were hanging out by the pool when just before lunch I had a couple of surprise visitors. Kathleen came over with Matt. She had a standing invitation to bring him over any time my folks were not around so it was no big deal.

I invited them to use the pool, but Kathleen was in a hurry. She had just two hours of free time left that day and wanted to spend every minute screwing Matt. I took them up to my bedroom and asked Kathleen if she explained the rules regarding the use of my bedroom to Matt? She said she did and he said he understood. I told them to strip and watched with anticipation. Matt had a penis that was the same size as mine and a nice crop of dirty blond public hair to match the shoulder length hair on his head.

To his credit Matt brought a condom with him, but this was my show and I was going to run it my way. Even though I already knew the answer I asked if he had ever done it with Kathleen before? He told me this was his first time with her, so I suggested he save the condom until he was ready to shot his load and let her experience the natural feel of his penis inside her. He loved my idea, but he did not know that I had an ulterior motive in making that suggestion.

Before I allowed them to get started I suggested that he allow me to lubricate his penis. I told him that Kathleen was not as experienced as I heard that he was and that the lubricant might make sex more comfortable for her. Matt agreed and allowed me to lubricate his penis with Vaseline. I liked the look of his muscular body, but he was not the kind of boy I wanted to play around with and he definitely did not lean in that direction. The real reason that I wanted to lubricate his dick was to embarrass him in front of Kathleen. I hated that she was wasting herself on a guy like him.

Matt was red faced as I lubricated his penis. It became stiff, so I jacked it a bit saying that I wanted to be sure it was hard enough to do the job for Kathleen. After I had both of them get on my bed I told them to get started while I sat in a chair and watched. Kathleen tried making out with Matt, but all he wanted to do was get inside of her just as I suspected. The look on his face was priceless as he entered Kathleen and suddenly realized that she was not a virgin! That took a lot of the wind out of his sail and quickly crushed his enthusiasm.

After just a couple of minutes he was ready for the condom, so I helped by sliding it on to his penis. In less than another minute he shot his load and then got off her as quickly as he had gotten on. Matt used the bathroom and got dressed in there. Kathleen was still laying on the bed expecting her lover to return when he stuck his head in the bedroom door and said that he had to be somewhere. In a flash Matt was gone.

Kathleen did not say anything; her tears did the talking for her. She was as devastated as I was surprised. I figured that Matt would have had the common decency or at least sense to make out with Kathleen and keep her interested in him in case he wanted more sex from her in the near future, but I guessed that he lost interest after he found out that there was no cherry for him to pop. He was a jerk and apparently did not appreciate used goods.

I knew it would have been useless to say anything to Kathleen at that point, so I just laid next to her in bed with my clothes on. She was facing away from me, but I pulled her close to me and just held her for a while. I rubbed her soft and freckled back until she began to settle down and talk to me. Kathleen just could not understand how Matt could be so heartless and act that mean towards her. I explained that from my experience the world was full of guys like Matt and that she was just lucky that she found out what he was like before she got too involved with him.

I was certainly no shining example of manhood when it came to my games or much else, but I tried hard to treat all the girls I knew with respect and was always there for them. There were times when I had to cut things off with a girl for one reason or another, but I never did it just because I wanted to screw them and move on to greener pastures. After having been used, cheated on and dumped by Lynn when I was younger I knew exactly how Kathleen felt.

I have always felt that emotional pain was worse than physical pain in many ways and sometimes took longer to heal. It was obvious that it would take some time for Kathleen to get over Matt and I was not going to try and take advantage of her during that period of time. I would wait and let her approach me if that was what she wanted. I knew that Robin would help her because Robin was the kind of girl who was always there for her friends.

I told Kathleen to take as much time as she needed in my room and use the shower if she liked, then I headed downstairs to shake off the sad events of that day and rejoin Rob and Rosemary in the pool. Rob gave me a look which told me that he had already figured out what happened with Matt. Rosemary was less interested in the situation having already made her feeling on what a trashy guy Matt was known to all. I was not about to gossip about what happened in my bedroom and just wanted to get it out of my mind.

Kathleen came down and hung out with us in the pool. I knew she was not quite ready to face Robin knowing that her friend would understand what happened, but embarrassed by the bad choice she had made with Matt. I was just thankful that he had not been her first. As we hung out together I felt Kathleen and I getting closer as friends and maybe more. By the time that Rob and Rosemary went inside to change into their clothes and watch TV, Kathleen was holding my hand in the pool. Before long we were making out.

I really liked Kathleen as a person and for her amazing body. After we got out of the pool we headed up to my room, got naked and had sex. I knew that this might have been a case of sympathy sex which is similar to eating comfort food after a traumatic emotional situation, but she enjoyed it all the same and so did I. There was a kind of silent understanding between us that this was probably not going to lead anywhere, but now Kathleen was a part of my game and

knew that she could do it with me without any guilt or commitment and more as friends than anything else.

Chapter Four: Jenny, Jimmy and Tommy

While I enjoyed the sexual opportunities constantly available from Rob and Rosemary as house guests and game players, I also liked doing it with my cousin, Robin, the twins, Patty, Kathleen and Mitchell. I loved challenges even more and looked forward to working on Robin's friend Jenny. She was next on my list and the new week brought an opportunity for me to take a shot at her.

Jenny was easily the most beautiful of Robin's friends. Her dirty blond hair, perfect physique and sweet blemish free face made her equal to any teen model I had ever see. She looked a lot like Christy Brinkley, however, in most ways she was actually more attractive! As much I craved Jenny for her beauty, she also had a wonderful personality and was extremely smart. Having a conversation with her always caused you to forget about how pretty she was and made you admire her intellect even more than her beauty and poise.

Jenny had an abnormal and and dysfunctional home life like most extremely beautiful girls I knew. It almost seemed to go with the territory. She was her mom's only daughter and never met her dad. He abandoned her mom before she was even born. Since that time her mom had many lovers, but few suitors and never remarried. To say that Jenny had trust issues was an understatement and little wonder why.

The good news was that Jenny was surprisingly upbeat and never bitter. Despite her mom's romantic pitfalls, she had a good paying job for a big company which meant that Jenny never had to go without anything. She was always well dressed and took good care of herself. She wore dresses instead of jeans and looked great in those. She had a great sense of humor and was well read for a girl her age.

Jenny's mom trusted her and she earned that trust by staying out of trouble. Although she was a latch key kid, Jenny knew what was expected of her and regularly checked in with her mom by phone. I knew that getting her into my game would be no walk in the park. She had all kinds of guys interested in her of all ages. None had even made it to first base with this dream girl, so if I did succeed with Jenny this would be my crowning achievement.

Jenny liked boys, but was either too smart or too emotionally immature to be boy crazy at that time in her life. I think it might have been a mixture of both. That made her an elusive target and one which I had to approach very carefully. Since she would easily see right through any of my more simplistic approaches I knew not to even waste my time on those. What I needed was a creative hook to catch this big fish and thanks to my cousin I found one.

Jenny came over to use the pool with Robin and her other friends a few days after the incident between Kathleen and Matt. When my cousin stopped by the patio to let me know she was heading out for the afternoon Jenny took notice of Ingrid and remarked how beautiful she

looked. Jenny loved using make up, but like most young girls was not adept at it. However, unlike the others she was smart enough to realize she needed more help with make up techniques than her friends or mom could offer.

Jenny asked my cousin if she could share a few make up tips with her sometime? Always friendly and helpful, my cousin invited Jenny over the next evening and said she would share some of her make up techniques with the young girl. That gave me an idea. I talked with Ingrid about Barbara. She was a make up expert who worked in the Beauty Salon at my father's hotel. Barbara taught Ingrid almost everything that she knew about make up and how to apply it. During her hippie days Ingrid did not use any.

After her clothing design business began to take off Ingrid needed to look more professional and had to begin wearing make up. My mom taught her what she could, then my dad sent her to Barbara who taught her much more. If she did that for Ingrid, why couldn't she do it for Jenny? Ingrid knew I was after Jenny and loved my idea. Her admiration for my plan was part selfish. She saw Jenny as the perfect young girl to model some of her clothes for younger teens.

After my cousin and I discussed the situation, Ingrid went to see Jenny the next evening instead of having Jenny came over to see her. My cousin explained her idea to Jenny and she loved it. They moved on to speaking with her mom about the situation and Ingrid got permission for Jenny to stay at the hotel for a few days the following week under her supervision. She basically sold her mom on the idea that Jenny would learn some basic make up, hair and modeling techniques from professionals which could be useful in many ways throughout her life, not just as a model.

She also got permission to use Jenny as a model for a reasonable fee and the promise of steering her towards more lucrative opportunities later on. By that time my cousin had built up a few key connections among some influential people in the fashion industry. Jenny thanked Ingrid for all of her help and the modeling job, but my cousin slyly gave me the credit for the whole idea. That got me a hug and kiss on the cheek from Jenny who stopped by our house that same night to offer her thanks to me as well.

While she was at our house Ingrid explained that since she was busy most of the time I would be staying with her in our suite in the hotel and keeping an eye on everything. My cousin made it clear that we would have separate bedrooms and that there was plenty of room for both of us to stay there without any moral compromises. Jenny was not about to question my presence and probably did not even give it a second thought at the time, so everything was GO for the lessons and hotel stay.

The following Monday Jennie's mom met Ingrid at the hotel with her daughter. She was introduced to my dad and the Beauty Salon staff. After taking a look at our suite and helping Jenny get settled in, her mom left to head out to her job across town. Ingrid took Jenny down to the Beauty Salon to begin her first day of lessons. My cousin stuck around long enough to watch the beginning of Jenny's transformation and take a lunch break with her new model, than left to go about her business just before I showed up. I made sure not to arrive until later that afternoon just to make sure that Jenny was not suspicious.

As I walked into the Beauty Salon I was stunned at Jenny's new look. She had a complete make-over which included a new hair cut, professionally applied make up and a custom designed outfit courtesy of my cousin. She was a vision! After she finished up at the Beauty Salon I took her to dinner. All eyes were on Jenny and I could see her new look was as big a hit as I thought it might be. As we left the restaurant and headed up to the suite women stopped her every few seconds to ask where she got her outfit or her haircut? She was a walking advertisement for my cousin's designs and the hotel Beauty Salon!

Jenny was using my cousin's bedroom in the suite during her stay. Ingrid was too busy to be there and depended on me to get her to where she needed to go for the next few days. Despite my own plans I had no intention of letting my beloved cousin down. That evening I sat around talking with Jenny and getting to know her better. Astonished at her new look and the response to it, she continued to be extremely grateful to my cousin and me for our efforts on her behalf. As much as I appreciated her gratitude, it was too early to take advantage of it.

After Jenny checked in by phone with her mom and friends to let them know about the excitement of her first day in model training, she went to bed. I followed a short time later sleeping in my own bedroom. I knew my time was limited because Donna and Alison were due back from camp that weekend. If I was going to get anywhere with Jenny it would have to happen over the next few days. Despite my limited window of opportunity I did not want to rush things. This situation would take some very delicate handling and I wanted to build up more good will with my new target before trying to have sex with her.

I guided Jenny through her second day of model training which included some more make up tips and a session with a local model and her photographer that my cousin used from time to time. Jenny needed to learn how to pose and act during photo shoots. Ingrid's business had progressed well beyond just taking a few photos of our friends modeling her outfits in our house or out on the patio.

Jenny learned to appreciate my attention to detail and the way I guided her through every step of her training. She also seemed to enjoy our evening conversations in the suite which were becoming increasingly personal as we both shared some of the things that happened in our short lives thus far. I even started to tell her about my adventures with Robin and some of the other kids. She was smart and already knew that we were fooling around with each other, but I think she liked hearing me admit to her. I did that to be honest, but also to build trust between us.

The third day of her Model boot camp was even more comprehensive then the first two and by the time we got back to the suite late that evening we were both ready for a break. With two more days to go before her training was complete I once again tried to kept things cool thinking that I did not want to rush her into my game. Exhausted by everything that was being hurled at her, Jenny sat down next to me on the couch.

We watched TV for a while, then she became sleepy and began to lean over towards me until she was partially laying over my lap when she finally feel asleep. I did not move fearing I would wake her and began to weigh my options. While I was still thinking about what I should do

Jenny suddenly woke up, realized the position she was in and apologized. Seeing an opportunity, I said that there was no need to apologize and told Jenny that I liked being close to her. I put my arm around her shoulder and pulled her back up against me.

Not wanting to appear too forward, I said that it was too bad that people could not just hold each other once in a while without making a big thing of it. She smiled and remained close to me as we continued to watch TV. At some point I asked Jenny if she was tired and wanted to go to bed? She said she was really comfortable sitting with me, so I took a shot and held her hand. She responded by squeezing my hand and cuddling up closer to me. Although I was a little surprised at her actions, I knew not to read too much into them or overreact.

After the show we were watching ended, I suggested we go to bed. Jennie agreed and began to head off to her bedroom. Before she went in to bed she turned around, came back towards me and gave me a sweet kiss on the cheek. Smiling as she walked off I knew this was a good sign of wonderful things to come. Little did I knew that fate would again lend a hand that would play out well in my favor.

Late that night a huge thunderstorm hit the area. This one was typical of a summertime 'window shaker' style Florida storm and I am sure that it woke everyone up who was staying in the hotel; which included Jenny and me. I got up to go and get a better view of the storm and the spectacular lightning displays it brought to us through the living room sliding door windows which looked out on to the beach and Gulf of Mexico beyond it. Before long I was joined by Jenny who ran into the room and glued herself to me in fear.

Seeing that she was upset and had no intention of going back to bed alone I walked her into my bedroom and suggested she lay next to me in my bed until the storm passed. She was too frightened by the lightning and thunder-boomers to worry about anything nasty that I might have had in mind and quickly crawled into my bed still glued to my side. As the storm went on I loved the feel of her soft skin and warm body against mine. We were facing each other and it was easy to feel her breasts making contact with my chest through her nighty and the tee shirt I was wearing.

Jenny was probably so scared that she did not even notice that I was wearing only a tee shirt and underpants. Even if she did notice it, she was still too frightened by the storm to let it bother her. As the storm finally begin to move away replaced by light rain we were still holding each other under the covers. Jenny snuggled against me and thanked me for allowing her to behave like such a little baby during the fierce display of nature's fury. I told her that I was glad she came to lay next to me in my bed and kissed her on the cheek.

Knowing this was an opportunity that might not come again I took a shot and slowly began kissing Jenny lightly on the lips. She allowed me to do that and responded in kind. Before long we were making out. I knew that was still a long way from having sex with her and was not really sure how to move forward? I could feel her passion for me through our kisses, so I decided to try some petting.

I carefully slid my hand up from the bottom of her nighty until it made contact with her breasts. At first she jerked back a little in surprise, but probably did not want to send me the wrong signal by totally resisting my advances and moved back towards me allowing my hand to fondle her breasts. As we French kissed I worked her nighty up until I was able to take it off over her head. At that point I took off my tee shirt and held Jenny close. I loved the way her ample breasts made contact with my chest.

I felt a bit like a masher as I petted her body, but I also knew that I had kind of earned the right to do what I was doing in a perverted sort of way. As far as I was concerned it was now or never so I decided to slide off my underpants and after I did began removing her panties. Once again Jenny jerked back away from me for a split second, then gave into my will and allowed me to slide off her panties.

Both of us were naked with only the night lights from outside the hotel window illuminating my bedroom through the few slits in the closed drapes. I gently pulled the covers off of us and began pressing myself against Jenny. I caught an occasional look at her crotch which sported a plentiful crop of dirty blond pubic hair. Apart from that she did not have much body hair that I could notice and I liked it that way.

Jenny tried to concentrate her efforts on getting me to make out with her. I assume she was trying to divert my attention from trying to have intercourse with her, so I backed off a bit and began to finger her. She had a relatively normal sized opening for her size with slight lips. I was able to slide a couple fingers into her before hitting her hymen. When Jenny was not looking I licked my fingers spreading some saliva on them to make it easier to get them in and around her opening and fingered her some more.

As I felt her hymen I was tempted to try and push my fingers all the way in and bust it out, but I decided to save that honor for my penis. Despite her best efforts to keep me making out with her, I eventually stopped kissing her and got myself lubricated and into position for intercourse. Jenny put on her best prefabricated smile as I mounted her and slowly pushed my penis inside her. My dick was really stiff and broke through her hymen with little resistance. Jenny shuttered a bit and took a few deep breaths as I took away her innocence, then laid back and allowed me to have my way with her.

Because Jenny was two years younger than me I knew she that sex was not something she might immediately enjoy as much as I would, so I took it slow and made sure that I stopped to kiss and hug her throughout our love making. The last thing I wanted was for her to feel like a sex toy for my penis. I handled the situation with as much kindness and gentleness as I could possibly muster. I sensed from her reaction that she appreciated my effort.

I knew that the main reason I was getting as far as I did was because of the modeling gig I got for her. She could have turned me down, but I sensed she felt like she owed me something. There was no doubt that Jenny liked me, but I suspect she would have liked to remain a virgin for longer than she had. I wanted to feel guilty, but I was enjoying myself too much for that and probably would have regretted not going all the way with her if I had held back.

After I shot my load into her Jennie gave me deep kisses until she finally had to get up and use the bathroom. I told her to go ahead and take a bath or shower if she liked, then rejoin me in bed. I think she was surprised that I asked her to come back to bed with me. I wanted her to know this was not just a 'wham bam thank you ma'am' situation. I had genuinely come to care about Jenny as a friend and maybe something more.

I hated just having sex for sex sake even with my list of potential game players always on my mind. I wanted relationships of some sort with my players and that took a lot of work considering how many there were. The good news was that my sexual encounters with Robin, Kathleen, Patty, Rob, Rosemary, the twins and the others were more about mutually enjoyable sex than anything else. I could have guiltless intercourse with them without worrying that they wanted anything more out of it. I could have treated the Jenny the same way, but I did not want to do that.

Jenny was more than just an extremely pretty girl to me, she was now a close friend and someone whom I had shared some serious conversations, sexual relations and feelings with. I had no idea how she really felt about me, so that would the deciding factor. If she wanted to be with me as much as I wanted to be with her, I was all in to that. If not, I guessed we would keep things casual and have sex when and if it was mutually desired.

After Jenny came back to bed we kissed some more without saying a lot. She was really into making out with me and I hoped that was a good sign that she wanted a relationship with me. We feel asleep next to each other. When I woke up in the morning I marveled at the beauty that clung to me throughout the night. I carefully separated myself from her to get up and shower. After I dressed I went out and got some breakfast for us from the hotel cafe. When everything was ready, I gently woke Jenny up and gave her a good morning kiss.

Jenny smiled at me as she headed off to get washed and ready for the days activities. After breakfast in the suite, it was back to the Beauty Salon. Ingrid arrived after lunch to have Jenny try on some more outfits for a photo shoot the next and final day of her training. I spent some time with my cousin filling her in on the intimate details of my latest sexual conquest out of earshot of Jenny who was trying on the various outfits that Ingrid brought with her.

Ingrid loved being a part of my game and appreciated getting an excellent young teen model for her clothes in the process. That happened over and over again with my cousin gaining pretty models or excellent workers as a result of our combined and perverted efforts. I was not necessarily proud of that fact, but it was a fact nevertheless and one that was appreciated by both of us. We were a team of the most vile sort, but I blamed myself more than my cousin for that. She may have had leanings towards the same games that I did, but I was the one who motivated her to actually play them.

The day again flew by and I did not have much of a chance to talk with Jenny, so I took her to a nice restaurant across the street in the hotel shopping center that evening. We had a great time, heard some wonderful live music and then headed back to the hotel. Before going back to the suite, we walked along the beach behind the hotel and watched as couples held hands. I offered my hand to her and she took it.

We talked about all that happened that week except for our sexual encounter and the possibility of a more romantic relationship between us. Fortunately Jenny found other ways of expressing her feelings towards me. She not only held my hand, but occasionally placed her arm around my waist. I told her that I was proud of her and even though I already felt she was a living work of art from the time I first set eyes on her, the make over and training had made her into a goddess.

Jenny blushed at my comments, so I took the opportunity to kiss her. She responded in kind and we found a quiet place to make out by some palm trees just off the beach. That sealed the deal for me. I knew she liked me and this was no longer just a 'thank you for everything' situation of Jenny giving in to me out of appreciation for all I did for her. It was something much more.

After a stop at the cafe for some ice cream we headed up to the suite and sat next to each other on the couch. We watched TV for a while, then Jenny surprised me by climbing into a position on top of me which was perfect for making out. Kissing Jenny was something special for me. I shivered a bit as we made out and felt myself falling head on into another serious relationship.

I was not going to even try and go for the gold again until Jenny sensed my hesitation and took off her top. I responded by taking off my shirt and undershirt while she took off her bra. Once again our bare chests touched each other. As we continued to make out I could feel Jenny's heart beat and breathing increase. I had managed to turn her on and there was no going back.

I carefully picked up Jenny and carried her into my bedroom. We both took off the rest of our clothes and got into bed. Before long our horizontal make out session turned into sex. Once again I was inside Jenny and this time she was wet. My penis slid in and out of her with ease and she really got into our session. Although I was surprised that my newest game player was so eager to have sex again that soon, I was not about to question her morals since she did not question mine.

Now that sex was becoming more comfortable between us, I led Jenny into different positions. At some point I ate her out. I really craved her opening and when I did begin licking her down there I found that she tasted clean and fresh. I could not get enough of eating her out and eventually moved on until I got around to her anus. That was also surprisingly clean and tasty, without a hair ring around it like there was on some other girls.

I did not push things to the point of asking her to suck me off or having anal sex with her, that would come later. At this point I wanted everything we did to be about passion and love making. We went on for over two hours between making out and actually having sex. After Jenny began to dry up and got sore, we stopped. We slept together and it felt great to once again wake up next to her in the morning.

After breakfast we headed down to the Beauty Salon so that Jenny could get made up for her photo shoot. Ingrid arrived after lunch to help her new model get fitted into the outfits they chose the day before. I was amazed at how far my cousin's business had progressed as I watched Jenny pose for the photographer. She was a natural and the camera loved her! I knew that Jenny's mom would arrive to pick her up later that afternoon, so I said my goodbyes to her and asked her to call me after the smoke cleared from everything.

Back at the house I began weighing my options. With Donna and her sister due back from camp the next day I wondered what would happen between us? I still liked Donna and did not really want to even think about giving up my relationship with her, but Jenny was a special girl who would require a lot of my time. I did not want to race into a relationship with her, but that was the way things worked out. I did not want to lose the opportunity to be with her because of anything else I was seeing regularly.

Now that Jenny had demonstrated a real desire to have sex, I wanted to be sure that she did not have to go elsewhere to fulfill her craving. I was under no illusion and understood that like all teenage girls and boys she would not be faithful for very long, but as long as she was I wanted to be with her and her alone. I would just have to wait and see what happened after Donna came back. I had not spoken to her in a long time due to limited phone availability at the camp, so there was no way to know where her head was at with our relationship.

Jenny called me later that night to let me know how happy her mom was with the way everything turned out. She had a phone in her room with her own number so we could talk freely. Both of us initially felt that telling her mother about any relationship we might have would be a none starter and if she ever found out that we were actually having sex we would both be finished.

Despite the obstacles we faced, it was obvious that Jenny wanted us to be together as a dating couple and to continue our physical relationship as much as I did. With those things in mind we decided to keep things cool for the weekend to avoid her mom's scrutiny and made a date to meet on Monday afternoon at my house. Ingrid needed some time with Jenny anyway, so it was the perfect opportunity to see each other again.

Sometimes I felt like Fate had my life on speed dial. With no need to worry about Jenny for the weekend, I was ready to face Donna on Saturday night. I called her late Saturday afternoon to find out if we could get together. She was anxious to see me, but seemed a bit disconnected from our conversation. I picked her up later that evening and as soon as I saw Donna I knew something was up.

Donna was dressed in a very conservative looking outfit instead of her normal casual style of dress. As she got into my car she asked if we could go to the ice cream restaurant in the mall instead of going to my house? I agreed and we did not say much to each other until we got into the restaurant. After we ordered, Donna told me that she and her sister had experienced a religious rebirth.

I knew that she was a part of a church that had a reputation for very conservative religious teaching, so her revelation was not really a huge surprise to me. After over a month of constant religious instruction anyone would likely revert to the roots of their faith and turn away from what they considered to be the temptations of the world. According to Donna those temptations included our relationship and my cousin's business. She no longer wanted to be a part of either of those things, but invited to join her world by visiting her local church the next day.

It might surprise you to know that I believed in God and loved him. I already knew the things that her faith offered and had embraced them in my own private way. I politely declined and after we ate I dropped her back home. I told her to call me anytime she liked, but that I really had no interest in visiting her church and had already made my own commitment to God. I knew she doubted me, but it was true.

My relationship with Donna and her sister was over. I cannot say I was unhappy about it considering what had recently happened between Jenny and I, and for the first time in a long time I felt free of being over-committed to girls. Even my relationship with Susan had cooled significantly. We still saw each other and continued our physical relationship, but the fact that I was also having sex with her sister, brothers and other kids made her less interested in me over time as a serious boyfriend and more as a friend and occasional lover.

Susan, Robin and her friends had replaced most of the other game players in my life. Even Rob and Rosemary were about to go back home to be with their dad. I was actually glad to see them go. Rosemary was emotionally immature and I worried that she would say or do something that could get both of us in trouble as long as we were sleeping under the same roof. Rob had really cooled off to me after the anal sex incident with Mitchell. The fact that I continued to have sex with him since we both slept in the same bed did not help things either.

I very selfishly made sure to have sex with Rosemary and Rob yet again over that final weekend of their stay. Rob was barely talking to me by then, but he still allowed me to have my way with him. He knew that he owed me some favors and did not want to build too big a wall between us just in case he had to stay over my house at some time in the near future. Rosemary liked me and the sex we had together, so doing it with her was a mutually satisfying experience without any relationship hassles.

As I ran errands for my cousin on Monday morning I began to think about the future. School was starting up very soon and I knew that meant many changes since I would be beginning my Junior year. I also needed a game plan to deal with Jenny. I was tired of sneaking around parents and hiding my relationships. I knew that I could never reveal everything I was doing to my parents or anyone else's, but if I was going to date Jenny I wanted that part of our relationship to be out in the open despite our age difference.

Regardless of her age, Jenny was wise beyond her years and who could fault me for wanting to date such a beautiful and intelligent girl? This is something I planned on discussing with her that very afternoon. I felt that if she agreed with me, my cousin could help run interference with her mom and convince her that there was nothing wrong with us officially dating. I hoped that she would appreciate our honesty and the fact that we would rather have her blessing than sneak around behind her back.

Jenny's mom dropped her off at our house after lunch. After Ingrid finished with Jenny, she changed into her bathing suit and we went into the pool together. Rob and Rosemary were packing up their stuff and getting ready to leave the next morning and none of the other kids were around, so it was the perfect time to have a serious conversation with Jenny about our

future. While she listened attentively to me and agreed with most of what I said, the idea of her mom finding out that we were dating scared the daylights out of her.

As much as I wanted our relationship to be on the up and up with her mom, I bowed to her concerns that telling her mother would be an extremely bad idea right at that time. We dropped the subject and made out in the pool. That lead to a trip to my bedroom and yet another sexual encounter. After we cleaned up and showered I told Jenny what happened with Donna just to clear the air. She tried to hide her joy, but it was obvious she was glad to have me pretty much all to herself.

Jenny confessed that she worried about me being around older girls which she thought were more desirable to me. Perhaps that explained why she seemed to want to have sex with me more than what I would have expected? Either way, I told her that she did not need to worry about my commitment to her. I made it clear that as much as I enjoyed having sex with her, I could not imagine being with anyone else for reasons that ran a lot deeper than our physical relationship.

After my folks got home from work Jenny joined us for dinner. Ingrid sang her praises and told my parents what a wonderful person and model she was, but my folks were already sold on her. She had manners, intelligence and was obviously more than a friend to me. My parents trusted me and were less concerned about what I was doing with Jenny and more impressed with her demeanor and the fact that she was as much against smoking, drugs and alcohol as I was.

After dinner Jenny and I made some plans for later in the week before Ingrid drove her home. We needed to put some space between our meetings to keep her mom from becoming suspicious. In the mean time I would do some shopping for school supplies and continue to help my cousin by trying to fill the gap left by Donna and her sister since they were no longer available to work for her. The good news was that Robin and Susan's folks had finally managed to convince some more of their relatives to come and help with their motel which meant that Susan could begin working for my cousin more frequently again.

Having Susan around was helpful in many ways. After Rob and Rosemary left she was in charge of things when neither I nor my cousin were around. She kept an eye on things and made sure that Robin and her friends respected the privacy limits of our house by staying out of the bedrooms and areas where they did not belong. Robin was coming over more frequently since her folks were always busy at the hotel. She did not like being at her house by herself or with her friends there and her parents not home.

I did not mind that Robin and her friends came over because they were respectful of our property and generally careful not to make messes or cause problems. Besides, I still enjoyed having sex with her, her sister, the twins and the others on a regular basis. I had backed off them a bit since getting seriously involved with Jenny, but I knew better than to slam the door completely on any opportunity to keep kids in my game.

By midweek I was already missing Jenny. Although we spoke on the phone at least once a day, I could not wait until Saturday to see her. My folks planned on spending that weekend at the hotel and that meant that seeing Jenny would be extra special. My cousin was already working on a

plan to have Jenny sleep over using her business as an excuse and considering the excellent impression she made on Jenny's mom, it was practically a done deal.

After I finished my work on Wednesday afternoon I was surprised to see Jimmy at the house with Robin and her other friends. I had not seen him for a while and it was unusual to for him to come around without Tommy at his side. It turned out that Tommy was away for a few days with his parents and that left Jimmy without much to do. Taking a shot at getting Jimmy into my game, I decided to try and get to know him better.

Jimmy and I talked for a while and after I felt he was more comfortable opening up to me, I asked him to stay for dinner. My parents were eating out that night and Ingrid was with her friends, so it was just me and Jimmy after the other kids left. I made us some terrific sub sandwiches, then we sat and watched TV for a while. I sensed that Jimmy missed Tommy and asked him if he wanted to sleep over? He was surprised at my invitation, but I was even more surprised when he accepted it.

Jimmy called home to get permission to stay over, then joined me in the recreation room to play some pool and listen to records. His mom stopped by with a change of clothes for him and after our game I invited Jimmy to join me for a dip in the pool. He surprised me again by coming into my bedroom and changing into his bathing suit in front of me. I knew that was a big step for him and it was obvious I had earned his trust. Jimmy had a nice penis with a decent shaft that was a little smaller than mine, along with a patch of very blond pubic hair. I loved the light freckles he had all over and the fact he had very little body hair overall.

Even with my parents coming home later that night I knew I had a shot at him when bedtime came around. They never came upstairs at night or bothered me once I went to bed. If worse came to worse I would wait until he was asleep and see if I could suck him off or play around with his dick while he slept. As we hung out and messed around in the pool I was surprised to see his penis become slightly stiff. I tried to ignore it, but Jimmy's woody was kind of obvious through his tight fitting swimsuit. Perhaps he was more like me then he or I thought possible?

After we played around in the pool for a while we got out and had some refreshments and a snack before heading up to my bedroom. Jimmy was having a good time and I sensed that I had helped to fill the gap that was created by his best friend's absence. That was something I could build on, but I needed to be careful. Jimmy was smart and after what happened to him and Tommy at the hands of the perverted photographer, he was unlikely to fall for any lame brained attempts to have sex with him.

Once we were back up in my bedroom, Jimmy took off his bathing suit and handed it to me so that I could hang it in the upstairs bathroom to dry along with mine. I made quick work of that chore and by the time I got back into my bedroom Jimmy was still naked and looking through what his mom had brought for something to wear to bed. Since I was as naked as he was, I decided to try the straight forward approach.

I went over to Jimmy and slapped him on the butt. He turned around and asked what I was doing? I smiled and said I was challenging him to a Greek style wrestling match which I

explained meant total nudity while competing. I started pushing at his shoulders playfully and Jimmy responded by smiling at me and pushing back. Probably thinking this was just innocent horseplay, he went along with what I was doing and wrestled with me in the standing position.

Before long I had Jimmy down on the floor and pinned. He said I cheated and we both laughed about it. Once again Jimmy was sporting a woody and this time I made mention of it to see what he would say or do. I laughed and said, "Looks like somebody needs some penal exercise!" while staring at his hard-on. Jimmy was a little annoyed that I pointed out his woody, but I told him it was normal for any guy making body contact with someone else to get one and admitted that it often happened to me. I decided to continue to pursue the subject hoping it would open the door to some sexual fun for both of us.

I asked Jimmy if he ever jacked off and suggested that would help him to avoid getting regular erections. He said he did, so I suggested that perhaps he was not doing it right or following through. At that point I could see that Jimmy was getting nervous. He was already digging through his overnight bag again for something to wear. Even while he was doing that I offered to help him with his problem by showing him how to get the most out of jacking off.

I was sure that Jimmy had heard about some of my sexual encounters with Robin and her friends and that may have helped to account for his concern about our topic of conversation. However, I was determined to have some fun with him so I decided to play the blackmail card. I reminded Jimmy about how upset Mitchell was when the rumor about him being gay spread around and wondered how he would feel if a rumor like that was spread around about him?

Jimmy stopped digging through his bag and asked me what I meant by that? I said that it would just be a shame if the other kids heard about the woody he got while we were playing around in the pool and wrestling. I said that no body needed to know as long as he allowed me to play around with him. Jimmy was upset, but not shocked. At that point he told me that he and Tommy both heard about me playing around with some of the other kids, but they did not know if it was true or not.

I admitted to Jimmy that the stories about my games were true and gave him a briefing on them. I said that if he gave my games a chance he might just have some fun. I also said that since he had probably never been with a girl, I could solve that problem as well. I told him that I could make sure that his first time with one was special and not just some quick 'stick it in and pull it out' in the back of some car.

As I spoke to Jimmy I lead him to the bed making sure that he got away from his overnight bag. I had him lay flat and said I would start by playing with his penis and balls a little until he got used to me touching him. Jimmy was silent and tried to act like what I was doing was alright with him even if it wasn't. He was fidgety as I began to touch his penis and feel around his balls, but he let me do my thing.

After a short while I lubricated his dick and began to jack him. He became stiff right away and looked embarrassed by that fact. I told him to relax and before long he shot a load on to his abdomen. I took a towel and cleaned him up, then said I wanted to teach him how to French kiss.

He sat up quickly and said he already knew how to do that. I could have cared less what he knew or did not know and told him to lay back down. I explained that he was going to French kiss with me whether he liked it or not.

I had hoped that my bullying days were over, but I was so into my game that it was sometimes a necessity. It also occasionally paid off for some of the kids I bullied into sex. A lot of them really wanted to play around and once they did were often better off for it. In Jimmy's case I was just too turned on by him to not go for the gold any way that I could get it.

Jimmy was red face embarrassed as we began kissing, but he eventually got into it enough to tell me he was not being entirely honest with himself or me about his sexuality. He obviously swung both ways as I suspected from his earlier hard-ons. After I finished kissing him, I told him that I was going to suck him off. By this time Jimmy was compliant and laid back quietly as I began to suck his dick. His penis got really stiff and I loved the feel of his long, thin staff in my mouth.

Once again he shot his load quickly and I sucked down every drop! Jimmy was really cute and I loved messing around with him. Just to exert my dominance over him I made Jimmy suck me off. It really did not take a lot of convincing and I suspected he enjoyed it more than he admitted. He did not swallow my load, but sucked on my dick until his mouth was full and that was more than I had hoped for.

After Jimmy washed out his mouth he came back to bed and asked me what was next? As I lubricated my penis, I said it was time to consummate our new relationship with anal sex. Once again Jimmy sat up quickly. He said that there was no way he was going to do that! I just laughed, pulled him into position and held him down as best I could while spreading his butt cheeks apart. I told him not to yell because even though my folks were not home yet, I did not want to wake up Ingrid who came in while we were doing our thing.

I said that if he was quiet and let me have my way with him I would do it slow and gently. If he tried to make noise or get away I would jam my stiff penis into him. Jimmy got the message and settled down as I started to push my penis into his slightly freckled buttocks. He had a decent sized hole so my penis went in without a lot of hassle. I eased it into him ever so slowly and tried to be as gentle as possible under the circumstances. Despite my careful approach, I could see that Jimmy was in pain and I just hoped it would ease up as his butt got used to my cock.

I began having anal intercourse with Jimmy and got really turned on by his very cute and lightly freckled back and buttocks. I loved the feel of my penis sliding in and out of him and it was not long before my dick was numb. Just as I was about to shoot my load I got an unpleasant surprise. I knew it was coming by the smell, but hoped I was wrong. As I shot my load on to his buttocks I saw that me penis was covered with his excrement.

I had a few incidents before that one when some excrement ending up on my penis, but never that bad. I immediately dragged Jimmy into the bathroom so that we could both get cleaned up. I told him not be worry about the situation and if there was blame to be assigned it was assigned to me for practically raping him. Jimmy kept silent and got cleaned up. After we were back in my bedroom I pulled him back into bed.

Jimmy was shocked that even after what happened I wanted more sex from him, but to tell you the truth it turned me on in a weird sort of way. I left his butt alone for the rest of our session, but sucked him off again and did some more French kissing before I allowed him to get into his underwear and go to sleep next to me. Even after he was dead asleep I pulled down his underpants and played with his penis some more. I was really attracted to his body and could not get enough of it!

I woke up before Jimmy in the morning. I was never a long sleeper and waking up early was like a ritual for me in most instances. I went downstairs and shared news of my my latest triumph with Ingrid. To my surprised she liked Jimmy's look as much as I did so I saw an opportunity. I asked her if she wanted to do it with him and she said she did. After my cousin went to work I formulated a plan in my mind and had it all ready by the time that my new player came down to breakfast.

I told Jimmy that I needed him to come back over on Friday evening and promised a nice female surprise if he did. I also dropped another bomb by telling Jimmy that after Tommy came back from his trip I wanted Jimmy to help me get his friend into my game. Jimmy was past being shocked at anything I said and just told me that he would try. I told him that he had better do more than try and left it at that.

With the extra work I had to do now that Rob, Rosemary, Donna and her sister were no longer available to help Ingrid the day flew by. Even with Diane and Susan helping out, we needed more workers. The problem was that I did not know anyone old enough that I could really trust to help out and do a meaningful day's work. Fortunately, a previous employee was about to resurface in my life. Late on Thursday afternoon I got a call from my mother who said that Jesse would be coming by that evening with Laura.

Yet another family spat had erupted and she was again at odds with her mom, dad and all of her other relatives. Jesse was coming to stay with us for another indeterminate period of time. Fate must have had a great laugh over that one. One set of house guests leave and another arrives right on their heals and just happens to be one who was an excellent worker and model for Ingrid. I missed Laura for many reasons and looked forward to her return. As soon as Ingrid heard the good news she could not have been happier.

Jesse arrived with Laura and a pile of suitcases around five that evening just before my folks got home from work. I already had the spare bedroom ready for her and got her settled in before dinner. We hugged and kissed and got caught up. Laura was no longer involved with Mark. All the family hassles and social pressures of the day pushed them apart. I was sad to hear that and had not heard from Mark for some time. I suspected he had enough of my game and was avoiding me, which I totally understood.

Laura was thrilled to be back at our house and we were glad to have her living with us again. After dinner with us I took her aside to find out if she could go back to helping my cousin again. She said she could and appreciated the chance to make some cash. That took a huge burden off

my back and made life easier for my cousin, Diane and Susan as well. Later that night after my folks and Ingrid went to bed Laura joined me in the pool.

It was hard not to be attracted to her, but I knew that getting back involved with Laura would really complicate my relationship with Jenny. I decided to leave that situation alone. If Laura came on to me I would do it with her because I liked her and did not want to create a wall of any kind between us. So far I did not get any hints that she wanted more than a friendship with me and I was fine leaving things at that.

Laura started playfully fooling around with me in the pool. I hoped it was just her enthusiasm at being back at my house and the fact that we had not seen each other for a long time, but I guess I knew better. Before long we were making out just like we used to. After we got out of the pool she ended up in my room and we had sex. Afterward Laura apologized for pushing me into it and explained her actions. She said she missed me and the things we did together. She had not had the same really close relationship with Mark that she had with me. Laura also gave me the impression he was not a very good sex partner.

I was honest with Laura explaining that although I still played my game, I was also seriously involved with a girl. I did not mind having a subdued relationship with her which included as much sex as she liked, but I could not offer more. She understood and my revelation did not seem to bother her at all. I wanted to keep her as a lover now that we had renewed our physical relationship and knew better than to close any door of opportunity, especially one as pretty as her.

Friday was an easier day for me with Laura helping out. My folks headed straight off to spend the weekend at the hotel suite without stopping by the house. Although Jenny had a family event to attend on Friday, she would be coming over on Saturday and staying for a sleep over until late Sunday thanks to my cousin's influence on her mom. Susan did some work for Ingrid in the morning, then we all had lunch at the house.

I took Susan out to the movies in the early afternoon and for some ice cream afterward. By the time we got back to the house it was late afternoon. We headed up to my room and had some much needed intercourse. We had not really been able to spend any quality time together for a while. I loved having sex with Susan and was probably more physically attracted to her than anything else.

After we got cleaned up, Susan had to go to meet her parents at the motel. She was trying to train some of her relatives who moved to Florida to give her folks a hand. They were planning to expand their motel on property they owned adjacent to it that was previously leased to a nearby attraction as a parking lot. I knew that would keep Susan busy even with the newly arrived helping hands and that was fine by me.

After Susan left I cleaned up the house and got ready for the arrival of Jimmy. I reminded Ingrid about her appointment with him. My cousin was ready and could not wait to get him into her. She and I shared tastes in boys and he was certainly tasty! Jimmy surprised me by arriving a little

early with his sleep over bag in hand and a surprise. He brought Tommy with him. I hoped that he did so because of my strongly worded suggestion to help me to get Tommy into my game.

Jimmy took me aside to tell me that he had spoken with Tommy and told him that I could get him laid if he let me see him naked and mess around with him. Could it be that simple? I knew that Jimmy was the leader of the two, but I did not think he had that much clout with his friend. Tommy was the kind of kid who thought of himself as tough, although not a bully. I could not see him just giving into me.

After speaking with Jimmy for a few minutes I got the impression that Jimmy had sold his friend on my game as a kind of training session for sex. That was fine by me and as long as I could deliver the goods, I figured that Tommy was already in my pocket. Despite my optimism, I knew that these things could not be rushed. I asked Jimmy if he could work it out so that Tommy would be able to sleep over? Jimmy was two steps ahead of me having already made sure that Tommy had permission to sleep over along with him on Friday night.

I knew that Robin would eventually stop by with some of her girl friends so I decided to put off most of what I planned to do with Tommy until later. I brought the two boys up to my room to stow their overnight bags and change into their bathing suits. I could see my influence on Jimmy already was taking affect. Not only did the boys arrive without their bathing suits on under their pants, but Jimmy told Tommy they should change in my room right along with me.

Once Tommy was naked I could see that he had a nice penis and set of testicles that was about the size of my own. His shaft was shorter than mine or Jimmy's, but he had a well defined crown and some dark shiny pubic hair above his dick. Like Jimmy he did not have much body hair. What he did have was a surprisingly shapely and very cute buttocks. It was larger than Jimmy's and I could not wait to explore it further. I also liked the fact that unlike on previous occasions, he did not seem at all shy about changing in front of me. Jimmy must have had a lot more sway over him than I previously counted on.

Tommy was naturally shy and did not talk anywhere near as much as Jimmy did. After Jimmy put in a good word for me Tommy opened up a bit more than I thought he would and that allowed me to begin building some trust with him. Tommy was shorter than Jimmy and although I thought he was good looking, I could see where his shyness easily got in the way of helping him to date or score with girls. That was where I could be helpful as long as he was willing to pay my price.

By the time we got into the pool Robin was at the door with Patty and Kathleen. They quickly changed into their bathing suits and joined us. I hoped to get Kathleen together with Tommy, so I asked her to get out of the pool and help me make some snacks for everyone. As we made sandwiches I told Kathleen that she should give Tommy a chance with her. I pointed out that he was a nice guy and would probably make a great boyfriend. Kathleen was interested, but still a little gun shy after her experience with Matt. I told her to let me work on it and she agreed to my proposition.

While everyone had some snacks I took Jimmy aside and asked him to watch over things while I took Tommy up to my room. With everyone taking a break from the pool and sunning themselves on the patio I knew it was a good time to get started with Tommy. I asked him to come and help me with something upstairs and he followed willingly. After we entered my room I locked the door and told him that it was time to do what Jimmy and he had talked about.

Tommy stood before me and made no fuss whatsoever when I asked him to take off his bathing suit. I could hardly believe what was happening and was thrilled to avoid all the usual hassles and double talk needed to get someone into my game. I sat on the edge of the bed and told him to come and stand in front of me. As he stood there naked I said I was going to lubricate his penis and jack it to see how well his dick responded to stimulus and how long it took for him to ejaculate.

I lubricated his penis with no complaint or comment from my newest game player. After I had him ready to be jacked off I told him to lay down in the bed thinking it might be more comfortable. Tommy laid down and allowed me to jack him off. As I went to work I asked Tommy if he liked Kathleen? He said he did, so I suggested he think about her in her bathing suit during our session. His penis began get even stiffer then it already was so it was obvious that he thought she was cute.

While I waited for Tommy to ejaculate I asked him if he would be interested in dating Kathleen? He said he would, so I told him that I planned to get her and him together before the weekend was over. With that seed planted I also asked Tommy if he felt comfortable with the idea of having sex with her and if he thought he was ready for that? He said he did want to have sex with her and was ready for it, so I promised to make that happen as long as he played along with me on everything else.

Before long Tommy shot his load on to his abdomen. I loved the way his penis quickly pumped out liquid. It did so faster than Jimmy's or even my own. I thought that maybe it was just because he was turned on by the idea of having sex with Kathleen, but either way I loved it and held on to his dick until the last drop came out. After I cleaned him up with the towel I said I was going to suck him off. I explained how that it would simulate sex with a girl.

I told Tommy that the oral sex was training to help him avoid premature ejaculation. I explained that girls hated it when guys shot their load after just a minute or two because it took girls longer to enjoy intercourse. I said that the goal of our exercise was to have him wait as long as he could to ejaculate, no matter how good it felt to get his dick sucked. Again, he was surprisingly on board with with what I wanted to do and made no protest.

I got Tommy into position and began sucking him off. Thanks to his shorter shaft I was able to fit his entire stiff penis into my mouth and I loved it. Although shorter, his shaft was as thick as mine and that meant it was thicker than Jimmy's making his dick a great one to suck off. Once again I told him to think about Kathleen and try to wait as long as he could before ejaculating. Tommy kept moving up and down and to the side a bit to try and keep from ejaculating, but his penis soon began to throb and before long I felt it jump in my mouth.

Tommy's dick quickly pumped a load of liquid out into my mouth. I loved the feeling of how fast his semen shot out and almost forgot to swallow it. My newest game player moved up and down as I sucked and swallowed. I could see he was in ecstasy and practically overcome by the sensation he was feeling as his fluid flowed down my throat and I kept sucking on his crown. Once he finished I gently sucked and licked his penis some more to put a cap on things.

After I cleaned him up with a moist towel and went and washed out my own mouth in the bathroom, I returned to the bedroom and asked Jimmy if he knew how to French kiss? He said he heard about it, but had never done it. I decided to use that opportunity to offer to teach him how to do it. "With you?" he asked surprised at my suggestion. That was the first time since I began our session that he appeared to object to anything we were doing.

I explained that I had already done the same thing with Jimmy and that it was no big deal. One mouth was the same as another and if he opened himself up to the experience, he could learn how to properly French kiss and might even enjoy it. Playing the Jimmy card immediately calmed Tommy down and he agreed to give it a try. I repositioned him for my French kissing lesson and joined Tommy on the bed. Both of us were facing each other with our heads on our pillows so that we were ready to get started.

I took things slowly by pressing our lips together and slowly pushing my tongue into his mouth. He resisted a little at first, but once I got him to reciprocate by shoving his tongue into my mouth he settled down and got into what we were doing. Just to make things a little more fun I began playing with his dick as we kissed. After I saw that had had gotten the hang of Frenching, I moved his hand towards my dick and told him to play with it. He obediently played with my penis which almost immediately began hard and very stiff.

I was more than a little surprised when Tommy shot his load as we were Frenching and he was jacking my penis. He was immediately embarrassed, but I quickly cleaned him up with a towel and said he had nothing to be embarrassed about. I explained that his ejaculation was a natural reaction of the stimulation he felt as we kissed and jacked each other. Personally, I loved the feel of his fluid flowing through my hand and kept jacking him until every last drop came out.

With things going so well I decided to go for the gold. I told Tommy that our final exercise of the day would be anal sex. He practically jumped up out of the bed when I said that and immediately wanted to know what I was going to do to him. I explained that I liked having sex with boys as much as I did with girls and planned to consummate our session by gently and carefully pushing my penis into his anus.

Tommy sat up on the bed quietly for a few seconds, than told me that he did not think he could do that. I said that I understood how he felt, but that it was going to happen one way or another. I suggested that if it bothered him to allow me to have anal sex with him, he could always get into position and then resist me. I would force myself on him and that would help to quell any guilt he might feel about letting me have intercourse with him.

While I lubricated my penis I was honestly surprised that Tommy had not grabbed his clothes and tried to flee my room. Instead, he willingly allowed me to get him into position for anal sex.

Robin and Patty had to leave, but I asked Kathleen to stay behind. She did not have to be home for hours yet which meant that right after dinner I could get things rolling. Ingrid joined us for the our meal on the patio and then surprised Jimmy by inviting him into her room. Jimmy smiled at me widely, so I guessed he was happy with my choice of female companionship for him. After Jimmy and Ingrid went off to enjoy sexual bliss, I knew it was time to create some of my own with Kathleen and Tommy. I told the couple to come upstairs with me and they willingly followed.

Once we were in my bedroom I locked the door and told them that it was time for a session of my game. Although Kathleen was a little shocked by my revelation, she went along with what I was doing. Tommy just stood by quietly waiting for my directions. I told the two future lovers to take off their bathing suits and although they both got a little red faced, they did as I had instructed. As the couple got ready for sex I put on some shorts and a tee shirt. I knew it would be unwise to be an active part of this session, so I decided to sit this one out and watch.

After the they were naked I told Tommy and Kathleen that I wanted them both to date. I said that I liked both of them very much and thought they would make a great pair. I said that the best way to break through the ice was for them to have sex. Kathleen giggled a little and said, "I guess so." Tommy just smiled widely at her and was obviously in agreement with my plan. I said that I was going to stay, direct and watch their first time together, but in the future I promised they could have intercourse in my room by themselves as long as my folks were not home and Tommy used a condom.

I had the couple lay next to each other on the bed and French kiss while I sat in a chair and watched them carefully. After just a few minutes they were passionately making out. Tommy's dick became very stiff, so I told Kathleen to play with his penis while they continued kissing. Knowing that Tommy was more then ready to penetrate his new girl friend, I had him lubricate his penis and got the couple into the right positions for intercourse.

I suggested they begin without Tommy using a condom and warned him to stop once he felt he was near an ejaculation. The couple fumbled around a bit, but soon found their groove and were screwing like the best of them. I loved watching Tommy shove his penis into Kathleen as their dark and shiny pubic hair met. They looked like a perfect fit for each other. I made them change positions several times and had Tommy put on a condom just in case. He did a pretty good job of trying to avoid premature ejaculation until Kathleen got on top of him. At that point he finally shot his load.

While the couple cleaned up together in the upstairs bathroom I felt satisfied that I had managed to play Cupid between Tommy and Kathleen. With my own love life always in some bizarre state of flux it was nice to know that I could still manage to help others with theirs. The downside of that session was that watching the two young lovers have sex left me horny and wanting some fun of my own.

After Kathleen went home I watched TV with Tommy for a while before we headed up to bed. Normally I would have went after him, but my taste was set for pussy after seeing Kathleen get naked and pumped by Tommy. My cousin would have been the perfect answer to my problem if

she had not been busy with Jimmy. I was sure they were still going at it and knew it would be unwise to even attempt to intrude.

I was too horny to go to sleep and knew that although I was trying to avoid her for fear of getting deeply involved once more, Laura was the answer to my problem. I quietly slipped out of my bedroom trying not to wake up Tommy and headed for the spare bedroom. After taking off my clothes I laid in bed next to Laura and began rubbing her back. Before long she began to wake up, turned over and smiled at me. The next hour with her was bliss and after we finished having sex I feel asleep next to her.

I saw Jimmy before he left on Saturday morning. Not wanting to say anything for fear of Ingrid hearing, he just smiled widely at me instantly conveying his satisfaction with no words necessary. Ingrid told me later that she really enjoyed herself with him. She also warned me to be careful and said it was probably just as much a mistake for her to have sex with an underage boy as it was for me to do with with kids younger than myself. I appreciated her concern, but with so many beautiful bodies of both sexes around it was hard to ignore them.

Tommy woke up and left not long after Jimmy. He already planned to see Kathleen later that day which made me happy. The original; plan was to have both boys sleep over Friday and Saturday nights, but with Jenny sleeping over I thought it might not be a good idea in case her mom showed up at the house for any reason. I did tell Jimmy that I wanted to see him sometime after school later that week. He already knew why.

Jenny arrived later that day and spent some time with Ingrid for business matters. By the time they finished up I was in the pool with Laura and invited her to join us. Jenny took the news that Laura would be living with us again pretty well. As good looking as she was, Jenny did not really have to worry about competition and I was not stupid enough to get things fired up with Laura again.

The first thing I did was to take Jenny up to the strip mall. I didn't say why we were going there, but after we walked into the jewelry store I guessed she knew something nice was coming her way. The clerk came out, brought her ring and she could not believe it. It was a beautiful ring and the most expensive one I had bought to date. Jenny cried, laughed and tried to stay still while the clerk fitted the ring on her finger. She left that store a happy girl.

As the day wore on Jenny and I ended up in my bedroom and once again had glorious sex. Once afraid of sex, it seemed like she could not get enough of it with me and I loved that. The only we faced now was explaining the friendship ring to her parents. For the time being she would say it was a gift from Ingrid and I for helping her with my cousin's business. That would keep her mom happy for the moment without arising too much suspicion or concern in her mind.

By dinner time I was a very satisfied guy and enjoyed a nice meal with Jenny, Ingrid and Laura. Jenny helped me clean up, then we sat on the couch planning the rest of the evening. I decided to take Jenny to the movies and for some ice cream afterward. She was not supposed to leave the house without telling her mom, so I knew I was taking a risk.

We went out around seven and returned around nine thirty to a total disaster. There was a police car in front of our house with its lights on. It was not Jenny's mom as I had feared, but rather my cousin. She became ill sometime after we left and had Laura call an ambulance just a half hour before Jenny and I came home. A police officer was talking with Laura to find out what happened. She told him that Ingrid started feeling really sick to her stomach and began throwing up constantly.

Fortunately, the police officer did not ask much about me or Jenny after he found out that we were all having a sleep over and Ingrid was the adult in charge. I promised to contact my parents after Laura and I checked in with my cousin at the hospital. I had to take Jenny home first. There was no way I could justify her staying at the house overnight without Ingrid present and if her mom found out that she was staying over without an adult present we would be finished.

Laura and I visited Ingrid in the Emergency Room after dropping Jenny home. The doctors believed my cousin had a bad stomach virus, but nothing more serious. I called my parents who also came to the hospital to make sure that my cousin was alright. With them on the scene my folks suggested that Laura and I go home. There was really nothing we could do anyway, so I drove us home. We both sat up for a long time watching TV feeling kind of helpless. When we finally fell asleep it was on the couch next to each other for comfort and nothing more.

By the next morning Ingrid was back home and feeling much better. We woke up to the sound of my folks bringing her in fresh from the hospital. After we checked in with her to be sure everything was alright, she called my Aunt Helen and gave her the scoop on what was happening. The truth was that even myself, Diane, Laura and Susan helping her part time, Ingrid was burning the candle at both ends when it came to her business and that could not go on forever. Fortunately, fate was about to send us a new helper that would benefit both Ingrid and myself.

My folks were back at the hotel as I had hoped and without Jenny around, I got into my 'get ready to go back to school' mode. I started getting all my school supplies together, slapped my newly acquired Student Parking Permit for that semester on my vehicle and put together some clothes I was going to wear for that week.

I wanted to give Jenny a ride to school, but I knew that was impossible. Her mom was already suspicious after she came home early instead of sleeping over. I suspected that her mom thought Ingrid was doing drugs and that was why she was sick. After she spoke with Ingrid on the phone to wish her well my cousin managed to discredit that theory and remain in the good graces of Jenny's mom.

Chapter Five: The Time of Terry, Mary and Jeannie

My first day back to school was actually just a registration fest. In that high school you had to request elective classes and hope they were not full. As far as the procedure went, it was like someone took boredom and made it a process. After I finished wading through the various forms and lines I finally got to my Guidance Counselor and was in for yet another surprise.

Thanks to the advanced education that I had received in New York I was still ahead of the curve in things like reading and most everything else. That left the school with no choice but to place me in a bizarre void between Junior and Senior High classes. I was told that if I took the right courses I could actually graduate a year early next June. Well, I was all in with getting out of school early even though I had no idea what I was going to do afterward.

My dad wanted me to take Hotel and Restaurant Management classes in college so that I could benefit from the relationship he had with his bosses. I was good at organizing things as my work with Ingrid and even some part time things I occasionally did at the hotel had already proven. I was on the fence about it and still too into my game to worry about anything as commonplace as real life past high school. Besides, with all the work I was doing for my cousin and being her unofficial partner I was already making piles of money along with her.

I had been casually aiming towards a career in hotel and restaurant management ever since my dad first mentioned it to me two years before. All the classes I took were heading me in that direction including high school Business Math and Business Law. I was already good at cooking and had a knack for problem solving thanks to all my relationships and my work with Ingrid, but my skills would soon be tested like never before in ways I could not even imagine.

While I was waiting in the huge cafeteria which was used for Registration Day I heard a familiar voice. It was Terry, a guy I knew from last semester's English class. I spoke to him occasionally at that time, but he was always in a rush and not the kind of guy I liked hanging out with. I only spoke with him before class while we were waiting for the teacher because Terry and his family were from New Jersey and that made us kissin' cousins with me being from New York.

When we did talk it was mostly about how much we missed the Northeast. Otherwise, we did not have a lot in common. Terry's parent's were into drugs and even got Terry into using pot when he was just twelve years old. I never hung around with people who did drugs, but Terry looked different now and even kind of cute. He had long dirty blond hair, was a few inches shorter than me and always seemed a little hyper. Last year he always looked like a mess, but now he looked better. I went over to say hello hoping that he had cleaned up his act. As it turned out, he had.

Terry's folks were arrested for dealing dope and sent away to jail. He was now living with his older brother who was a straight shooter and worked as a Chef. His brother was single and that left plenty of room for Terry in the three bedroom house owned by his parents now that they were away in prison. Terry told me that he was also caught up in the drug mess and placed in foster care for a few months.

While he was in foster care the court sent him to a special drug and behavior rehabilitation program which forbid its participants from socializing with any of their former friends or family members that did drugs. That accounted for just about everyone that Terry knew, even his parents. His adult brother was the sole relative with a completely clean record and excellent reputation, so he got regular visits from him. When it came time for the placement hearing, the court placed Terry with his brother.

Knowing my feelings about drugs, alcohol and smoking, Terry must have seen me as a very friendly port in the storm of his life at that time. As we talked I found out that he had almost no friends and for a social kind of guy like him that was punishment most cruel. Beginning on that day we started hanging out together. Before the week was out I had him over to my house. I wanted to know more about what was going on in his life before I placed him on my game list or got too further involved with my new friend.

The day that Terry came over after school he arrived on a cheap motorcycle that his brother bought for him to get around. He needed it to get to school and work. For him work was bussing tables a couple of nights a week at the hotel restaurant where his brother worked on nearby Treasure Island. He hated that job, but his brother figured it would put a few dollars in his pocket and keep him out of trouble. Terry never had any money and was always riding around on fumes. The day he came over he was out of gas, so I bought him gas to fill up his cycle so he would not have to be embarrassed by having to call his brother.

I invited Terry to ride around with me that afternoon as I completed a bunch of errands for Ingrid. Afterward we planned to go out to my dad's hotel for a nice dinner so we could catch up. As we drove around from place to place picking up or dropping off stuff, Terry saw how busy and stressed I was and asked if I needed any help? I said I did and that we could talk about it over dinner. With school in session again I had less time to do my cousin's errands, but just as many errands to do.

When we finally got to the hotel to have dinner I spoke to Terry about possibly working for my cousin. I already knew she needed the help and that he needed the cash, so I invited him to join me again the next day to see if he could handle the work load. After dinner we brought a can of gas back to the house for his cycle, then he went home. He had a nightly curfew and even though his brother was working most nights, he still called to be sure Terry was home.

It was just after eight and I was surprised to see Jimmy in my pool with Ingrid. An even bigger surprise was that he had brought a girl along that he introduced as his sister. Mary was a year and a half younger than Jimmy, but just as cute. She had more freckles than he did, dark shiny hair, beautiful pale skin and an extremely cute face with half moon eyes. She was thin with an athletic build and small breasts. Mary looked a lot like a young Cheryl Tiegs and I was instantly smitten by her looks and knew this meant trouble.

I got on my bathing suit as fast as I could and joined the others in the pool. I saw that Jimmy and Ingrid were getting along really well, so I went over and started talking to Mary. She was a little shy, but opened up more after we talked for a while. Before she and Jimmy left I made him promise to bring her around again in a day or two. He probably knew what I was up to, but I doubt he cared. Jimmy did not really have much of a relationship with his sister and only brought her along to my house that time because their parents were busy and did not like having her left in the house alone.

I was so busy trying to impress Mary that I forgot to call Jenny. When I did I explained that I was catching up with Terry and explained who he was. Jenny and I had a nice conversation and planned a get together that weekend when Ingrid needed her for some outfit fittings. I hoped that

this one would turn out better than the last when Ingrid became sick. No overnight stay this time around, but at last we would be able to spend some time together.

The next day after school I got with Terry, brought him to my house and had him meet Ingrid. I already explained his situation to her and she did not care about his past as long as he was clean in the present. Ingrid was a kind soul who believed in giving everyone the benefit of the doubt and a second chance if they needed one. She told me to take him and show him the things that needed to be done. If he could do them, he could use her car while I used mine.

With another worker things would get easier. Laura was so good at sewing and such that Ingrid needed help with in house that she was too indispensable to be used for errands and outside work. Susan was becoming less and less available to help Ingrid, The relatives that arrived to help her parents with their motel took some of the pressure off of her, but they needed training and were slow learners.

Terry caught on to the tasks I performed easily and before the day was over he was hired. He would now be making over a hundred bucks a week for working just a few hours each weekday and on some weekends. He proudly told his brother about his new gig and ffter his brother came over early the next day and talked with Ingrid to be sure everything was on the up and up, he gave Terry his blessing for the new job. Terry's bus boy days were over.

Just because Terry was off the hook with his brother did not mean he was not on the hook with me. I planned on keeping a close eye on him and if there were any signs of drug use I would immediately cut him off from the job and my friendship. I wanted Terry to be more to me than just a friend or coworker and that could not happen if he was getting high.

After a few days of watching him at school and at work, I was certain that Terry was clean so I invited him to stay over the next Friday night. My folks were attending some big charity gig at the hotel and would likely stay overnight at the suite and maybe even the next night as well. While I was busy working for my cousin and getting ready for an interesting Friday night with Terry another opportunity came my way on Thursday evening.

Once again Jimmy came over. He brought Tommy and Mary with him. Robin, Patty and Kathleen also came by. Laura was also hanging out with everyone. At that point I had already gotten what I wanted from Tommy and with Jimmy busy screwing with Ingrid, that meant it was now open season on Mary. Before I got busy trying to lure her into my web, I got Kathleen and Tommy settled into my bedroom so that they could have some private time together. My folks were out for the evening with some friends and would not be back until late.

We were all hanging out on the patio and taking dips in the pool. Even though it was early September, the Florida weather was still very warm. Mary was getting into hanging out with the rest of us much to her brother's annoyance. She would never rat on him and knew how to keep her mouth shut about things that did not concern her, but he worried that the thing he had with Ingrid might somehow get under her skin. If it did she might pressure him to cut it off and he liked my cousin.

Jimmy and Mary stayed later than the others. As long as she was with her brother at our house, her parents let her stay out late. They knew that Ingrid was there all the time and trusted that she would keep everyone in line. They could even sleep over just about anytime they liked as long as they let their folks know and got to school on time the next day. Their parents were always working or going out anyway, so Jimmy and Mary were really classic latchkey kids often left to their own devices.

Jimmy was relieved when I invited Mary to go to the mall with me for some ice cream. He wanted some bed time with Ingrid and it looked like my cousin wanted the exact same thing from him. For all her talk about avoiding relationships with younger or underage kids, she was certainly not following her own advice! But that really was not my business. I loved Ingrid and anything she did was fine with me as long as it had nothing to do with smoking, drinking or drugs.

Mary accepted my invitation to go to the mall and seemed to be warming up to me. By that time she was talking a lot more and shared her desire to become an actress with me. She became interested in acting as a little girl after seeing a bunch of old Shirley Temple and classic American cinema films. They used to play a lot of that stuff on broadcast TV in those days before all those classic movie and Retro TV cable channels came along years later.

As soon as Mary heard that a major film needing local kids was being shot in the central Florida area she made her mom take her to an open house for local talent. After Mary got her photo taken and read a few short lines she was hired on the spot. The movie might have been something like a Tom Sawyer movie or some other well known American story told on film, I just cannot recall the title. Mary said it took a little over a month to film and that even though she was just an extra, she was there on the set and part of the production for at least three weeks.

Since acting in that film she had been involved with school plays and such, but she wanted much more and was always reading the newspaper to see if any new movies were being filmed nearby which might need her age, looks and talent. It appeared odd to me that she wanted to act because in her private life she seemed so shy. At least that was my first and apparently incorrect impression.

I loved people with ambition and drive, and Mary had plenty of both. I could see her accomplishing anything that she wanted to and her acting fever opened a big door for me. Thanks to my dad I just happened to know a well known character actor named J. Carroll Nash who worked in a pile of classic Hollywood films during the time of the studio system. Now retired, he hung out regularly at the hotel and kept a boat at the hotel marina across the street. He was a good friend of one of the hotel owners.

I had no idea if this guy could help Mary get started in the acting business, but I was certain that he could offer her some sound advice if I could get my dad to arrange a meet up some time in the near future. Mary already mentioned that she loved older films and as soon as I mentioned his name she knew exactly who I was talking about. I promised her a possible meeting with him at some point in the near future and she was thrilled at just the suggestion.

As much as I came to like Mary, I knew she was going places and all of those would eventually be without me. Jenny was my dream girl. I wanted Mary for her looks and personality and hoped that we could be friends once I brought her into my game. I was being more selfish then ever when it came to sex, but I hoped that I was still no where near as bad as Matt. I did offer friendship and help when I could to my players and that was more than he ever did for his victims.

After we left the mall we headed back to my house. When I got home I invited Mary up to the recreation room and went to use the rest room while she listened to records. The presence of Jimmy's clothes in the upstairs bathroom meant that he was still busy having sex with my cousin in her bedroom downstairs. That gave me some more time to try and get somewhere with Mary. Up to that point we were friendly, but because she was younger and so enthused about explaining her acting ambitions to me I had not been able to decide whether she actually liked me as something more than a friend.

Since Jimmy was still busy with Ingrid and we had been having a good time, I thought I would take a stab at trying to get Mary to stay overnight. I knew it was a long shot, but if I wanted to get anywhere with her before I was busy with my other players this was it. I went downstairs briefly to speak with Laura. If I could convince Mary to sleep over, I needed for Laura to tell her parents that she would be sleeping with her in the spare bedroom. Laura had come to know me and my game very well by that time. She agreed to my deception. Now all I had to do was to convince Mary.

I went back up to the recreation room and told Mary that her brother was still busy with my cousin. She already knew about them, so my revelation was no surprise. I suggested that if she went home without him it might cause trouble which neither of them needed. Mary knew that having the freedom to hang out with her brother and stay out late was a privilege that could be revoked at any time and that was not something she wanted to have happen. I suggested an alternative.

I told Mary that if she called her folks and said she wanted to sleep over, Laura would get on the phone and say that she was sleeping with her in the spare room. I would cover for Jimmy and that would be that. Without giving it too much thought, Mary was on board with my plan and made the call. Luckily, her folks did not ask to speak directly with Jimmy being satisfied with what Laura and I had to say about the sleep over. After we promised to get her to school on time the next morning, they gave their permission.

Once we were off the phone Laura went to bed. I asked Mary if she wanted to take a dip in the pool with me since it was too early to go to bed. She said she did and used the downstairs bathroom to get changed into the bathing suit she wore earlier. I still had no idea how Mary might respond to a romantic come on from me, but I also knew that there was only one way to find out.

After we got into the pool I asked Mary how she felt about skinny dipping? She said she never tried it and did not want to. I countered by saying that if she ever wanted to be a serious actress, she might have to take off her clothes for a movie part. A lot of recent movies featured nudity in

them and she knew it. Even the movie she was in as an extra had a scene where young boys swam naked in a river with their butts showing as she and the other extras watched from the shoreline.

While Mary was giving my argument some thought, I pointed out that Ingird, Laura and most of my other friends often skinny dipped in my pool because none of the neighbors could see into our back yard. It was good practice for times when we had to be nude in front of others our age, as in the case of physical education class during showers. Mary admitted that she was a little shy when it came to her body and disliked showering in front of her classmates as much as I and some of my friends did.

I asked Mary what she felt the worst thing about getting naked in front of other people was for her. She said it was taking off her clothes. I suggested a solution for that: I said that I would take off my bathing suit, then come over and help her take off hers. Mary nodded, was red faced and turned away as I removed my bathing trunks. Even with the pool lights it would have been hard for her to see my private parts clearly even if she were looking, but she was still embarrassed.

Once I was naked I waded over to Mary. I said I was going to take off her swimsuit from the back so that she did not have to look at me and went to work. I carefully unhooked Mary's bathing suit top and allowed it to fall off her small breasts until it was in the water. I scooped up her top and threw it on to the cement which surrounded the pool. Mary instinctively crossed her arms to hide her breasts even though I was still behind her and would not have been able to see them anyway.

Next I bent down and slowly pulled off her bathing suit bottom exposing a very shapely buttocks that I thought was one of the cutest I had ever seen. By then I was sure that Mary wondered what the heck she was doing, but I tried not to allow her the time to think about it. After throwing her swimsuit bottom up on the concrete near her top piece, I came around to Mary's front and slowly eased her arms down exposing her cute little breasts.

Even though they were small, her breasts were well rounded and had little red nipples which I thought were adorable and just begging to be sucked on. Looking down I could see that she had an ample patch of dark shiny pubic hair which although blurry in the water was still very obvious. Mary had no hair on her legs and probably shaved what little she did have. She had some light colored hairs on her arms, but hardly enough to even notice. Her freckles and beautiful green eyes captured my attention more than anything else and I loved the look of her naked body.

As we stared at each other I said, "There, that wasn't too bad, was it?" Mary shivered a bit and said, "No, I guess not." I'm sure she was praying that she would never have to do a nude scene in a movie and was obviously not very uncomfortable being naked. There was not much I could do to quell her fears or make her feel more comfortable, so I just went ahead and hugged her slightly. Mary backed away and said, "What are you doing?" I said I was just hugging her.

Mary was not expecting my onslaught, but after I again faced her and began rubbing her shoulders she stood still and allowed me to massage her that way. As she stood there I told Mary

that I liked her. She said that she also liked me, but felt she was too young for a boy friend; especially one my age. I was a couple of years and change older than she was. I reminded Mary that her brother was much younger than Ingrid and they still got along really well.

The message about Jimmy and Ingrid was not lost on her. Mary knew that if she turned me down it would cause a snowball effect for everyone involved. She asked, "Do you just want to go out with me?" I explained that I wanted her as a friend, but also more. It wasn't like she had to be exclusive to me, just available and ready to play my game.

As I explained my game to her she was more than a little surprised. She already knew that her brother and his friends were not just coming over to my house to use the pool, but she had no idea they were doing all the things I told her about. Rather then go into deep detail, I gave Mary a good thumbnail sketch about what we did and why we did it together.

I told Mary that I was going to help her out of the pool, dry her off and take her up to my room. She asked me if I was going to do anything really bad to her? I answered her by asking if I had done anything to hurt her or insult her since we met? She said I had not, so I told her not to worry. I don't think my words comforted her, but she played along with what I was doing seeing few other options. After all, her brother was in the house and if things got really bad she could call out for him.

After we got out of the pool I dried off Mary and myself, picked up our bathing suits, retrieved her clothes from the bathroom and walked her upstairs to my bedroom. Once inside I closed and locked the door explaining that I did it just for privacy. Mary said she had to use the bathroom, so I gave her our bathing suits to hang up in there and let her out of the bedroom. I knew she would not bolt unless she planned on running around outside with just a wet bathing suit on. While she was out of the room I lubricated myself.

She came back into the room wrapped in a towel. I told her to think of me as the guy she was talking to just an hour before at the mall. I was not the devil and had no intention of hurting her or making her do anything she did not want to do. I said that I liked her a lot and wanted to make love to her. Before she could say anything I pulled the towel off her and gently pushed her on to my bed.

I began kissing her on the lips and worked my way up to Frenching. It was obvious she had never done that before and although she tried to resist, I kept going and before long had her responding to the thrusts of my tongue into her mouth. I kissed her breasts and sucked on them a little, then began to finger her down there.

Mary had a very small opening which meant that both of us were in for some work and pain. To make things easiest, I pulled her down to the edge of the bed and got into a standing position. I knew that Mary wanted to object to what I was doing. I guessed that she was conflicted about losing her virginity so young, wanting to try something new and worried that turning me down might start too much trouble. However, I was in no mood to take 'NO' for an answer and soon began pushing my penis into her.

Everyone had a weak spot. Sometimes I could use the knowledge of what it was to score with kids and even bring them into my game. Terry's weak spot was cash. He needed the job with Ingrid and any extra money he could get. Even though his brother made a pretty good living, he had a lot of bills. He had to pay for everything after his parents were hauled off to jail and also care for his brother.

Terry wore cheap tee shirts, shorts and sandals most of the time. With winter coming and school again in session he needed a whole new wardrobe. I took him out to a clothing store for young people in the Tyrone Square Mall which was owned by a teacher at the school. Despite his objections, I bought Terry a pile of clothes and told him that just by working for my cousin every day he was paying me back.

We dropped the clothes off at Terry's house, then headed back to mine. Terry was a smart guy. Despite his family situation, he did well in school without really trying. If he had put forth some real effort he could be have easily been a straight 'A' student. There was no way he was going to fall for some stupid or hookey reason to get naked and mess around with me. Since he was all about cash, I shamelessly used that as a lure.

Terry was attractive to me in a weird way. He talked a lot about having sex with girls his age and younger, but he was in my physical education class. One story he liked to tell was about 'balling' a girl in a phone booth at the beach. He said that he got up right in front of her and pulled down his bathing suit and hers enough to stick his dick into her. Well, I knew that was a hard thing for anyone to do, let alone him.

Terry was not shy about himself. Whenever he came out of the shower area in P.E. class he had his towel over his shoulder proudly walking along and showing off his private parts. His penis was small to medium sized at best and bounced around rapidly as he walked. He had a short shaft and testicles that were as unimpressive as his dick. That made his 'balling' story an unlikely reality, but his shortcomings also made him attractive to me.

After we got back to my house we went into the pool for a while. As we swam around I told Terry that there was more to me than meets the eye and that I liked playing games. After I began describing the games, he laughed. He took me seriously, but thought the idea of what we were doing at the house was crazy and funny to him at the same time. I explained to my new friend that my game was also a chance for him to make some extra cash.

I told Terry that if he allowed me to do whatever I liked to him once a week that I would make sure he got an extra twenty dollars in pay. He looked at me and asked if I was kidding? I said that I was not and that he should think about my offer carefully. I told him that the only reason I was willing to pay him for what everyone else gave me for free was to help him out financially.

High School was different than everything that came before. Things cost money, there were no free lunch programs and costs went beyond just lab fees and such. There was the cost of taking girls out. I mean, how many phone booth sex partners could he find at the beach? Unless he

wanted to date girls that were disease factories, got paid for doing it or traded drugs for sex, he would have to eventually pony up some cash to show a decent girl a good time.

My arguments made sense and I knew that Terry was paying attention to them, but I also knew he was surprised at my cash offer and was not sure how to respond to it. I helped him by explaining that I would not mention the money again. As long as he did what I wanted, he would get the money without anything being said about it except on weeks when we did nothing together. I even sweetened the pot. I said that if he brought me new players and I liked them, I would pay a him a twenty dollar bonus. That included girls and boys. I knew he would quickly figure out my taste in kids and the entrepreneur in him would produce at some impressive results.

Knowing that enough had been said, I extended my hand to seal the deal. Terry took it and shook it. I was kind of surprised that Terry actually accepted my offer, but then nothing had been done yet and as far as I was concerned the deal was not actually sealed until the fun was had. With that in mind I got out of the pool, made us some snacks and brought some cold soda out to the patio. Terry got out of the pool and joined me for a break.

After our snack fest, I figured it was time to head up to my bedroom. With Ingrid and Laura already in bed, I checked to be sure the house was locked up for the night and escorted Terry to my room. Once inside I closed the door without locking it to make him feel more comfortable and told him to take off his bathing suit. Terry laughed a little, shook his head and slipped out of his swimsuit. I guessed that he still could not believe what he was about to do.

Terry asked me what was next as I stared at the nice crop of dirty blond pubic hair above his package. I asked him if he ever played doctor while growing up? He said he didn't, but he came from a weird family that moved around Jersey a lot. I doubt he was in one place long enough to get to know the kids well enough to try anything with them even if he wanted to. I explained that my game was just like playing doctor, except it was for older kids and told him to lay on the bed next to me.

I took some Vaseline and lubricated our penises a little, then began jacking him off. His small penis came to life and I loved the well defined crown he had. Each time my hand slipped over it I felt shivers down my spine. Like most of the boys I played around with he was circumcised and that made his dick seem even smaller than it was when it was not hard, but after his penis got stiff it did not look or feel so small anymore. After a while I led his hand to my dick and had him jack me at the same time.

I could see where Terry would make a decent sex partner for most girls unless their opening was as large as the Grand Canyon down there and revised my opinion of his penis somewhat. Either way, his dick was perfect for me and I loved jacking it. I knew that Terry was nervous about what we were doing and doubted that he would ejaculate anytime soon, so I got him into position for oral sex, explained what I was going to do and began sucking his dick. It felt great in my mouth and fit all the way in even when it was fully erect.

When Terry finally shot his load he was embarrassed about it. I told him that he had to stop letting his hang ups about sex with me get in the way of his fun. I said that over time I could get him laid with girls as often as he liked, as long as he calmed down and played along with my game. Terry loved the idea of not having to hunt for his sexual prey and settled down.

I knew that although he was with me in this thing, I needed to exert my authority to really get him into my game. That meant it was time for him to suck me off. I got into position and told him to get busy. He was slow and awkward at first, but finally realized there was no escaping the inevitable. He began sucking my dick and while he did I reminded him that there was no cheating! He had to suck and swallow.

I shot my load which Terry very reluctantly sucked down his throat. After he cleaned out his mouth, I lubricated my penis and got him into position for anal sex. He knew what was coming having read some of the same nasty books and magazines that I did which carefully illustrated boys having anal sex with each other. His brother kept some in the house and Terry sneaked a look at them from time to time because they also had pictures of girls getting screwed by boys.

I rubbed Terry's back a bit to try and keep him calm, then began separating his butt cheeks and getting my penis into position. As I did Terry asked, "Do we have to do this?" I said we did and told him that he would get a turn on me next. I knew that wouldn't really help to get him into what I was going to do, but thought I would give him a heads up just the same. This was one of those rare occasions that I would allow a guy to penetrate me. I just had to know how it felt to have his small penis inside me.

Terry had a decent sized ass for a thin guy of his short statue. His hole was average sized and I was sure that it could handle my penis without me doing too much damage. I gently began pushing the crown of my penis into him, then my shaft. He moved around a bit, but did not make any noises apart from a few muted grunts and groans. I could see that he was determined to take what I was giving him and do it without wimping out.

Once I was all the way inside I began having intercourse with Terry like there was no tomorrow. I don't know why I found him so desirable, especially since he was not my usual taste in boys. All I know is that I enjoyed having sex with him. I pulled out my dick just in time to shoot my load on to his buttocks. At least he did not give me the kind of nasty surprise that I got from Jimmy!

After cleaning up, I lubricated Terry's dick and got into position for him. He was really nervous, but I talked him through what needed to be done until he managed to slide his dick into my anus. It was a little painful at first because I was not used to it, but once he had his dick inside me I liked it. He did a pretty good job of screwing me and after a short while pulled his penis out and shot his load on my buttocks.

We cleaned up, then got back into bed. I was still horny and decided to suck him off once more before we went to sleep. He had a smooth body for the most part so sleeping naked next to Terry was nice. The next morning I was up early and found my cousin already in the kitchen having

breakfast, We exchanged stories about our recent sexual triumphs and I could tell she was already getting bored with Jimmy. The good news that Diane was interested in him.

My stories about Terry's small package intrigued my cousin and that meant he was next on her list. I was sure he would have no problem with that. Any guy would love to have sex with my cousin, but she was selective and less interested in guys her own age then they were in her. All the talk about sex got us going and we actually ended up having intercourse in her room after breakfast.

I was not looking forward to telling Jimmy that his time with my cousin was up, but there were other fish in the sea, or at least in my pool, that he could have fun with including the lovely and always desirable Diane. I knew that Robin would also like a roll with him, as would Patty. I would start that process going as soon as he came over later that day.

After Terry got up and had breakfast, I drove him home and paid him for the work he did that week and added my promised extra pay for a job well done. Ingrid did not need him again until Monday, so the weekend was his. However, I told him to stop by on Saturday night and visit with my cousin. I explained she wanted a tumble with him and he was instantly glad he had gotten involved with both of us.

After I got back to the house Ingrid told me that Jenny called. I called her back and found my weekend plans completely disrupted. She and her parents had to go out of state for a few days to help make funeral and other final arrangements for an uncle who died suddenly the day before. I was disappointed, but understood and wished the family well.

I wanted more of Mary, so I called Jimmy and told him to bring his sister with him when he came over later that day. By lunchtime Jimmy, Mary, Tommy, Robin, Patty and Kathleen were at the house. With my parents gone it was yet another fun weekend. I took Mary upstairs and had sex with her. She was still a little gun shy from our first encounter, but played along and seemed a little more into what we were doing than before.

After I got through with Mary, I brought Jimmy up to my room and gave him the bad news about Ingrid. He did not take it well and even though I mentioned Diane, he still made a fuss and that started to piss me off. I explained that he was lucky that my cousin even looked his way in the first place, let alone slept with him. He was still being a jerk, so I told him that he owed me some fun time and made him strip naked. He gave me more grief, so I reminded him that I had other girls for him and could easily cut him off if I wanted to.

While Jimmy got ready for me a terrible thought crossed my mind. I said I had to use the bathroom and after I did and before I came back to my room, I went and got Mary. She was surprised to find her brother naked in my bedroom when she walked in. He quickly tried to cover himself up by getting into the bed and pulling the covers over his private parts, but I told him to get out of bed and face his sister.

I closed and locked the bedroom door, then told Mary to get naked. She was upset and cried a bit, but I said that her brother had really pissed me off and it was time for both of them to pay the

piper. She hesitated, so I pulled off her bathing suit until Mary was as naked as her brother. I asked if they had ever seen each other naked before? They said they had not since they were much younger.

I made the siblings stand in front of each other naked, then had Jimmy lay on the bed while I positioned Mary for sex. I had intercourse with her while I made Jimmy watch and play with himself. After I finished with Mary, I sucked off Jimmy in front of his sister and made her watch. Once I finished with both of them, I had Mary and Jimmy lay next to each other and made him finger her while she played with his penis.

The siblings were afraid of me for various reasons including the fact that I get them in huge amounts of trouble if I wanted to without getting myself in as deep. I had the backing of all the other kids, as well as my cousin, so anything they said about me would be their word against everyone else's. On the other hand, anything I said about them would be everyone else's word against just theirs.

After I got tired of watching Jimmy and Mary just touch each other, I again positioned Mary for sex and got Jimmy ready to have intercourse with her. He tried to resist, so I forced him into position and told him that if he did not do it with her I would have anal sex with him in front of his sister and then force him to do the same to her. Jimmy decided to cooperate and began reluctantly pushing his penis into his sister.

I loved watching the cute pair have sex, and even more so because they were brother and sister. I watched carefully as Jimmy shoved his penis into his sister over and over again. He kept doing it with her and did not want to shoot his load into Mary, but I made him do it at least three times. I finally pulled him off her and once again stuck my own dick into his sister. With all the semen in her she was really wet and it felt good to me. I shot my own load into her and then let her take a bath while I kept busy with Jimmy.

I lubricated my dick and shoved Jimmy into position for anal sex. He struggled with me, but I penetrated him and this time there was no chocolate surprise. I shot my load into his anus and left him to deal with the clean up after Mary came back into the room and saw us finishing up. She was freaked, but I warned her to calm down and keep her mouth shut. I knew she would anyway, I mean who would admit to having sex with their brother?

After we all cleaned up I had one final nasty trick up my sleeve. I made Mary suck off her brother while Jimmy sucked me off. I squatted over his face and shoved my penis into his mouth over and over again while he laid flat on the bed. I loved shoving my penis into his cute freckled face! His sister laid across the bed on her stomach and sucked her brother off. I shot my load into Jimmy's mouth and even though he choked a bit, he managed to suck most of my semen down his throat.

After I finished I moved back to where Mary was to be sure that after Jimmy shot his load, she sucked it down her throat. She did the dirty deed pretty well and I said I was proud of her. As a reward, I had her get on her knees and suck me off. I rubbed her dark and shiny hair as she

sucked on my penis. Even though I had just shot my load into Jimmy's mouth, I somehow found enough reserves to shoot a few more drops into Mary's mouth as well.

That was the worse thing I had done to date, but I enjoyed doing it. I was sick of pussyfooting around. People were either all into my game or they were out and would no longer be able to enjoy the sexual benefits I offered to them. I was amazed that not only had I done it with both siblings, I had done it with them at the same time and had them do it with each other as well!

After they cleaned up I had Jimmy dress in my room and Mary get back into her bathing suit. I warned the siblings to keep their mouths shut. I said that their bodies now belonged to me and just to be sure that they listened, I let Jimmy go on his way and kept Mary with me for a while. I was not done with her yet. I again pulled off her bathing suit and had her lay naked in the bed next to me. She had cried a bit during the previous ordeal, so I tried to comfort her as best I could by rubbing her back and kissing her shoulders. I eventually turned her towards me and made her make out with me. I loved Mary's tight hole and planned to have more of it later that night after I recuperated from all the sex we already had.

After a while I let Mary put her bathing suit on and told her she was staying over that night. I called Jimmy and made sure he squared it with his folks. He was very cooperative knowing what I had done and could still do. As a reward I arranged a meet up between Jimmy and Diane for later that night at her place. After I called Jimmy back with the good news about Diane, I think he suddenly realized that despite my behavior that day, he had made the right decision by doing what I said and staying in my game.

With Mary now at the house for a sleep over, I yearned for the days in New York when I would go out together with my many girlfriends to the movies and such. I decided to take Laura and Mary out to the movies that night, with a stop at the ice cream restaurant on the way home. After Mary and I rejoined the others by the pool, I spoke with Laura who was a 'go' with my idea to head out for some fun later that evening. She liked hanging with me and the feeling was mutual.

After speaking with Laura I noticed that Tommy and Kathleen were gone. She told me that she overheard them talking and discovered that they decided to go to his house and screw there instead of at mine. With no one home, I guessed that Tommy figured it was the perfect time to introduce Kathleen to his bedroom! As long as they kept using condoms and did not get caught, I was fine with whatever they did together.

Patty had to leave, so our crowd was definitely thinning out. Robin stayed around and looked a little glum. As cute as she was, she had not been able to hook up with Colin. She really liked him, but his drug problem kept getting in the way and Robin was smart enough to steer clear of that stuff. I knew that Robin needed some company and with her Susan and her folks busy at the motel, I asked her to stay overnight and go out with the rest of us.

Robin was thrilled at my suggestion, so she called her parents and they gave her the go ahead. They hated having her home by herself and she was always bored at the motel, so staying over night at our house with Ingrid and the rest of us around was almost always fine with them. I

knew that Ingrid wanted some personal time with Terry that evening, so when I told her we were going out she was all the more happy and said she would cover for us if need be.

We had originally planned to eat at the house, but I thought it would be more fun to go out for Chinese Food. There was a place downtown that was built like a Chinese style house and served the best Hunan cuisine I ever tasted. As we ate Mary began to open up again and settle down from all that had happened that day. She saw that as perverted as we all were, we could also have honest and non-sexual fun together and got along really well. She knew that she was now a part of our group and there was no going back.

We went to see a movie. It was some weird film that I cannot remember, but I do recall us all having fun by constantly changing seats with each other, pretending to screw in the aisle, throwing candy at the other theater patrons and almost getting kicked out twice! After the movies we went to the ice cream restaurant and ordered a gigantic trough of ice cream. It had everything in it and five different flavors to boot. We kept putting the whipping cream topping all over each other's faces, throwing cherries at a table full of college girls that were annoyed by us and made a terrible mess by the time we finished and left.

After we got home we found Ingrid and Terry skinny dipping in the pool, so I told everyone to strip and we joined them. My cousin thought we were idiots, but she loved the fun and mayhem we created. After a while she and Terry left for her room, while the rest of us swam around and played a few sessions of naked pool volleyball. Mary was actually enjoying herself by this time and probably even forgot that she was naked.

By the time we decided to call it quits in the pool, we were all exhausted and it was late. Laura said good night and headed off to her room. She said that either Robin or Mary could sleep with her if they liked, but I had other ideas. After we dried off on the patio for a while and locked up for the night, I took the girls upstairs. We all hung our bathing suits in the bathroom, then headed into my bedroom.

I laid on the bed on my back and told the girls to join me. Mary got one one side and Robin on the other. I kissed both girls and made out with them for a while, then had Robin start kissing Mary. She was really uncomfortable with that, but Robin was gentle and did not push things with her. Eventually I had them making out and hugging each other. I knew that Mary was not really into it, but she had to learn to try new things if she was going to hang with us.

I played around with the girls and got Robin giggling. I fingered both girls at the same time and Robin thought that was hilarious. She settled down after I had her finger Mary and Mary finger her. I had them hug and make out so that their breasts met, then made then rub against each other's private parts as best they could. I saw these positions in my books and could not wait to see if they really worked. They did, but with Mary's tiny pussy options were limited.

I had Robin mount me and began having intercourse with her while Mary made out with me. I switched them out by having Mary lay on her back as I penetrated her tiny hole and had Robin kneel over her and kiss me at the same time. By the time we were finished I had eaten each girl out as best I could, gotten a blow job from Robin, tried every position I could imagine with them

and shot my load into Mary. It was one of the best sessions I ever had. I was glad that Laura had decided to go to bed because if she had joined us I think I would have been a dead man!

I knew that in many ways Mary might have been too young physically and too immature emotionally to play my game, but she was beautiful and exactly my taste in a girl. There would have been no way that I could have refused her. An after seeing her screw with her own brother, I knew that I wanted to be with her for as long as I could be. She was mine to play with as I pleased and play I would!

The next morning my folks called to see how things were and I said everything was fine. They were invited out on a last minute fishing trip by one of the owners of the hotel and would not be back until Monday night. I said that was fine and that there was plenty of food in the house thanks to a shopping trip that Ingrid and I made earlier in the week. After Mary and Robin got up, Mary prepared to go home.

As I drove Mary home I stopped the car a few blocks away to give her a last kiss. That turned into a short make out session and showed me that much to my surprise, Mary was becoming quickly acclimated to me and my game. She genuinely liked me despite the things I had done to her. In the end it was all part of my game with no malice intended and I think that she was beginning to see that.

By the time I got back to the house fate had another gift for me. Robin called and said that a huge bus tour that was booked at another motel suddenly ended up at her parent's place. The other hotel where they were originally booked had some sort of a plumbing problem which resulted in no running water for the rooms. The bus driver pulled up to their motel and the Jensens found room for everybody, despite a heavily booked weekend.

With the extra guests, it was every hand on deck. Susan, her folks and the other relatives working there were locked into staying at the hotel for the next three days to accommodate all the guests. Robin and the twins would be alone at the house and that was not what their parents wanted. Robin said her folks asked if Ingrid could call them to see if John, Jerry and her could stay at our house until Tuesday night.

I was more than fine with the idea and after speaking with my cousin she was on board with it as well. She knew that I would take care of our extra house guests and handle things while she was busy working. Anyway, with Terry being her new boy toy I was sure she was into that more than anything else socially speaking. He would be over again on Monday to work after school and who knows what else?

After speaking with Robin's parents on the phone, she and the twins were at our door with overnight bags in just minutes. I got the twins settled into a downstairs room that we sometimes used as an extra bedroom and placed Robin in with Laura. She didn't mind because she was a house guest herself and got along really well with Robin. Meanwhile, I hatched yet another game plan that would either work well or fail miserably. It if failed I might have a problem, but if it worked I would have scored yet another first for my game.

Robin found out that I was fooling around with the twins some time ago. As in the case of Jimmy and Mary, she did not really care about that as much as I though she might. Susan was her sister, but the twins were just long term house guests to Robin. They were the same age as her and they all barely tolerated each other. If my plan worked, Robin and the twins were about to get a lot closer!

I loved messing around with Robin. The previous night have been bliss, especially with Mary added to the fun. Robin was a bit of a wild child, but she was also a straight shooter when it came to certain things. I had no idea how she would react to the idea of having sex with her adopted brothers. I was not even sure how to bring that about? But I was certainly working on it!

The weather was still beautiful so I decided to change the scenery by taking Robin and the twins to the hotel. A day at the beach always loosened everyone up and with my folks on a fishing trip, the suite was available. I had everyone pack some stuff up and we headed to the hotel. After we got settled into the suite, I treated everyone to lunch at the cafe and then we headed back to the suite to change into our bathing suits.

I decided to test the waters by having everyone change in my room. I said that since we had all already skinny dipped together in my pool, seeing each other naked should be no big deal. Robin and the twins went along with it and no one looked particularly uncomfortable as we all got naked in front of each other. The twins were always a little shy, but they knew better than to let it show and ruin our day.

The Gulf was as warm as bath water, so I rented a couple of power skiis. Robin and Jerry rode on one, while John and I shared the other. We had a wild time and then ended up being invited to play volleyball with some kids staying at the hotel for some kind of a nearby softball competition. There were some really cute thirteen to fourteen year old boys and girls in that group, but that was not the time or place for new recruits. Besides, they were all from out of state.

After the volleyball game we made a stop in the hotel pool and then dried off laying on the chaise lounges that surrounded it. We played some games in the game room, then went back up to the suite to get dressed for dinner. I took my guests to the restaurant where we enjoyed live music and a wonderful meal. After dinner I treated my friends to a movie across the street in the hotel shopping center and that finished up our day.

After we got back into the suite, I told the twins that they could sleep in my parent's room. I had Robin in with me. Before we went to bed we all sat around watching TV for a while. The hotel had cable TV and although it was not what it is today, that meant great reception and a few extra channels. As we sat on the couch together I said that I was in the mood to play a game.

I admitted to Robin that I wanted to play around with the twins much to their horror and her surprise. I had not been with them for a while and missed their cute little bodies. However, I said that I really enjoyed my time with her the night before as well. I suggested that we all have some fun messing around with each other at the same time. Robin started laughing, while the twins just sat quietly probably hoping that I was just kidding. I was not.

Even with the curtains wide open and a fabulous view of the Gulf, no one could see into the suite. We were upstairs anyway so unless you stood pressed again the window no one would be able to see you. I told Robin and the twins to take off their clothes. They looked at me strangely, but seeing that I began undressing they followed my example. As we undressed I told them all to just think of it like skinny dipping inside. I doubt they were amused or comforted by my attempt at humor, but this was my game and I really did not care how they felt about it.

After we were naked, I told them that we should all begin by making out together. I made out with Robin and told the twins that I wanted to see them make out with each other. They reluctantly obeyed me knowing how my games worked. After a while I decided to try and get Robin to make out with Jerry while I made out with John. Again, they all played along probably not wanting to rock the boat. I played with John's penis and told Robin to play with Jerry's. She reluctantly obeyed me and then we switched out.

After a while I got up and had the others follow me into the bedroom. I told Robin to lay on the bed and had the twins sit opposite each other next to her. I told them to play with each other's dicks while they watched me have sex with Robin. She was surprised at what I was doing, but still compliant. I pushed my penis into her and watched the twins jack each other off as I did. After changing positions with her a few times, I told Jerry to come over to where I was.

Everyone was shocked when I told him to get on top of Robin and put his dick into her. Robin tried getting up, but I told her to lie still. I said that it would be cool to see them have sex since they were really not brother and sister in terms of actual blood relations. Robin laid back down probably figuring she was in a 'no win' situation and Jerry knew better than to disobey me.

I loved watching him jack his small dick to get it hard enough to put into Robin. Once he was in her, I could hardly believe what I was seeing. I sat with John and jacked his dick while he jacked mine as we watched Robin and Jerry having intercourse. After a few minutes he shot his small load into her, then I had the twins switch places and it was John's turn to get a piece of his sister.

John had a hard time getting his dick hard and was very nervous, so I helped by lubricating and jacking it for him until it was stiff enough to enter Robin. Once he got going he actually did a better job of screwing her than his brother. He really got into it for some reason and I could see that Robin actually seemed to be enjoying his penis inside her.

After John shot his tiny load, Robin went to into my parent's bathroom to clean up. The boys and I used the bathroom near my bedroom and also got cleaned up. After we were all back in my room I told Robin that I wanted to see her suck off John and Jerry. By this she was immune to being shocked any further, but before she could make any protest I got John on the bed and told her to start with him.

While Robin sucked off John, I again stunned everyone by getting Jerry into position for anal sex and shoving the crown of my penis into him. I held back from sticking my dick all the way into Jerry because I knew that neither of the twins would be able to take the full length and breadth of my penis without doing some real damage to them. After I saw Robin make a face which said

that John had shot off his load, I stopped screwing with Jerry and had everyone get cleaned up a bit.

It was Jerry's turn with Robin and she did a great job of sucking his little dick. By this time I think she was really getting into it. I stuck the head of my penis into John as we watched his twin brother get sucked off by his sister. It made me really hard and I wanted desperately to shove my penis all the way into John's cute buttocks, but I managed to hold back. After Jerry shot his small load into Robin's mouth we all took a break again.

Next I had the twins get on top of each other and face in opposite directions for oral sex as I had on previous occasions. Robin was as amazed as I had been the first time I watched the two perfect copies of each other perfectly suck the other one off at the same time. As they had oral sex together Robin asked me what it felt like to have anal sex with them? That was the wrong question to ask!

I told Robin that if she meant on the receiving end, I could show her and had her turned around on the bed before she knew what was happening. I quickly got her into position and began to slowly shove my penis into her anus. She begged me to stop saying that she was just curious, but I kept on until I was all the way into her. She had a decent sized anus so I knew she could take my dick.

I was not rough with her, just determined. I slid my dick in and out of her anus a few times and then stopped. I did not want to push things further than I already had. Robin smiled as she wiped some tears from her eyes. I guessed that she did not want to appear weak in front of the twins. I figured that enough was enough and told the twins to go to bed. After Robin and I cleaned up again, I told her to lay next to me in bed and we made out quietly.

Robin was very passionate and said, "I want to be with you. I need you." I was floored. My wildcat was actually just a soft kitten inside and had fallen for me. I knew that meant trouble, but I liked Robin all along and always secretly wanted to be with her. Despite our slight age difference, she and I were made for each other. It just took both of us longer then anyone would have thought it would to discover that fact.

I told Robin I was hers if she would be mine and she smiled widely. My new girl friend immediately jumped on top of me and kissed me even more passionately then before. She got on top of me and screwed me until I practically begged her to stop. After she did, she slid down a bit and sucked me off to finish the job. She swallowed every ounce of my semen and sucked it so hard and fast down her throat that I begged for mercy.

Robin and I had one big thing in common; we were both very determined people. After we finished having sex she told me she would help me with my game and do anything I asked her to do as I long as I stayed with her. In many ways this was a blessing in disguise. As much as I liked Jenny, I knew she was out of my league and once she got a little older I would be left behind in the dust. Mary was too young and immature to take seriously and Susan was too involved with her parent's business and school to do much else.

In the end Robin was the perfect choice for me. She did not care how perverted I was as long as I was with her. I knew this was a relationship made in Heaven (or elsewhere) and that we would have a lot of fun together. We stayed up and talked for a long time. I loved the fact she she liked to talk and converse as much as I did and I knew it was time for another trip to the jewelry store.

Things have a way of working out for me. A few days after my day with Robin and the twins Jenny started to become harder and harder to reach. Thanks to my cousin she was suddenly busy with local modeling assignments and word came through her folks that a big modeling agency in New York was interested in her. Within two weeks she was gone. She and her mom headed to New York and planned to stay there while they finalized things with the agency. We still talked on the phone occasionally, but I knew things were over between us.

Over the those next three weeks after Robin and I got together things changed a lot. Kathleen had a pregnancy scare. She was not pregnant, but I found out that Tommy was not always using protection. I barred him and her from doing it at my house, although they were still welcome as guests as long as they behaved themselves.

The Kathleen-Tommy situation also took care of itself after Kathleen decided that being with Tommy was not worth taking a chance at getting in trouble with her family, especially her dad. They broke up and I only saw Kathleen once in a blue moon. Her folks had tightened the leash on her rightly suspecting she was seeing boys behind their backs. Tommy was embarrassed and upset with the whole thing and just stopped coming around.

Jimmy was busy with Diane and had found a real soul mate in her despite their age difference. Ingrid was having fun with Terry, so I let him out of his agreement with me and allowed him to be the sole property of my cousin. He remained a great worker who showed up every day on time. After a while Ingrid bought him his own car and he made good use of it by working even harder and helping her to expand her business. He remained clean and made his brother proud.

By the end of the first week that we were together Robin had the very best friendship ring I had ever purchased. By the end of the third week she was also sporting a beautiful necklace I bought for her. Despite all of our wild talk, Robin and I had become complacent when it came to my game. We suddenly found ourselves happily exclusive to each other and I had not messed around very much with anyone since that night with her and the twins in the hotel suite.

We did play around with Mary because I thought that the three of us made a fun threesome for sex and Robin liked it as well. Mary loosened up a little and started enjoying our sessions more and more. We also played around with Laura. Robin and her became good friends and my new girlfriend did not mind sharing me with her as long as she got to participate. As far as Robin went, she was off limits to other guys and the only girls I did it with were Mary and Laura when Robin was involved.

Everything was finally coming together for me. I had the perfect girlfriend, I was helping my friends and doing well in school now that a lot of the pressures that plagued me were gone. I was still playing my game and having fun, but not in a way that brought too much attention on me.

Robin, Mary and Laura were surprisingly discreet and did not blab about our sessions together. That kept us all safe.

As Christmas approached my parents were busy attending parties and such. There were thousands of tourists in town staying there because they liked the beach even in the dead of winter or because they found it less crowded than Orlando or Kissimmee. Those places probably had an extra half million people filling their hotels during the holiday season at that time and everything always cost double during peak periods like that one. Because it was not a particularly long drive to places like Orlando (home of the Mouse House) or Sarasota (home of the Ringing Museum) from St Pete and our room prices were better, most of our hotels and motels were super busy and so was my dad, as well as the Jensen family.

Robin was staying over my house again with the Twins to avoid being home alone with her folks and Susan working overtime at the motel constantly. I loved having Robin over and her brothers over. To keep things right with her, I did not mess around with the twins anymore. I had my fill of those boys anyway and between Robin, Laura and Mary, I was kept mostly satisfied.

I did miss fooling around with guys like Jimmy, Tommy, Terry and Mitchell, but going after them was no longer practical. Jimmy was with Diane, Terry was with my cousin, Tommy was dating some new girl I did not know and Mitchell was also out. He told me that he was no longer available to mess around with me because he still worried about being pegged as gay.

Christmas vacation was wonderful. I suspected that Robin's folks and my own knew that Robin and I were an item, but they were too busy to worry about it. Both sets of parents trusted me and knew that I was a straight shooter who would not get her into drugs or anything else really bad. It was kind of like a 'don't ask, don't tell' situation which both Robin and I were O.K. with. Ingrid also took a shine to Robin in a friendly sense. She had a couple of beautiful custom outfits made for her as a reward to me for all the help I gave my cousin with her business.

Robin looked better than ever and even though I guess you could say we were in the 'honeymoon' stage of our relationship, we really did become close during those days and had every intention of staying that way. We were already friends, so that was not a hurdle we needed to jump over and I think that was one of the reasons we got along so well. Another reason that I think our relationship blossomed and we got so close was because of our friends.

Robin, Mary, Laura and I started going out together and really enjoyed each other's company. Mary was too young for a traditional boyfriend, so I guess I kind filled the gap for her in a bizarre sort of way. Laura was having trouble finding the right guy despite her good looks so I was also a kind of 'fill-in' boyfriend for her as well. Robin knew she was number one with me and did not worry about competing with the other girls. We were all one happy and somewhat perverted family with Robin and I playing the parents more or less.

Christmas came and went and we had yet another big New Year's Eve Party while my folks spent their New Year's with the hotel bosses in another state. Many of those who came to last year's party were not present this time around having moved on in one way or another, but those who came like Robin, Laura, Susan, Patty, Terry, Diane, Mary, Jimmy, Tommy, the twins,

Ingrid and myself had a great time together. Apart from my relationship with my cousin which was special and constant, Robin, Laura, Mary and I represented a new core group and became very close to one another. Oh yea, and then there was Jeannie.

Jeannie was my age, attended the same high school I did and worked at the ice cream restaurant in the mall. She began to warm up to Robin, Laura, Mary and myself as we visited the place more often and always managed to attract attention with our sometimes loud voices and always stupid antics. Most of the servers hated us, but Jeannie thought we were a barrel of laughs and was always glad to take our orders and it was not just because we tipped unlike many students. I suspected it was our uniqueness, togetherness and fearlessness that attracted Jeannie to us.

As soon as Christmas break began we spent more time at the mall and the ice cream restaurant. One day while we were eating Jeannie heard us talking about a kid I casually knew from a class at school. He died suddenly of a drug overdose. Jeannie came over to offer her condolences and explain that although did not know the boy, she heard about his death from the gossip going around our high school. Once on the subject we discovered that she was against smoking, drinking and drugs as much as we were and that made her instantly O.K. with me!

One day during on of our Christmas break visits to the ice cream restaurant we invited Jeannie to hang out with us that evening after her day shift ended. She was kind of hesitant about accepting our invitation at first, but after we told her that we were just going to hang out in the mall she was happy to join us and met us there later that evening.

I could see that Jeannie had trust issues which went beyond what I would have expected from the average person. I chalked those up to the fact that she was a very pretty girl who probably got hit on a lot and had to watch her back when it came to invitations to hang out with people she did not know. After all, she could end in in some house or apartment where she might be accosted and unable to leave. The mall was familiar, public and safe for her.

Jeannie was my age, just about my height and thin with strawberry blond hair, freckles and an adorable face. She had a perfect figure and a terrific personality once you got to know her. Originally from upstate New York, she told us that her dad was a career military officer and her mom was an executive secretary turned homemaker. Her parents had Jeannie late in life several years before her dad retired from the military and the family moved to Florida. She had two sisters and a brother that were much older then her and did not live at home.

We all had a blast together at the mall. We went to the arcade, the movies and even had the nerve to go and see Santa at a big department store. We took turns sitting next to him so he would know what we wanted for Christmas. We were a little too big for his lap! Even my new somewhat cautious friend Jeannie played along and took her turn with Jolly Old Saint Nick. We all got nice little bags of candy for spending a few minutes with Santa and left him with peace on earth and good will towards men.

Jeanne was fascinated by us and later told me that she originally thought that we were part of some Commune or something like it because we all appeared to be romantically involved in one way or another. I didn't know that it showed that much, but I did not care either. I loved my girls

and they loved me. Despite the strange relationship we all shared, Jeannie did not judge us and enjoyed our company.

When we first met Jeannie I figured she had lots of friends, but I soon found out that there were only two other girls her own age that she was even slightly close to and they were more classmates at school than anything else. There were lots of girls she spoke with casually at school and at work, but none which you could call her close friends. That seemed odd to me for such an outgoing and pretty girl, but since she did not judge us I was not about to judge her.

I normally would have jumped at the chance to be with someone like Jeannie, but I was trying to stop getting involved with fast and loose relationships for Robin's sake. I wanted to stick with our core group and was not looking for new recruits. However, despite my best attempts to avoid any further romantic entanglements, Jeannie was just the kind of girl I liked and I found it hard to resist her. Apart from wanting to be involved with Jeanne for selfish reasons, I also felt that she would make a great member of our group and bring a lot to it if I could get Robin on board with my feelings on the matter.

After Jeannie started hanging out with us some more over that Christmas break she eventually felt comfortable enough to go other places with us besides the mall. She did not have a car, so I always picked her up and she rode with us in mine. We went bowling, dancing at a local youth center and saw a Christmas play together. Despite the fact that we were getting closer to her and visa versa, I knew that Jeannie was not yet yet ready to go to my house or the hotel. She was very careful about everything she did and about the places she went. Despite her somewhat odd behavior, I really liked her and finally decided to approach Robin about trying to get her to officially join our little group.

While we were planning our New Year's Eve Party I spoke to Robin and the others about Jeanne. I suggested that we could all benefit from having her as a part of our core group in more ways then just platonically. Robin already knew that she was my cup of tea, so there was no need to try and mislead or lie to her about my desire to add Jeannie to my wish list. Robin also knew that my commitment to her was now absolute, so she did not worry about me falling for our new friend as a replacement for her. She and the others agreed that we should try and get Jeannie to join our core group as more than just a casual observer.

After Robin and I got seriously involved I was not embarrassed by our age difference and hung out with her at school. I took Robin to dances, sporting events and any other school activities where couples were welcome. None of the members of our little group worried about peer pressure because we had all already been victims of it. We hung out together and enjoyed each other's company. We were different and proud of it!

By the time that Jeannie came along all of us had fooled around with each other together and separately making us more than just a group of friends, but Robin was still my girl. She had also become my partner in the game and was a willing player who seemed to enjoy running it as much as I did. The other girls were close friends and obviously more as well, but none of them had any hope of replacing Robin with me as far as I was concerned.

Jeannie was as different as we were and that is exactly why I knew she would fit in with us. She not only stayed away from drinking, drugs and alcohol, but was a very unique person as I was about to discover. With older parents, no other siblings at home, no boy friend and no really close friends other than us, she accepted my invitation to our New Year's Eve Party. After I introduced her to the others at the party that she did not know, I kept her close to Robin and I throughout our shin dig to be sure she felt comfortable. I was laying the groundwork for my invitation to join us which I hoped would come in the very near future.

The party started to break up around one in the morning. Ingrid and Diane headed out to spend the night at Diane's house with Terry and Jimmy. Susan drove back to the motel to help her parents out with a full house. The twins got tired and went to bed in the extra downstairs room they were using as a bedroom while they stayed with us. Before long only Robin, Mary, Laura, myself and Jeannie were left. We all watched TV, listened to music, played pool and talked for a while really enjoying each other's company. All of them were sleeping over except for Jeannie.

I could have tried to get Jeannie to spend the night, but the instincts I had developed for playing my game successfully over the years told me to wait and be patient with her. I suspected that there was more to Jeannie then met the eye and before I made any provocative moves on her, I wanted to find out what it was. Seeing that she was getting a little nervous about the time, I offered to drive Jeanne home around two thirty and she accepted. She did not really have a curfew and as long as she called home every once in a while her parents left her alone.

Jeannie lived in a quiet neighborhood in a nice house near the mall. We first met her parents one night while she was hanging out with us at the mall. They were shopping and seemed like a nice couple in their early fifties. Although Jeannie indicated she was close with them, her parents did not seem overly concerned about who she was hanging out with.

When I asked Jeannie about the situation with her folks she explained that they trusted her implicitly. She said they knew how much she hated smoking, drugs and alcohol, and how careful she was when it came to the people she chose to associate with. Her parents were Morman and had made personal choices not to smoke, drink or take drugs.

Jeannie attended church with her parents when she was younger out of necessity and continued to do so out of respect for them into her adolescence, but she was not really interested in their Faith. She stopped going to services after they wanted her to get more involved with their religion, but occasionally visited other churches much to their chagrin.

Jeannie was smart and well read. It seemed liked she was always searching for answers and I really enjoyed the conversations we had together about anything and everything. As I dropped her home that night after our New Year's Eve Party I felt sad that she was alone, but I knew that if she got involved with our group she would find companionship and more.

It was hard to wrap my head around the fact that a beautiful girl like Jeannie did not have a boy friend. However, the more I got to know her, the more obvious it was that she was very choosy about the people she brought into her life. I saw guys hit on her all the time when we ate at the ice cream restaurant, but none of them appeared to attract her interest.

At one point I thought that it might have been possible that she swung the other way except for the fact that she never put the moves on Robin, Mary or Laura; and all of them were really cute. I guessed that she was not boy crazy and willing to wait for the right guy whoever that was as far as she was concerned. Except for my commitment to Robin, I would have ordinarily tried to be that guy.

It took a lot of self control to keep from making the moves on Jeannie and even more to stay focused on my relationship with Robin with this new and very cute girl in our midst. I mean, it wasn't like I was going to dump Robin for her or anyone else. It was just difficult not to want to be as close as possible to a girl with the looks, personality and brains of Jeannie. The trick was to get close without offending, hurting or abandoning Robin. That was what was good about our core group concept and the game. We could enjoy the best of each other in every way without getting hung up on jealousy or back stabbing one another.

We still had a few days before school started up again, so I began to think about how to initiate Jeannie into our group. I worried that saying or doing the wrong thing would frighten her away or give her the wrong idea about us. We were kind of perverted, but in a good way as far as I was concerned. That was a concept foreign to most so-called 'normal' people even in those days of free love and sexual experimentation.

Robin and the others chimed in with some suggestions, but none of them seemed any more workable then my own ideas. What we needed was some kind of a major ice breaker that would let Jeannie know what we were all about without cornering her. If it was summer or the weather was warmer the easy answer would have been a skinny dipping session to see if she was into that for a start, but the weather was still a little chilly at night, unpredictable and no where near suitable for nude bathing even with a heated pool at my house. Anyway, I suspected that getting Jeannie naked in front of us might be more of a challenge than we originally hoped it might be.

Jeannie dressed modestly in jeans, pants suits and knee length dresses. She never wore short skirts, low cut blouses, tight fitting jeans, hot pants or halter tops. As much as I would have loved to see her in a bikini at some point, I doubted that would ever happen and began to wonder if I would ever actually see any more of her body than I already had?

Most girls in those days that dressed modestly did so because they were either religious, ashamed of their bodies due to excess weight or hair issues, trying to cover up huge or tiny breasts or were just legitimately modest. Jeannie did not seem to fit into any of those categories as far as I could tell. She was thin, did not have excess body hair judging from the hair on her arms which was almost non-existent, was not overly religious and not extremely shy.

My new friend was becoming more of an enigma by the day and even though I thought she would be a good fit for deeper and more intimate involvement with our group, perhaps I was wrong? I expressed my concerns to the girls, but they still felt we had a shot at getting her into the game. At some point we even considered talking to her as a group. The problem with that idea was that I believed it would put too much pressure on Jeannie all at one time and might make her feel outnumbered.

Robin sensed my frustration with the Jeanne situation and made a final recommendation. She told me that I should either drop the whole thing and just let her hang out with us as a friend, or take on the job of getting her into the game myself. She said, "You're the guy who created the game and you're also the one who is always saying that you are the Master of it." Robin was mocking me a bit, but she was also right. If I could not find a way to get Jeanie more involved with us, then we might just have to let her hang with us as a friend and go on with things the way they were.

With just Friday night and the weekend available before school started up again on Monday, I was feeling the pressure to do something about the Jeannie situation. I knew she was a serious student who got good grades. Between her studies and the part-time job at the ice cream restaurant, I doubted that she would be as patient or susceptible to indoctrination into our game as she might be before the next week began. If I could get her into it before school started up on Monday, it would be easy to move ahead with things like sleep overs and group get togethers afterward. However, I still needed that ice breaker and could not seem to find one.

My old friend Fate came to my rescue once again giving me a belated Christmas present. On Friday evening just around six o'clock I went to see Jeannie just as she was finishing up her shift. She seemed out of sorts and upset, so I offered to drive her home. She normally caught a ride with one of her coworkers who worked the same shift that she did and lived two blocks from her, but she immediately accepted my offer and I was sure she wanted to talk.

I waited in my car outside the mall entrance nearest to the ice cream restaurant. Jeannie came out with a huge overnight bag in her hand and began crying as she got into my car. I asked her what was wrong and she told me that she had a huge blow up with her parents earlier that day. They had been putting a lot of pressure on her to get involved with their church and always seemed annoyed with her about one thing or another.

She said that she was tired of all the hassles with her folks. Before heading off to work that day she packed a few things that were important to her and told them she was leaving. They were concerned, but not enough to stop her and said that she could do whatever she liked because she would do that anyway. She planned to go to a cheap motel about a mile from the mall, but I had a better idea.

I told Jeannie that we had a small downstairs room which we never used accept for overnight guests and that she was welcome to stay there until things could be better sorted out. Robin and the twins had gone back home the day before after staying with us over the holidays and that freed up space for her if she wanted it. I said that I would take her to and from work and that she could ride with me to and from school, so transportation was no big deal. I also pointed out that Laura and my cousin would probably more than welcome her company. Besides, I doubted the motel would accept her as a guest because she was underage and had no adult staying with her.

I understood this was not an easy decision for her, but Jeannie knew that Laura was staying with me and that Robin and the twins had also spent time at my house and none of them seemed to have any concerns or issues with their stays or with me. Knowing that a motel would cost her

more than she made each week and that the one she had in mind was not the most desirable place for a teenage girl to stay even if they did allow her to stay there, Jeannie accepted my invitation.

After I got back to the house I explained the situation to Laura and Ingrid. They welcomed our new guest with open arms and I gave her a quick tour of the house. While Jeannie was getting settled into the spare room I called my parents who were still out of town and explained the situation to them. They said she could stay with us, but wanted to speak with her parents. After they called Jeannie's folks, they called me back a half hour later to let me know that her parents had no problem with her staying at our house.

I thought it was a little weird that Jeannie's parents gave their permission for her to stay with us so quickly, but then it was pretty obvious that their relationship with her had never been super close and was now badly strained. From my standpoint the situation could not have been better. With Jeannie staying at the house there was more time to try to ease her into our group activities. Robin could barely believe it when I gave them the news and was as thrilled as I was. Mary reacted the same way when she found out.

After all she had been through Jeannie slept until well after nine on Saturday morning. She did not have to work that day and probably needed the rest. I got before her and talked with my cousin before heading out to do some errands for her. Even with Terry, Diane, Laura and me helping her out, Ingrid was falling behind on her orders. She needed more help at the house now that Susan was working at her parent's motel most of the time and I suggested that Jeannie might be perfect for that job. I had no idea how Jeannie would feel about it, but Ingrid was all in with my suggestion. She trusted my judgment because I had already found her so many good workers. Now I just had to convince my new house guest.

By the time I got back to the house it was after lunch. Jeannie feeling a lot better thanks to the news that her folks were allowing her to stay at our house. I offered to take her over to pick up the rest of her things and she was grateful for my help. I brought Laura along and after just a few minutes, we had everything that Jeannie needed from her house in the car. Laura and I greeted her parents when we came into help Jeannie retrieve her things, but she said nothing at all to them and they remained silent as well.

After we got back to the house I gave our new guest time to settle in while I did some cleaning and the wash. Ingrid was still busy in her workroom, so Laura and I did the weekly shopping that afternoon. When we got back Jeannie came out to help us get everything into the house. After we put the groceries away I did all I could to make Jeannie feel welcome and made sure she knew that she could take whatever she wanted from the kitchen and use the washer and dryer anytime she liked.

I knew that having Jeannie stay with us would be an adjustment for her, Ingrid Laura and I, but there was plenty of room and we were used to house guests. My parents were almost never home anymore so I knew that Jeannie would not run afoul of them even if she turned out to be a brat (which I knew she was not). My dad's responsibilities at work had grown along with the property and his salary. He was doing a terrific job and the bosses loved him. My mom was now

fully licensed as a Registered Nurse in Florida and had switched to a better job as a Nurse Supervisor at a private hospital not far from my father's hotel.

My parents had grown even closer then they were before as a result of our move to Florida, so I never resented their absence. They enjoyed spending time at the hotel suite together and my father's constance presence on the property had been the catalyst for the hotel's successful growth and expansion. Besides, they knew that my cousin and I were inseparable and trusted us to keep things going smooth at the house. As long as we stayed out of trouble, we had Carte Blanche to go pretty much as we pleased.

Jeannie turned out to be a very pleasant and helpful person to have around. Before she came I made dinner every third night with Laura and Ingrid switching off the rest of the time. I enjoyed cooking and found my new house guest to be a good and willing helper as I prepared that night's feast. She offered to cook or help with whatever else we needed her to do around the house. I said that we appreciated her offer and would gladly take her up on it.

Jeannie really knew her way around the kitchen and we had dinner ready in no time. After we all ate, I sat down to have a private chat with Jeannie. Before I said anything Jeannie offered to pay us a weekly rent for her room, but I told her that was not necessary. I knew she liked paying her own way and was not surprised when she insisted on giving us something for her stay, but I had a better idea.

Jeanne already knew about my cousin's business from hanging out with us. I told her that Ingrid was now busier than ever and had trouble keeping up with orders. I explained that Diane and Laura had become indispensable to her as far as sewing and getting patterns cut, but she needed someone to help with with phone calls, correspondence, general secretarial work and miscellaneous tasks. I said that if she was tired of working for peanuts at the ice cream restaurant, she could work for my cousin and made some real money.

I could see that Jeannie was excited about the opportunity, so I also told her that if she took the job it would really help us out and that she would not have to work any more hours than she did at the mall. It could be an after school job on weekdays and part time on weekends. Knowing it would help us out, put money in her pocket and that I would not have to drive her back and forth to the mall everyday, Jeannie quickly accepted my offer. I took her into Ingrid who welcomed her to the family business.

Robin, Jeannie and Laura rode to school with me everyday. Mary was still in Junior High and took the bus. Things at the high school were becoming complicated for me. Unlike most of my fellow students my social life did not revolve around school. I hung with the three girls, Terry and the other guys I knew from home and my game. I felt like I had already plowed the field as far as potential friends or game players went, so apart from attending the usual social and sports events to show at least some school spirit and keep the girls happy, I was disinterested in most anything that was happening on campus.

Some of our classmates thought we were part of some cult or something because the girls and I tended to stay close to one another and the others we knew from the game or home, but none of

us cared what any of them thought. The only bad thing was that sometimes I felt like I was holding Laura back from finding a real boy friend. Although I felt the same about Mary, she was still in Junior High so there would be plenty of time for her to find Mister Right. Robin and I were happy together and although Jeannie enjoyed hanging with us, I had the same concern about her.

Now that she was an informal part of our group, Jeannie hung out with us more than she did with the few girls who occasionally talked with her before or after classes. She had already met most of the guys I knew either at home or at school. She was cordial with the boys we knew and did not mind taking the time to talk with them when they were around her and the rest of us were in classes, but she showed no romantic interest in any of them. Even with Jeannie living in my house, she was still largely an enigma to me.

I kept my grades up and began looking into business programs at some local colleges, but I had no intention of leaving Ingrid or my girls after I graduated High School that June. Laura already decided to attend a local Junior College, while Robin was still over a year away from having to worry about even applying to colleges and universities. To be honest, I think she was beginning to get interested in my cousin's business.

Robin changed a lot since becoming involved with me. She was still impetuous, but not as wild as she had been. I tried not to cramp her style too much because I liked my little wild child. However, I think that Robin was catching the maturity bug from me. Because her parents felt she was too young to work at the motel, she had shied away from asking me to get her involved with my cousin's business.

Robin came along and helped me run errands for my cousin every so often, but I think she lacked the confidence to take on a regular part time job. That began to change after she saw Jeannie step in the position my cousin gave her and easily pick up on the work Ingrid had for her. Robin had a definite sense of style. I knew that if she did try and work with Ingrid she would certainly catch the fashion bug and do really well.

After Jeannie had been with us for almost a month Robin asked my cousin if she could work with her. Ingrid liked Robin and immediately put her to work helping Laura with her in house duties. Robin hated asking her parents for money and although I loved buying her things, she rarely allowed me to purchase any clothes or personal items for her. This job would allow her the freedom to earn her own money and buy the things she wanted without having to ask anyone for them.

It was getting close to Spring Break and things were beginning to change again. Jimmy's folks knew that he was hanging out with my cousin. They were not particularly worried about the age difference because they liked how that Ingrid was responsible and successful, but they began to set more limits on how much time he could spend with her. He had been neglecting his school work a bit and that was a non-starter for them. Despite the limitations, Ingrid and Jimmy stayed together. She still thought of him as more of a boy toy than anything else, but as long as she was happy so was I.

Knowing that Mary was also spending a lot of time at my house with me and the other girls, her folks worried more about her than Jimmy. I was sad to learn that they had cut most of her free time to the point that she would no longer be able to be a part of our group in a practical sense. They also decided to put her in a private school effective next September. We all got the message loud and clear. Due to her young age, none of her were prepared to rock the boat. For her own good and ours, we had to bid farewell to a much loved member of our core group.

Ingrid gave me a lot more responsibilities as far as her business was concerned. Truth be told, by that time I was an almost equal partner and helped to run it behind the scenes more than my parents or the other kids knew. My dad hoped that I would come and work at the hotel during the upcoming summer tourist season. However, after seeing how involved I was with my cousin's business and how successful she had become with my help, I guess he decided not to rock the boat and retracted his offer.

With Spring Break looming and school beginning to wind down for me, I decided to place more effort into the Jeannie situation. Although Robin, Laura, Ingrid and I were careful not to do anything to frighten her off, Jeannie began to see that we were all a lot more than just close friends. Ingrid did not fool around with the girls, but she and I made out and had sex frequently enough to be noticed.

One night Jeannie saw my cousin and I kissing and fondling each other on the living room couch, although she did not know that I saw her watching us from the kitchen. The good news was that it did not seem to bother her. That gave me hope that she could still be brought into our fold as more than just a friend or casual observer. There were also times when Robin and Laura (and Mary when she was still with us) joined me in my room with the door closed. I was sure that Jeannie must have noticed that as well.

It was getting warmer out and we were already taking dips in the pool. It would not be long before some of our pool time would be clothing optional and I worried how Jeannie might respond to that. I really liked having her around and enjoyed our conversations. My cousin found a skilled and dedicated worker in our new friend. She got along with all of us extremely well, so the last thing I wanted to do was mess it all up with some clumsy invitation to join our group.

Robin and Laura had become like sisters and although I was Robin's boyfriend, she did not mind sharing me in a sexual sense with Laura or other girls including Susan when that situation occasionally presented itself. Robin swung more towards guys than girls, but she liked making out and playing around with Laura as long as I was present. I had no idea how adding Jeannie to the mix would play with her, but my two girls were still all in with getting Jeannie into bed with us.

My own relationship with Jeannie was a good, but somewhat complicated one. Sometimes she made me feel like a very close friend. Other times I felt like an older brother even though we both the same age. We always got along, talked a lot and sometimes as we sat with each other on the couch she would snuggle up close to me. I knew not to read too much into that because I saw her sit close to Robin and Laura when they were all on the couch watching TV. Still, there were

times when we sat alone that I sensed Jeannie was just moment or two away from kissing me before she caught herself and pulled back.

I guessed that Jeannie liked me as a friend, a benefactor and perhaps more. It was the 'more' part that was hard. She knew how dedicated I was to Robin and probably did not want to come between us. If I could just get the message to her that she would not be coming between us, but joining us. There was the rub and even with the ice breaker of her living with us, I was still unable to find a way to get that message across to her in way that would not blow her mind.

With Spring Break beginning and the pool season starting I decided to just be honest with Jeannie, explain our group situation and invite her to join us. There was nothing else I could do. If she was not comfortable with taking her friendship with us to a new level, I would let her know that it was alright to leave things as they were. Either way, I definitely wanted her to stay in our lives and in my house.

I waited until the Saturday before Spring Break began and my parents were gone out of state for the weekend to have my little talk with Jeannie. I asked Jeannie if I could talk with her for a few minutes in the late afternoon after we all finished our work and the others were not home. As we sat at the kitchen table, I began by telling her how much the girls and I enjoyed her company. I also stated the obvious by saying that she might have noticed some strange goings on between me, my cousin and the other girls.

From that point on I laid out a thumbnail sketch of my relationship with my cousin, the girls and the story behind my game. Jeannie sat quietly and did not seem at all upset about my revelations. I finished off by extending an invitation for her to join our little group in a more active and intimate way, pointing out that there was no pressure and that if she wanted to leave things as they were we were all fine with that as well.

Jeannie said she was fine with everything I told her about us. She said that she knew we were different and now that I explained the situation, accepted our unique relationships with one another. She also told me how much she enjoyed being around us and felt like she wanted a more intimate relationship with us, but she was not sure if she would fit in. She said she liked guys, never tried anything with girls and was open to new experiences. She told me that the problem was not us, it was her.

Before elaborating on her situation Jeanne offered me a compliment. She said, "Guys ask me out all the time. Most of them see me as a walking skirt and don't look beyond what they see in front of them. I can't deal with guys like that. You're different. I see it in the way you treat the girls around you and the way you've treated me. I wanna be with a guy like you. When we're sitting close to each other I want to hug and kiss you. I didn't want to get between you and Robin or the others. Now that I understand how things are with you and the girls I still want to do those things, but there is something that I think you should know about me first. "

Jeanne summed up her situation by saying, "I am not your typical girl." She choked up, looked around the kitchen as if she was searching for something and then continued her explanation. She began by saying, "I was born different. I was born with, well, female and male sex organs. I

mean, I am a girl, not a guy! I look like a girl and feel like one. I have a vagina, but I also have a small penis and ball sack with a vagina that cuts into the sack."

I was stunned. When I was a kid I heard about this because one of the other kids who went to my doctor had this issue and was always the talk of the waiting room after he left. I never gave it much thought because I never expected to actually meet someone who had this condition. I understood the condition to be very rare, but here I was sitting across my kitchen table from a hermaphrodite!

Me being me, Jeannie's condition did not turn me off, it turned me on! The possibilities were endless. While I took some time to mull over the situation she continued on by saying, "I was always very much of a girl. That was never in question. What I wondered about was what would happen when I became a teenager. Would I have female type breasts, a period and so on? Well, I have breasts and what my doctor says is a uterus. I experience a period and may even be able to get pregnant."

I told Jeanne that she did not have to prove her femininity to me! She looked and acted all girl and I admitted to being very attracted to her. I said that I could not speak for the others, but that her condition would not bother me in the least and I doubted it would bother the girls either because we were all just as different as she was, but in a more behavioral sense.

Jeanne smiled at me, so I got up, took her by the hand and lead her to the couch. We sat next to each other and I said, "Let's do what we both have been wanting to do for a while." We began making out, but I was careful not to push the envelope. Jeanne apologized for being a little clumsy as I tried to French kiss with her. She admitted that she had never even kissed a boy before.

I could not even begin to imagine how lonely Jeanne must have been over the years. Both of us were now sixteen and as I thought about all the experiences I had, I wondered how she got along without any type of romantic or physical contact at all. The good news was that she was making up for lost time. Once Jeannie got the hang of French kissing, she made the most of it. We passionately kissed and hugged each other for what seemed like an hour.

While we made out I tried to avoid touching her breasts just in case that might make her feel uncomfortable, but Jeannie pulled my hands towards them in an almost instinctive manner. As I fondled her breasts and made out with her, my new convert just melted in my hands. I felt the same. I did not even give her medical condition a second thought and wanted more.

I asked Jeannie if she wanted to come up to my bedroom and she said she did. I closed and locked the door to my room, then asked Jeannie to lay on my bed. I laid next to her and we continued the make out session we began downstairs in the living room. I took off my shirt and undershirt to see how she would respond. She took off her blouse and unhooked her bra.

Before I knew it we were both topless. Jeannie had a beautiful set of breasts that were the perfect size for her body, not too big or small. Our chests met as we kissed and I loved the feel of it. I

fondled her breasts slightly, then kissed and gently sucked on them. I could feel her body temperature rise and she moved in a way which told me it was time to move forward.

I knew that I was treading on fragile ground, so I slid out off my pants without removing my underpants. Jeannie unsnapped her jeans and asked me to help her take them off. I did so carefully and made sure that my hands felt her legs as I pulled down her jeans. She had on panties, but I did not look at them. The last thing I wanted was for Jeannie to feel like a freak in some carnival act because I was staring at her unique private parts.

We went back to making out until my penis was very stiff. I took off my underpants and moved her hand towards my dick. I got her to begin jacking me and I could tell that she liked doing it. She seemed to be thoroughly preoccupied with my private parts. She not only jacked me, but felt all over my penis and balls. She even asked me if she could go down and get a closer look at them! I told her to go ahead and enjoy herself.

Jeannie touched my private parts all over, eyed every part of them and lifted my testicles to see what they looked like underneath. At some point I said, "My turn." I knew I was taking a chance at spoiling the intimacy of our session, but it had to happen sometime if we were ever to actually have sex. At that point she moved away from my balls to lay flat on her back on the bed, took a deep breath and said, "Go ahead."

I pulled down her panties. Once they were off I saw that she had a nice patch of strawberry blond pubic hair above a small penis about the size of the dicks that the twins had. It was shapely with a nice crown. Below her penis was a small set of testicles that eventually parted into a normal looking female opening with slight lips and a medium sized hole.

I had a million questions that I wanted to ask Jeannie, but I knew that this was not the time or the place. I just said, "Your body is just as beautiful as I thought it would be and began kissing her again. She melted in my arms, then stopped making out with me a few minutes later to ask, "Aren't you any more curious than that?" I answered, "No, I just want to make love to you. Are you ready?"

Jeannie took another deep breath, laid back on the bed, spread her legs a little and asked, "If this alright?" I told her it was fine, opened the bedside nightstand drawer with my trusty lubricant in it and got ready for action. I asked Jeanne if she would like to lubricate my penis? She smiled and stuck her fingers in the Vaseline jar. She loved lubricating my penis and feeling the stiffness of it. I wiped off our hands with a towel, then explained that what we were going to do might hurt a little. I said that the Vaseline should help and privately wondered if she even had a Hyman?

The presence of her penis was not a distraction and actually turned me on. I was tempted to touch and jack it, but once again I stopped before I even started thinking that doing that might break the mood. That kind of stuff would come later if Jeannie allowed it. After all, despite having a dick through an accident of nature, Jeannie was very much a girl and beautiful one at that!

I loved her strawberry blond hair, cute face, freckle covered body and kind spirit. I kissed her all over before getting into position for intercourse, only avoiding her small penis and muted ball sack. I spread her legs a bit more pushing them up out of the way, then slowly slid my dick into Jeannie. Rather then stare down at her private parts, I looked into her eyes and smiled at her as I penetrated her opening.

My penis fit perfectly inside of Jeannie and soon hit her Hyman. As I slowly pushed through it she cringed a little and took several deep breaths. Once I was all the way inside her, I began having regular intercourse with my new goddess. We kept at it for a long time until I finally shot my load into her. She went to use the bathroom while I wiped myself off with a towel. After she came back into bed with me, we made out and I positioned her for doggie style sex.

Jeannie loved doing it that way. We tried several different positions and each time her insides got a little wetter. She even got on top of me and by the time we finished I was shocked to see that two hours had gone by. I must have ejaculated at least three times into her, but Jeannie did not care about that. The one thing that she did know was that she could probably not get pregnant; at least that was what her doctor said and what she told me before we got started.

Even after we stopped having sex we made out some more and it felt like we could not get enough of each other. Once we finally stopped Jeannie put her clothes on, went downstairs to the bathroom and showered. I showered in the upstairs bathroom, got dressed and ready to make dinner. While Jeannie was still cleaning up and dressing I called Robin to tell her the good news. I said that there was some things I needed to tell her about Jeannie and that I still had some work to do with her, so I suggested she not come over the next day. Robin agreed and sounded excited that Jeannie was now a part of our core group.

Jeannie helped me make dinner so that by the time that Ingrid and Laura got home we were all ready to eat. We enjoyed a nice meal together, then Jeannie offered to clean up. Ingrid said she would help and that gave me time to talk with Laura privately in her room. I told her everything about Jeannie. Laura was surprised, but it did not really bother her.

As a group we had already broken through so many traditional courtship and sexual walls that having someone like her involved with us was a natural. Laura was happy to have Jeannie in our core group and understood my need to prep her a little more before we all shared a bed together or the girls got a shot at her separately.

I decided that Jeannie and I needed some privacy and time to ourselves. After taking Ingrid aside and filling her in on the situation, I told Jeannie that I had a surprise for her that night. I told her to dress up, pack an overnight bag for one night and get ready to go out. Before long we were all dressed up and headed to the hotel suite. After we arrived and got us settled in, I took Jeannie for a show at the nightclub in the shopping center across the street.

We watched a couple of show bands perform, had some snacks and soda, then headed back to the hotel. I asked Jenny if she had a bathing suit, but she left it back at the house. She rarely swam unless it was in her own backyard pool and she was alone. I took her to the hotel store and

bought her a swimsuit, then convinced her to go swimming with me in the indoor hotel pool after hours.

The indoor pool closed at ten, but I got the night supervisor to open it for Jeannie and I. We were able to swim comfortably without Jeannie having to worry about anyone looking at the slight bulge in the bottom part of her two piece swimsuit. I barely noticed it and knew that I was looking at someone who was all girl and a good looking one at that. I was really beginning to feel close to Jeannie and just hoped that our new relationship would not ruin things with Robin.

Jeannie and I had a great time in the pool. After we went back to the suite and changed into our underwear, Jeannie kissed and hugged me saying that she had never met anyone as nice and considerate as I was. As we held each other I told her that I really liked her a lot and that I was glad we had become involved with each other. I lead Jeannie to the couch, turned off the lights in the suite and opened the drapes so that we could look out on to the moonlit beach and gulf beyond.

With such a romantic setting as the perfect backdrop, we began making out on the couch. Jeannie climbed up on to my lap and French kissed with me like there was no tomorrow. Before long we got up, headed into the bedroom I used at the suite, got naked and climbed into bed. We made out some more, then Jeannie asked me if I wanted to touch her other sex organ? She was no dummy and knew that I was curious. She was honest and said that her penis got hard and could even ejaculate.

I began playing with her penis and it instantly got hard. I decided to try licking her pussy while I played with her penis. Jeannie told me that it was hard for her to differentiate the feelings between her sex organs. She could really only feel one sensation at a time, so I ate her out and then began jacking her off. I asked Jeanne if I could suck on it and she said I could.

He dick was stiff and soon shot a load of semen into my mouth. She tried apologizing, but I said that I loved it. She knew that I fooled around with boys as well as girls from my previous confession about my game earlier that day, so it was no big deal with Jeannie that I wanted to suck her off. After I washed out my mouth and got back into bed, Jeannie said, "My turn!" and went down to suck me off.

This was another first for her, so it took Jeannie a while to get used to sucking on my penis. I told her she did not have to keep my penis in her mouth while I ejaculated, but she insisted and managed to suck all my semen down her throat. I knew she had not really wanted to swallow, but did so as a 'thank you' for all I did for her. I returned the favor by screwing the daylights out of her for the next hour and a half. I loved having sex with Jeannie and not just because she could offer a lot more than most girls.

Chapter Six: Just The Four Of Us and Greg

The night at the hotel suite was special for both of us. The next morning we headed back to the house. With Spring Break now on Jeannie had some shopping to do, so I took the opportunity to

have Robin come over. I explained the situation to her and she was as surprised as I was when I first heard the news about Jeannie. Robin immediately saw the same opportunities and extra added benefits of having Jeannie as a part of our core group that I did.

Laura joined us after a few minutes, so I decided to fill them in on all of my exploits with Jeannie the day before. I made it clear that they should treat her the same way we all treated each other and go out of their way to make her feel welcome. Most importantly, they needed to remember that she was a girl. If they wanted to mess around her and she was good with that, no problem. They just needed to let her make the first moves in bed as far as what sex organs she was willing to share with them.

Laura and Robin were smart and got my message loud and clear. They knew better than to do anything to screw up our relationship with Jeannie. I suggested that since Jeannie and Laura were closest thus far, Laura should invite our new member into her bedroom that night and see where things would go from there. Sometime later I would arrange it so that Robin would have an opportunity to be with Jeannie in my room. The girls were with my plan and the stage was set. That night Laura invited Jeannie into her room and the two spent the night together.

With my parents still out of town, Robin's folks busy at their motel and Jeannie shacked up with Laura for the night, I asked Robin to spend the night with me. She brought the twins over as well. They slept in the recreation room on cots while Robin slept with me. After all that happened with Jeannie I really needed to reconnect with Robin. We had a great night together, making out and making love.

The next day after I finished my errands for Ingrid and got back to the house Laura took me aside and said that Jeannie and had a great time the night before. Jeannie opened up and even used her penis to have sex with Laura. I knew that Robin was also chomping at the bit to have sex with Jeannie, but moving too fast would be a mistake. I planned to get them together later in the week. For now I had a nice surprise for the newest member of my game.

On Monday evening I took Jeannie to the jewelry store in the mall. I went there earlier in the day while running errands for Ingrid and picked out a beautiful ring that I knew would drive her crazy. The jeweler in the mall had more choices than the one in my neighborhood. My choice was impeccable and Jeannie went crazy as soon as she saw the ring. The jeweler fitted it on to her finger while we were there so that she could leave wearing it.

Jeannie cried like a baby for several minutes. We sat on a bench in the mall so that she would have time to settle down and let everything sink in. She hugged and kissed me, then thanked me profusely. After we got back to the house Jeannie showed off her ring to Laura and Ingrid. Both of them also had rings from me, so there was no jealousy there. Instead, they treated her like a long lost relative come home. We all enjoyed each other's company and I was happy to see Jeannie fitting in with us so well.

After the others went to bed Jeannie made it clear that she wanted to sleep with me that night. With my folks not due home until the next day, that was fine by me. We made out, got naked and had sex, but the best part of that night was just having her sleep next to me. Jeannie was

beautiful, but I think it was the fact that she was so different that made her so very special to me. After all, I was also very different and had been for as long as I could remember.

The next day after I got done with my work for Ingrid I came home to find Ingrid, Laura, Robin, Diane, Terry, Jeannie the twins and their friend Greg all in the pool together. That was a big deal as far as I was concerned. Jeannie was very careful about showing off her body to others. Just the fact that she was willing to get into the pool with the others wearing the two piece swimsuit that I bought for her at the hotel was a milestone. It meant that she now felt comfortable with us and that it was time for my new convert to spend some private time with Robin.

With my folks due home the next day I knew this was the perfect opportunity to get Robin and Jeannie together. Just before dinner I asked Jeannie if she would feel comfortable spending the night with Robin? She said that as long as Robin came to her room it was fine. I got with Robin and she could not have been more excited. She called her folks at the motel to let them know she and the twins would be sleeping over. I was excited because the twins would be sleeping with me that night and another opportunity came with that.

The twins had not changed much since I first met them even though time had passed. They had a little more pubic hair down there and their penises had grown a little larger, but their dicks were still small even for their size and that was good news for me. I loved their bodies and the fact that they were twins. I still had my eye on some of the other boys, but most of them were now preoccupied with girls. I did not want to push any of them too far for fear of exposure. The one exception was a kid named Greg.

Greg was a friend of the twins. He lived around the block having just moved to Florida with his parents the previous summer. It took him a while to hook up with the twins, so we only recently saw him at our house. The twins brought him along on this visit to swim in our pool. They tried to shield him from me this time as they had done before, but I got a chance to talk with him a few times and began to set the stage to have some fun with this new kid.

Greg was cute and friendly just like the twins and had a great personality. What I really liked about him was that he had pure blond hair, very white skin, a few freckles on his face and body, and not much body hair for a boy who was fourteen. He was a little bit taller than the twins, but a little more filled out as far as a body type goes and not as thin as they were.

Greg was originally from Pennsylvania and had an ethnic background of being Pennsylvania Dutch. His folks had both left the strict religious sect years before and lived apart from the kind of primitive lifestyle most Pennsylvania Dutch endured. They were now as modern as anyone else, just a lot less rebellious. No tobacco, alcohol or drugs. The same could be said of Greg who was always polite and had a relatively short hair length for the time. I guess you could say he even had a slightly minimized "Dutch Boy" haircut.

Greg was an only child and yet another latch key kid. His dad was a skilled cabinet maker and carpenter, while his mother was a practical nurse. Both worked and were saving to try and open some sort of business in Florida sometime in the next several years. After Greg started spending

time with the twins his parents got to know the Jensen Family. Before long he was having sleep overs with the twins, but with their folks rarely home those became few and far between.

The Jensens introduced my parents to Greg's folks and that's when he started coming over our house more often. I had been so busy with the girls that I had not tried to take advantage of his visits up to that point. Now that things were settled with Jeannie and the others it was time for a new boy to be added to my game. In fact, I figured that evening was the perfect time to get things started with him.

I knew a dirty little secret that would help me get better access to Greg. The twins had Greg sleep over at least a couple of times every few weeks, but I knew for a fact that during some of those occasions the Jensens and Susan were staying at their motel. That meant that Greg and the twins were home alone and even though they were right across the street from us if they needed anything, I was sure that if his parents found out that would be the end of the sleep overs.

I took the twins aside and made sure they understood that I was wise to what they had been doing. After they admitted that Greg was supposed to be sleeping over their house that night with no adult supervision, I told the boys that they needed to tell Greg that since their parents were not home and Robin was sleeping over my house, he would also need to sleep over in my room along with them. I made sure that they understood that I had every intention of bringing Greg into my game and that I needed their help.

I hated trying to bring anyone into my game in a 'cold turkey' kind of way. I like doing some finessing first, but with my parents returning home the next day and Jeannie busy with Robin that night it was a golden opportunity to try and take a shot at Greg. With the twins and their friend sleeping in my room, I could always shut down my plans if Greg saw what I was doing to the twins and did not like or accept it. Being their friend I was fairly certain he would keep his mouth shut about what we were doing either way.

We had a real community meal that night with Jeannie, Robin, Laura, Ingrid, Terry, Diane, the twins, Greg, Jimmy, Diane and me present. The way I looked at things the meal was a big plus. It helped put Greg at ease seeing how all the people that either worked for Ingrid or hung out at our house got along so well. The more at ease he was, the better chance I had to get into his pants.

Terry and Ingrid were going out after dinner while Diane was being picked up for an evening out with her new boy toy Jimmy. Laura was exhausted from doing extra work for my cousin that afternoon and could not wait to get to bed. That left more than enough privacy for Robin and Jeannie in her room, and the boys and me in mine.

After Ingrid, Terry and Diane finally left, Robin, Jeannie and I watched TV together for a while. The twins were up in the recreation room playing games and listening to records with Greg. Knowing that would also help to make him feel welcome and be caught off guard, I was all for what John and Jerry were doing with him. Things would have been even easier if they had played around with Greg during those sleep overs at their house in the first place, but I knew better.

The twins did not mind occasionally messing around with each other if they were in the mood, but they were not really interested in playing my game with their friends at that point. They had almost been caught playing around with each other and some of the other neighborhood kids several times when their parents came home unexpectedly. That put them off to trying anything with others unless it was at my house and supervised by me. I understood their situation at home, but now that they were over my house they knew what I expected of them.

Near nine thirty Robin and Jeannie were ready to had to Jeannie's room, so I went upstairs to see what Greg and the twins were doing. By that time they were watching the TV in the recreation room. I sat with them for a few minutes until the program they were watching ended, then I told them that it was time to go into my bedroom. I did not say it was time to go to sleep!

I managed to quell most of the rumors or loose talk that occasionally circulated around the neighborhood about my games thanks to a few big mouths that had played my game in the recent past and decided to try and spread rumors about me. They were all unsuccessful and for that reason I doubted that Greg had heard about my games or been at the house enough times to figure out that something strange was going on there. That meant that I needed to start from scratch with him.

Once we were all in my room I closed the bedroom door and told the three boys to sit on my bed while I sat on a desk chair and faced them. I asked Greg if he had ever played doctor? He said that he had not. I asked him if he knew how the game was played? He said that he thought it was something like a deal where some kids got together and showed off their private parts to each other. I congratulated him on knowing the basics of the game.

At that point I calmly explained to Greg that the kids who lived in or visited my house all played a version of that game. I gave him a brief explanation of how I first got involved with the game and how I made some changes to it to include sexual experimentation with both boys and girls. So far so good. Greg did not appear upset or overly concerned, so I went on with my diatribe.

I went into all the stuff about how my game made it easier for kids to deal with things like taking showers in gym class and getting to see each other naked if they were curious. I also said that playing the game gave guys a chance to enjoy being jacked off instead of just jacking off themselves off and even have sex if they wanted it. I told Greg how that boys got to learn more about how to correctly have sex, and that my game gave both girls and boys a chance to have their first sexual encounter in a nice atmosphere with friends instead of somewhere disgusting.

After going through all the hoops about why my game benefitted all who played it, I told Greg that the twins wanted me to invite him to play it with us. Before he could respond to the invitation, I told Greg that John an Jerry were prepared to give him a demonstration about how the game was played if he was willing to participate. He looked at his friends and they nodded in agreement.

I said that since he was sleeping over anyway and had probably already seen the twins naked when they all changed clothes during previous sleep overs or maybe even in physical education class at school, it should be no big deal for him to get naked with them. I said that would be

Having Greg's penis in my mouth was awesome. It fit perfectly with room to spare and throbbed continuously. He moved around a bit so I knew his dick was sensitive and that made the situation even better for both of us. He watched John give Jerry a blow job while I gave him his. Before long he shot his load and I sucked every drop down my throat as my new player moaned and moved around in the kind of painful ecstasy that guys feel while ejaculating during a blow job.

After getting Greg cleaned up, I had John lay down on the bed and got Greg into position to suck him off. I got Greg to put his friend's penis into his mouth and walked him through how to suck John off. I was sure he would stop sucking as soon as John began to ejaculate, but Greg surprised me. He sucked John's semen down his throat like a pro and seemed to enjoy doing it.

I began to wonder if Greg was holding out on me? Even if he had done some some of this stuff before, that was not the time to try and find out. Things were going well and the last thing I wanted to do was to rock the boat. I asked Greg if he would also suck off Jerry and he said he would. He went to work on Jerry and sucked him off the same way. At this point I took off my clothes feeling comfortable enough to join the party. Greg stared at my package and seemed awe struck by my dick.

I had the twins get into position for anal sex. Jerry was the more passive of the two so I had him lay across the bed with his feet on the floor while John stood behind him. I lubricated John's penis explaining what was happening to Greg, then had John penetrate his brother. After John pulled his dick out and shot a load on his brother's buttocks, I had them switch places. Jerry did his thing, then I told Greg to take a turn on Jerry giving him no choice in the matter.

After I lubricated Greg, he quickly penetrated Jerry who was in some pain due to his friend's thicker and very stiff penis. Greg ignored Jerry's moans and shoved his penis all the way into his friend time after time. He was a natural at anal sex and appeared to be enjoying himself a lot. He kept on for quite a while until he finally pulled his dick out and shot his load.

I could see that Greg was into what we were doing, so I decided to go for the gold. I got into position for anal sex without saying anything to him. I guess he thought that one of the twins would be taking a turn on him, but imagine his surprise when I came up behind him and began pushing my sixteen year old penis into his anus.

Greg started squirming and saying, "I don't think I am ready for this!" I told him to relax and very slowly penetrated his anus with my crown. He had a larger hole than the twins, so there was no way I was not going to push my dick in all the way. Like so many others he gave off muted cries into the pillow, then settled down as I moved my penis in and out of him.

After I finished and cleaned off Greg's buttocks, he got up and had some tears in his eyes. I told him to lay down on the bed so that I could comfort him. While he did I had the twins demonstrate French kissing with each other as I rubbed Greg's back while he watched them. After a while I turned him around and told him I was going to teach him how to make out and French kiss.

Greg went along with what I was doing and eventually got into the French kissing. While we made out I played with his dick and had him play with mine. He appeared to enjoy jacking me more than I thought he would. I switched him out with the twins and had Greg take turns French kissing with John and Jerry. After the kissing practice, I had the twins suck each other off again while I laid down on the bed and told Greg to suck me off.

My newest player was a little hesitant leading me to believe he preferred messing around with kids his own age or was just scared of my dick, but I got him to comply. Once he began sucking me his whole attitude changed and he really got into it. He sucked me off really good and even swallowed my semen. I decided to have anal sex with Jerry while Greg took on John's buttocks. This time he appeared to take the frustration he must have felt at being screwed by me out on John. Once again I saw Greg watching my penis as it went in and out of Jerry.

Greg really went to town on his friend and all but shot his load into John, pulling his penis out after some had already been deposited into poor John. I finished with Jerry about the same time, so we all took showers. John and Jerry showered together, then Greg and I took our turn. Once again I saw that Greg liked looking at my penis and that was goo news for me. I knew right then and there that we would be a team for some time to come.

While we showered together I told Greg that I would get him with some girls very soon and thanked him for playing the game. He did not say much and I could tell that despite the fact that I had boned his buttocks so hard, he liked me and what we had done with each other and the twins. While we got ready for bed the twins laid down on some cots I had in my room. Greg joined me in bed where we laid right next to each other in our underwear.

I asked Greg if he was sure he had never sone any of this before and he swore he had not. He did admit that seeing boys naked in gym class sometimes made him horny and that he had tried to play around with both the twins while they slept. He also admitted to playing around with a couple of younger relatives, but only while they were asleep staying over his house. With strict and still very religious parents he was scared to death of being caught or exposed if he played around with other kids while they were awake.

So Greg was a player! An inexperienced one, but I would take care of that. By that time the twins were asleep so without saying anything else I slipped off Greg's underpants and sucked him off once again. After he ejaculated, I had him suck me off. This time he seemed really into it and again sucked every drop of my semen down his throat.

After we finished up and cleaned up, I play wrestled with Greg for a while and then began making out with him to see what he would do. He did not object, Frenched with me passionately and actually started playing with my dick while we kissed. He was fascinated by my penis and I loved the attention he gave it!

After we stopped making out I showed Greg the dirty books and magazines I had in my nightstand drawer and said he could read them any time he came over as long as he did so in my room and put them away right after he finished. he began checking them out and I fell asleep while Greg was still reading them.

The next morning we all got up and joined the others for breakfast. Robin and Jeannie were smiling, so I knew things went well with them. I found out later that they really got into each other, did all kinds of cool stuff together and that Jeannie used her penis to screw Robin several times. I could not wait to get both of them together in my bed! That would happen very soon, but right now I was really into Greg.

Robin and the twins went home after breakfast. I asked Greg if he wanted to go with me as I run errands for Ingrid. He surprised me by saying he did, so while we ran around town in my car we talked about some of the things in the dirty books and magazines. I loved the way that he talked so freely about sex and knew I had an important new player for my game. Such dedication deserved a reward.

That afternoon Kathleen and Robin came over while Jeannie was still busy helping Ingrid. The twins were hanging with some other friends. I took Kathleen aside and asked her if she thought that Greg was cute. She did, so I asked her if she wanted to join me, Robin and Greg up in my bedroom? She said she did knowing what i had in mind and we all headed upstairs for some fun before my folks got home later that evening. Kathleen liked me a lot, but I knew that getting her too involved with the game would be a huge mistake with her parents now watching her like a hawk most of the time.

We all got naked, then I had Greg make out with Kathleen for a while while I got into it with Robin. I placed Greg into position with Kathleen and he soon had his first sexual encounter with a girl in the comfort and privacy of my house just as I had promised him. While he screwed with Kathleen, Robin and I got sexually reacquainted and did it on the other side of my bed. I saw Robin watching Greg have intercourse with Kathleen while we did it and instantly knew he was on her radar, so I decided to give her what she wanted.

After Greg and I shot our loads and everyone cleaned up, I asked the girls if they wanted to switch partners? Robin and Kathleen giggled, then said that was fine with them. Before long I was again having intercourse with the lovely Kathleen while foxy Robin was really getting into having Greg's short, thick penis stuck into her over and over again. I really liked doing it with Kathleen and was glad that things had worked out so well.

After we all cleaned up, Greg had to leave. I invited him back on Friday for another sleep over when my folks would be away again. He quickly accepted my offer and why not? I had already got him laid twice in one day by beautiful teenage girls. As soon as Greg left the girls ganged up on me and the three of us had sex together. It was really nice, but I could not help wondering if I had created a bunch of monsters with my game? Either way, it was nice to be with Robin and Kathleen again.

I spent the remainder of the day cleaning up the house to be sure that everything was perfect by the time my parents got home. They were impressed with the way we kept things as they always were after returning from a trip. I collected the dirty laundry from my folks and everyone else. By the time I finished the laundry that evening I was really beat. My fun with Greg, the twins,

Robin and Kathleen had worn me down to nothing. I fell asleep fast and did not wake up until around seven the next morning.

All morning long I thought about Jeannie, Robin, Laura, Kathleen and my new boy toy Greg while I ran errands and did some paperwork for my cousin. Jeannie made lunch for everyone and as she, Ingrid, Laura, Diane, Terry and I sat down to eat I was still distracted. Had I again bit off more than I could chew? I felt like the King of Chaos ruling over a Kingdom of my own design. On top of my still very complicated girl situation, I was now second guessing myself about Greg.

Although it seemed like Greg was on board with everything I was doing, he was still a new comer and that made my latest player a bit of a wild card. I needed to talk with him some more about being discreet. Even though I was certain that he would be as careful as I was because he feared his folks would find him out, I had to be sure. Once again I caught myself over-thinking everything and realized that I needed to just settle down and enjoy ruling over my bizarre land of sexual perverseness.

I knew that Jeannie had fun with both Robin and Laura during their recent one night flings. I also knew that she was dying to get intimate with me again. I felt the same, but needed some space to keep myself from becoming too involved with her. As much as I liked Jeannie, I did not want to blow off Robin or even give her the impression that I was no longer as involved with her as I had once been. The answer to my problem was a threesome between myself, Jeannie and Kathleen.

By leaving Robin and Laura out I could have fun with Jeannie, keep her happy and use Kathleen as an excuse for the sex session. Kathleen was amazingly cute and I could not imagine Jeannie not being into doing it with her and I together. After we all finished working that day I took Jeannie aside to ask her how she felt about having a session with me and Kathleen? I was honest saying that I worried about having sex with her alone because I did not want to send Robin the wrong message.

It was not like Robin was the jealous type. We all had fun with other people, but that usually happened when the rest of us were there or knew about and approved of it in advance. The girls tended to run everything intimate they were planning by me first to avoid the appearance of impropriety. I tried to reciprocate as often as possible. Even within our always promiscuous group there were rules.

Because Jeannie and I talked so often and spent so much time together, I wanted to be sure that when we did want to have sex apart from Robin we did not piss her off. The time would come and was not far off when Robin, Laura, Jeannie and I would share a bed, but that would not begin until my parents next trip. Trying to sneak a session that big by them made no sense and was far too risky.

There was a method to my madness and a certain bizarre perverseness involved with my plan to connect the dots between Jeannie, Kathleen and myself. The truth was that my freckle fetish was kicking in and I really just wanted to have a private session with two beautifully freckled girls. Not only would that give me more time with Jeannie, but it would provide an excuse to have them all to myself with Robin's blessing! All I had to do was explain to her my desire to satisfy

my fetish. Robin always bent over backward to keep me happy and I tried to return the favor whenever possible.

The only problem with my plan was that Kathleen did not know about Jeannie's unique sexual identity. We all promised her, and each other, to keep our mouth's shut about it. If I told Kathleen about Jeannie, I was pretty sure she would not blab about it. However, was always the possibility that she would have a slip of the lip while talking with one of her friends. I did not want to be the one responsible for outing Jeannie to the world. She had enough to deal with and I wanted her association with myself and the girls to be a positive one.

I decided to bring Robin and Laura in on the conversation explaining that Jeannie and I wanted to have a session with Kathleen. Before we discussed it together, I took Robin aside and said it was really all about my love of freckles. She laughed and immediately understood that it was an opportunity too good for any freckle lover to ignore. Robin trusted me and was fine with the situation. She even volunteered to explain Jeannie's situation to Kathleen. They were friends long before I ever met either of them, so that was a no-brainer. Laura agreed with Robin and Jeannie gave us to go-ahead to tell Kathleen.

Later that day Robin went over Kathleen's house to talk to her. Once inside Kathleen's room and out of the range of her mom who was always wondering what Kathleen was up to, Robin spilled the beans to her friend. Kathleen was as stunned as we had been when we first found out, but not upset or turned off by the situation. Both girls had been getting along fine with each other ever since they first met at my house after Jeannie moved in with us. To Kathleen it seemed like Jeannie was just another young person hanging out, playing our game and staying there due to family issues.

Robin asked Kathleen how she would feel about having sex with just Jeannie and I? Kathleen liked me a lot more than she admitted or Robin knew, so she was more than alright with the idea. To make it all work Robin got permission for Kathleen to stay over at her house the next night. When my parents were home and Robin's were at the motel overnight with Susan, we occasionally had sessions in her room. On this occasion Jeannie, Kathleen and I would be using Robin's room, while she was sleeping in my bedroom across the street.

As long as Kathleen's parents did not come into Robin's house to check on her, we would be safe. Even if they did, her folks knew that Robin, Kathleen and her other friends often came over to my place to use the pool or socialize at all hours. With Ingrid being a responsible adult who was always around, that did not seem like an issue; especially since Robin's folks sometimes had to go out to their motel at all hours to deal with one problem or another.

Kathleen could always answer the door if her parents stopped by while Jeannie and I stayed out of sight. All she had to do was tell her parents that Robin was across the street at my house visiting with Ingrid for a few minutes with she picked up something she left there earlier in the day. Meanwhile, I would call my house to alert everyone to the situation and our deception would remain intact. I would square Robin staying at the house with my parents by telling them that I was spending the night with the twins at her house to give her a break from babysitting.

Kathleen's parents were willing to give her some more freedom as long as she stayed out of trouble and away from romance with boys. They knew that keeping her home all the time and apart from her friends was a bad idea. She had not done anything that they knew about to deserve so many restrictions and the last thing her folks wanted was for her to rebel against them because she felt like they did not trust her.

Robin saw an opportunity there. She and Kathleen had been friends for a long time and there was nothing she wanted more than for Kathleen to become a more active and permanent part of our core group. She was smart and knew that I liked Kathleen as much as she did. As far as Robin was concerned bringing Kathleen into the fold would be a win-win situation for all of us.

As much as I liked Kathleen and wanted to keep Robin happy, I worried a lot about Kathleen's parents. If they found out what we were all doing together I would get the majority of the blame and could actually end up dead! Her dad was very serious about keeping his daughter pure and wanted her to be a virgin on her wedding night. Anyone who got in his way was dead meat and I did not want that to be me.

After Robin spoke to Kathleen at her house, her parents let her join me, Jeannie, Robin and Laura for a trip to the Chinese restaurant. We ate in a little side room off the main dining area so that we could talk about things in privacy. All of us agreed that Kathleen would make a wonderful addition to out group, but I made it clear that she would have to keep up appearances, as well as her grades, if this was going to work.

The moment her folks suspected anything and found her naked with me or anyone other member of our group when she was supposed to be at Robin's house or somewhere else, we would be finished. I also pointed out that it made sense for all of us to be more careful anyway. We were getting a little sloppy when it came to our sessions and despite supposedly living in the days of free love and sex, we all faced the Generation gap between us and our parents. For them there was no free love and sex.

It was official. Kathleen was now a full fledged member of our core group. I cannot say I was not happy, just concerned. We also agreed on the plan to have Jeannie, Kathleen and I sleep together at Robin's house the next night. Laura jumped in by adding that if Robin was game, she would like to have Robin sleep in her room instead of mine. I knew that Laura liked Robin as a friend, but also more. Since Robin and Laura were friends, my parents would not think anything was up with them having a sleep over. Robin agreed and the situation worked out for everyone.

The next night I was a little nervous about the idea of being in Robin's house, but after Kathleen met Jeannie and I there around eight I felt better. We all stripped, then got into Robin's bed. We made out with each other while Kathleen did her best not to stare too much at Jeannie's unique anatomical situation. Jeannie told Kathleen not to be afraid to touch her penis. Kathleen laid down and played with it while Jeannie sat next to her and I ate Kathleen out, then had intercourse with her. Jeannie was next.

As I was began having intercourse with Jeannie doggie style, Kathleen sat with her legs spread over Jeannie and made out with me at the same time. I loved doing it with these freckled beauties

and they loved doing it with me. These were two girls who once they got into sex, were unstoppable! We traded positions and had sex with each other for what seemed like hours. Then came the grand finale.

I asked Jeannie if she wanted to use her penis to have intercourse with Kathleen? She seemed enthusiastic about it and even if she really did not want to, she was willing to do it to keep me happy and show that she was a willing member of our core group. The same was true of Kathleen. Even if she had reservations about allowing Jeannie to insert her penis into her, she did not say anything wanting to keep me happy and show she was earning her way as a new member.

I watched as Kathleen laid down on the bed, spread her legs and Jeannie got into position to have intercourse with her. I was amazed as I watched Jeannie penetrate Kathleen. It was not like watching a guy have sex with a girl, it was soft and beautiful. I guess you could say it looked like two girls gently and passionately kissing and touching each other.

Even more amazing was watching Jeannie pull her penis out of Kathleen at the last second and shoot her load onto Kathleen's ample patch of dark shiny pubic hair. Jeannie was fairly certain that she could not get pregnant, but less certain about whether or not she could get other girls pregnant with her penis. Talk about weird and bizarre!

After we finished and got cleaned up we were a little nervous. Every time a car drove by we thought it might be Kathleen's parents, so while Kathleen waited at Robin's house Jeannie and I went back to mine. While Jeannie went to her room I woke up Robin who had obviously finished messing around with Laura by that time, got her out of Laura's room and walked her back to her house to spend the night with Kathleen just in case anyone came by. All was right with the world again and despite doing it with my two freckled beauties in strange digs, I had one of the best sexual sessions of my game.

It was Friday and I was about to close out a Spring Break week of sexual adventures with at least one more memorable intimate encounter. Greg was due over that evening to spend the night. After my parents came and went, Greg arrived in the late afternoon with a surprise. He brought along a boy named Timmy. Timmy was his age and about the same size with very white skin and very dark red hair. He also had loads of freckles on his face and body. I was instantly smitten!

Timmy lived in another part of town, but his parents and Greg's folks were good friends. Their dads worked together and the boys originally got to know each other casually, but now they were friends. Timmy's folks both worked just like Greg's parents, so the boys spent a lot of time together at one house or the other so that neither would be home alone. Timmy was an only child just like Greg.

Now that Greg was a friend of mine and welcome at my house, he thought that Timmy might enjoy coming over since we had more room and stuff to do. However, there was more to his visit than that and I knew it. Greg asked me if Timmy could spend the night along with him? I put my cousin on the case and had her call both sets of parents just to be sure it was alright and that everything was on the up and up.

After Ingrid came back to me with the good news that the boys had permission to stay over, I was thrilled and made both of them feel right at home. Greg and Timmy brought some clothes and bathing suits with them anticipating my approval of Timmy's stay, so we were all set for a fun and very interesting sleep over experience. Ingrid and Diane had to go shopping, so they left us to our adventure.

Greg was a lot smarter and more with it than I dared think possible. He wanted a piece of his friend, but was afraid to try anything at either of their houses for fear of being caught or exposed. My suspicions were confirmed when I took Greg aside to ask him about Timmy. He told me that he really liked the boy and it turned out he was as into freckles as I was. He just was not sure how to approach his friend or get him to play along.

Greg obviously swung both ways the same as I did. That was fine by me, but I was a little worried at being under the kind of pressure that Greg created by bringing his friend over with no prep work and just one night and a day to work with. I knew nothing about the kid, had never met or spoken to him before and worried about what would happen if he decided not to play our game, got freaked out and bolted.

I forced the negatives of the situation to the back of my mind and decided to concentrate on the positives. That meant starting with the simple things like seeing how Timmy reacted to getting naked in front of Greg and me. I gave Timmy a tour of my house and brought him upstairs so that he could stow his stuff in my room. At that time I suggested we go swimming. Greg and Timmy with all in with that, so I closed the door to my bedroom and said we could get changed in there.

Greg knew what I was up to and immediately began taking off his clothes. I did the same while Timmy fumbled through his bag for a bathing suit. Once he had his swimsuit in hand, Timmy began taking off his clothes without any hesitation. Greg and Timmy did not go out of their way to look at each other while they changed, so I guessed that the boys had already seen each other naked during previous sleep overs at their homes.

As soon as Timmy was naked I saw that he had a nice crop of dark red pubic hair above a large penis for his size. It was not overly thick, but really long. He had some fuzz for body hair, but not very much and you could barely see that with all the freckles that covered his pale white skin. Little wonder that Greg wanted to play around with this amazingly good looking boy who had a cute face and a great body!

Timmy did not seem particularly concerned about getting naked in front of us. That was a good sign and gave me something to think about while I tried to figure out the best way to get a piece of this kid for Greg and I. Once we were all ready for the pool, we went back downstairs. While Jeannie made dinner, Laura joined me and the boys in the pool. Robin and Kathleen were busy elsewhere and had not come over that day. Laura took one look at Timmy and the large bulge in the front of his swimsuit, then smiled at me. She knew he was definitely my type and instantly figured out what I was up to with the boys.

After we swam and played around in the pool for a while it was time for dinner. Jeannie, Laura, Greg, Timmy and I feasted on a really tasty meal courtesy of the lovely and talented Jeannie. I sat next to her at the large picnic style table on the patio. It was hard to focus on the task at hand with Jeannie around. We occasionally rubbed our sandaled feet together under the table and smiled at each other. We were becoming closer by the day and although she was a distraction on that particular occasion, she was certainly a lovely one!

After dinner the girls went to watch TV in the living room while Greg, Timmy and I played badminton on the grass near the patio. After working up a pretty good sweat, we went back into the pool for a while. The good news was that by that time the three of us were getting along pretty well. The bad news was that I still had no idea how to even begin to get Timmy into my game.

With the girls just inside and Timmy having such a large penis, I knew that the nude wrestling angle would not be appropriate for this occasion. I needed something else that would get me to first base with the new kid. After we got out of the pool we sat on the patio and talked for a while as we dried off. I found Timmy to be friendly and well mannered just like his friend. That gave me the idea that the straight forward approach might work as well with him as it had with Greg.

We went back upstairs and changed into our clothes, then hung out in the recreation room. While the boys played pool I went downstairs to spend a few minutes with Jeannie. She was sitting alone in the living room and watching TV. Laura was tired and went to bed early. I sat next to Jeannie and held her hand. I worried about my special girl. She put up a brave front, but I knew that she was a lot more fragile from an emotional standpoint than she let on.

I made sure that Jeannie knew I was there for her. With her parents being so distant and her siblings mostly disinterested in her, I hoped that staying with me and being a part of our little clan would provide her with some sort of stability. She appeared to be happy and Jeannie was definitely a welcomed presence in our home. She brought us all joy on many levels and made me personally very happy. The only downside was that I found myself falling in love with her and that had nothing to do with her anatomical uniqueness.

Jeannie knew what I was up to with Greg and his friend, so she understood when I had to head back upstairs. I did promise to take her out on Sunday for some time between just the two of us. That brought a smile to her face and I suspected she felt as strongly about me as I did about her. I felt guilty because I also cared deeply about Robin, so I tried to balance my time with both girls not wanting to lose or hurt either one. At least that was what I told myself to excuse my new feelings for Jeannie.

By the time I rejoined Greg and Timmy they were finishing up a game of pool. We were all tired so after a quick trip to the kitchen for some cold soda, we headed back up to my bedroom. Timmy said that all he had to sleep in was his underwear. I said that would be fine and that we should all just sleep in our underwear. While we were getting out of our clothes I asked Timmy if he liked playing games? He said he enjoyed playing pool and board games. I told him that Greg and I had a game that we liked to play and wondered if he wanted to join in?

I explained to Timmy that this game was one that everyone who hung out at my house or slept over played. Timmy looked puzzled, but not concerned so I continued my explanation. I asked him if he ever played doctor? Timmy said he had a friend named Donald that used to play doctor with him. He told Greg and I that Donald almost always made him be the patient and that he had to take off all of his clothes. I asked Timmy if that bothered him? He said it didn't because all Donald did was look at him naked for a while, then tell him to get dressed.

I asked Timmy if Donald got naked when he was the patient? Timmy said he did, so I asked him how he felt about seeing his friend naked like that? He said that it was alright and helped satisfy his curiosity. Timmy told us that at the time they played doctor the two boys were just around twelve years old. At that time neither of them were in Junior High and did not take showers in school yet. That meant he did not really have a chance to see other boys his age naked.

Timmy said that he got pubic hair down there when he was just eleven years old. Being an only child and without seeing other boys naked at that time, he wondered if his classmates at school also had pubic hair? After seeing Donald naked and finding out that Donald did not yet have any pubic hair, Timmy got kind of embarrassed about his pubic hair. He even admitted to shaving it off during his first year in Junior High. He also stopped playing doctor with his friend because of it.

Seeing that Donald did not have any pubic hair when they played doctor together, he did not want to look like a freak during showers in physical education class in case the other boys did not have any either. He felt he had made a good decision to shave it off when he went to shower with his classmates for the first time and saw that only a few of the other boys had pubic hair and most did not have anywhere near the amount that he had.

I told Timmy that I could relate to how he felt and did pretty much the same thing when I started Junior High. I also explained that we also played a kind of 'doctor' game, but that ours was more hands-on. The good news was that no one had to be embarrassed about how they looked down there and everyone had fun. Another difference was that we experimented with sex and that girls were also involved.

Timmy appeared surprisingly calm after hearing my explanations, so I told him that if he was willing to give our game a try that night he could count on playing it with more boys and girls later. Rather than wait for an answer I asked the boys to take off their underwear and get naked. Once again Greg was Johnny on the spot and immediately slipped out of his tee shirt and underpants. Timmy saw what Greg was doing and followed suit. I remained in my underwear for the moment.

After the boys were naked I told them that we would start with a short body massage. The truth was I could not wait to get my hands on Timmy's beautiful freckled body. I explained that I would give both boys a brief massage, then let them take turns giving each other one. I started with Timmy and had him lay flat on his stomach. I figured that doing his back and buttocks first would be less upsetting than going for his package right away.

I had Greg stand next to me and watch while I massaged and gently rubbed his friends arms, back, legs and buttocks. I could feel Timmy moving up and down as I massaged his buttocks, so I knew that what I was doing was giving him a hard on just like it had when I did the same thing to other kids in the past. By the time I turned him over, Timmy had a huge boner. His penis was as stiff as a board and at least seven or eight inches long.

While I began massaging Timmy's arms, shoulders and chest from the front he tried to apologize for his hard on, but I told him that there was never a need to feel embarrassed or sorry about anything in our game. I said that what happened to him was natural and that the more he got into our game, the more comfortable he would feel about sharing his body and the bodies of other boys and girls.

I saved Timmy's penis for last. Before I touched it, I explained that I was going to put some Vaseline on his dick for lubrication. As I lubricated his big dick I told him that as part of the massage I was going to jack him off. I said that he could ejaculate without feeling guilty or bad and placed a towel on his abdomen so it would be ready for when he did. With a penis his size and well formed testicles, I did not even have to ask if he ever played with himself or ejaculated before. I knew he did.

Just to make Timmy feel more comfortable, I had Greg sit next to him on the bed. I also lubricated Greg's penis and had Timmy begin to play with and jack it right after I began to jack his. Timmy's dick remained very stiff and almost immediately began to throb. Before long he shot out a huge load which actually flew past the towel I had in place and all the way up to his chest until some drops almost reached his neck. Timmy let go of Greg's dick, so Greg did not yet have a chance to shoot his own load.

I held on as Timmy pumped out semen and did not stop jacking him until he was finished. From his movements and the look on his face, he enjoyed the experience as much as I did. After I cleaned him up, I had Greg lay flat on the bed and got Timmy to massage him. Timmy was a little shy about touching his friend at first, but by the time he got down to Greg's buttocks and began massing it he seemed thoroughly into our game.

When Greg turned over to let Timmy massage his front, Greg had a boner that was just as hard as Timmy's. Even though Greg's penis was smaller, he made up for its size with stiffness and a lot of enthusiasm to play my game. Greg let Timmy massage him and was completely relaxed even after his friend began touching and massaging his thick little dick.

Timmy seemed almost hypnotized by Greg's dick and appeared to really enjoy jacking his friend off. He was so enthusiastic that I had to ask him to go a little easier on Greg's penis to avoid hurting him. Timmy's own penis got hard again as he jacked his friend which meant that Greg had hit pay dirt with his friend and that I got the deed to the gold mine with both these boys. Before long Greg shot his load. Timmy held on to Greg's dick just as I had showed him and kept jacking it until every drop came out.

Greg took a turn massaging his friend. When Greg got around to jacking Timmy, both boys appeared to be fine with what was happening. Timmy even took an additional step of touching

and playing with Greg's pubic hair, penis and testicles while his friend jacked him off. Before long Timmy started pumping out semen again as Greg held on to his friend's stiff dick until he finished.

While the boys cleaned up I went and got us some soda, then explained that the next part of our game involved sexual experimentation. While we took a break and refreshed ourselves I said we were going to begin our next session with oral sex. I had Timmy lay flat on the bed and told him that Greg and I were going to take turns putting his penis into our mouths and sucking on it until it ejaculated (if possible). I also pointed out that he could so the same thing with us if he liked it. At that point I slipped off my underwear just to show I was playing the game right along with the boys and started sucking off Timmy.

His penis did not fit all the way into my mouth, so I took as much as I could and jacked the base of it occasionally with my hand. I loved looking at Timmy's beautiful body while I sucked his dick. Sensing he was into what I was doing, I reached out and took hold of his hands which were at his sides. I gently squeezed them and he reciprocated. Rather then be selfish, I relinquished my dick sucking duties to Greg so that he could experience any ejaculation if it occurred. Timmy managed yet another ejaculation and Greg dutifully sucked down and swallowed every drop.

Greg was next. After he laid flat on the bed, I told Timmy to take a turn sucking off his friend. Timmy acted like he could not wait to get at Greg's penis and immediately began sucking him off. Greg's penis fit all the way into his mouth and Timmy loved it. He did a great job and before long Greg shot a lot. Even though it was his first time, Timmy managed to awkwardly suck in and swallow his friend's semen.

After cleaning up and taking another break, I told the boys the next step was the final one for this session since we were all tired and had done so much with each other. I had Greg get in place for anal sex and described what I was going to do for his friend's benefit. Timmy was a little freaked out or surprised, it was hard to tell which, but he watched carefully as I lubricated my penis and began gently pushing my dick into Greg's anus.

Greg moaned a bit, but took the experience better than the last time knowing that he would soon have a shot at Timmy's buttocks. After I ejaculated on to his butt, I cleaned off Greg and asked Timmy if he wanted to take a turn? Greg looked a little disappointed that I did not immediately let him have a go at Timmy's butt, but anal sex was a lot difference from jacking or sucking someone off. It was very personal and often painful. It took some finessing for one boy to let another boy shove his dick into his anus.

Greg got back into position while I enjoyed lubricating Timmy's penis. Timmy seemed to like me touching him. My lube job got Timmy's dick hard enough so that he was ready to penetrate Greg. I helped Timmy get into the right position to go for Greg's anus and even guided his penis into Greg's hole with my hand. Timmy's stiff dick slowly went inside Greg. Greg was probably in a lot of misery as Timmy pushed his long shaft into his friend. Luckily for Greg, Timmy's dick was not as thick as his own or mine.

Timmy's length would cause major discomfort for any boy on the receiving end of it, but no where near as much as it could have if his long and stiff dick were a lot thicker. Greg tolerated the pain well and managed to get through the experience. Timmy pulled his penis out after doing with his friend for at least three or four minutes and shot a small load on to Greg's buttocks.

It was finally Greg's turn. Timmy dutifully and somewhat nervously allowed his friend to have a go at his freckled buttocks. After I lubricated Greg, he began to slowly push his small, stiff dick into Timmy. His friend moaned and said it hurt, but stuck it out as Greg penetrated him all the way. Timmy was lucky in that Greg was so excited that his session only lasted a minute or so before he had to pull his penis out and shoot his load on to Timmy's buttocks.

Seeing that Timmy was as sore and tired as Greg, I decided to save my own butt safari with him for a future session. After we cleaned up, we all climbed into my bed and went to sleep. I made sure that Timmy slept in between Greg and I so that I could enjoy looking at him in the darkness and perhaps occasionally play with his dick and testicles if the opportunity presented itself during the night and I happened to be awake at the time.

Sometime in the early morning hours I woke up and went to the bathroom. Just as I was returning to bed, Timmy got up and did the same thing. After he crawled back into bed between Greg and I, he faced me. I loved looking at his freckled face and green eyes. He looked right back at me in a way which told me to try something, so I moved my hands towards his underpants and gently worked it inside.

I began feeling Timmy's penis and jacking it. Just as it was getting hard, he began moving slightly and surprised me by pulling down his underpants and taking them off. After he laid back down I began playing with his penis and testicles again. As I did he surprised me again my trying to play with mine. I pulled down my own underpants and took them off to give him better access to my package.

Before long we were playing with each other and jacking each other off. This was a big surprise for me. He was almost two years younger than I was, but he seemed to really like me for some reason. I was not bad looking and most girls were attracted to me, but not many boys. I felt like fate was again offering me a wonderful opportunity and there was no way I would refuse it.

Timmy was not the first boy to cooperate with me as far as my game went, but I am sure he was the first to really get into it with me on a personal level. As we jacked each other I sensed an amazing connection with my new friend and it was one which I had never previously felt with a boy. I sensed his frustration and that might have been one reason for his sudden desire to play around with me.

I could just imagine what it must have been like for him to play doctor with Donald and get into it, only to find that his friend was not as well developed as he was, did not take full advantage of them both being naked and also had to deal with the fear of exposure. Donald was a novice at playing doctor. He did not even want to make physical contact with his friend. For someone who seemed to be as passionate as Timmy, that could not have been pleasant.

I decided to test the waters some more to see if the player that I awakened in Timmy would respond to more aggressive moves. I stopped jacking him and pulled Timmy's body very close to mine. I put my hand around his head and moved it towards mine to see if he would French with me. I had not even tried that earlier with either of the boys due to time constraints. I wanted to get to the crux of the game and leave the peripheries for later.

I quietly told Timmy that I wanted to teach him how to French kiss so that when I got him with a girl he would be ready. It was a thinly veiled excuse to kiss him, but necessary this early in our relationship. I asked if he had ever Frenched before? He said that he had never made out with anyone, so I told him to just relax and give it a try. He agreed and allowed our lips to touch.

Everything happened so quickly that I barely remember it all. One minute I was just barely touching his lips, the next we were kissing like devoted lovers. It was really bizarre! Even stranger was the fact that I was certain he loved it as much as I did. While we kissed we again began playing with each other's dicks. Timmy's penis suddenly exploded all over me. I held on and let it pump out on to my private parts.

Timmy was immediately apologetic, but I told him that was not necessary. We got up and sneaked quietly into the bathroom still naked from our little session. As we showered together I washed myself and him off, then we quietly went back to bed. There was no mess on the bed, so we laid next to each other. I initiated yet another make out session and Timmy responded just as enthusiastically as he had before.

We were more horny than tired, so after we Frenched for a while I got Timmy up and lead him to the edge of the bed. After lubricating my penis, I slowly and carefully began pushing my dick into his anus. I was really surprised that he let me do it without even saying one thing. Before long I had fully penetrated Timmy and was having amazing intercourse with him. I was surprised that we did not wake up Greg, but then again he seemed dead to the world.

We went on for a while and I was more than a little surprised that Timmy did not ask me to stop, but I figured that enough was enough. I pulled my penis out of him and shot my load on to his buttocks. After I cleaned myself and him up, Timmy surprised me yet again by asking me to lay flat on my back on the bed. Before I knew it he was sucking me off. By that time my dick was stiff and numb so when I did not ejaculate after a while I tried to make it up to him. I asked Timmy if he wanted to have anal sex with me?

Timmy was new to everything we were doing and it was easy to forget that fact considering his enthusiasm. He told me that he was tired and doubted he could perform well enough to give me anal sex. I understood and left it at that. I finally managed an ejaculation and he sucked me off to perfection. After that we cleaned up and went back to bed. Timmy and I slept right next to eah other and that was a real turn on for me.

Actions are always easier than words. It was Saturday, but there still errands to run for my cousin who now busier than ever as far as business was concerned. Greg and Timmy got up for breakfast before I went out, so I invited them to spend another night over. Both boys told me it

Robin gasped as he penetrated her. Seeing how long and hard his penis was, I guessed she felt like someone was jabbing her with a sword. I began making out with Robin while Timmy kept shoving his dick into her. Even though Robin was attracted to Timmy's overall look and probably liked the idea of getting screwed by a penis that long, she quickly soured on their session because she was feeling the pain of his very long and stiff dick constantly pushing its way into her. As we made out she whispered to me that she needed him to stop. Before I could act on her request nature intervened.

Following instructions I gave him before they started, he pulled his dick out before long saying he was ready to shoot his load. Instead of putting a condom on him and letting him go back to screwing her, I told Robin to suck him off and she did. Even though his dick did not fit all the way into her mouth, she did a good job of sucking him off and he seemed to enjoy it. While Robin sucked off Timmy by leaning over the edge of the bed where he was laying, I came around in back of her and shoved my own penis into her.

By the time that Timmy shot his load into Robin's mouth, I was also ejaculating my semen into her. Just watching Robin suck off Timmy made me hard and horny. Judging from her response, Robin preferred my thick and normal sized penis to Timmy's obscenely long and thin dick. That was fine by me because I really did not want her becoming infatuated with any other guy, even though our group was definitely in need of more male members.

I figured that was enough for the present because I had plans for Timmy and I to connect up with the twins later that night in a far more serious way. After we all cleaned up and Robin headed downstairs, I asked Timmy how he liked being with Robin? He told me it was great and seemed happy with the outcome, so I guessed that he was as good being with girls as he was with boys. However, he had yet another surprise for me.

We allowed Robin to shower by herself, so by the time she was finished cleaning up, dressed and headed downstairs, Timmy and I were still drying off from our shower together in my room. As we did I noticed that Timmy's penis was stiff. He made sure that I saw it by drying his hair first leaving his body uncovered by the towel. Timmy looked at me and said, "I think I'm ready for what we were talking about last night." I knew he meant anal sex, and even though I thought his timing could have been better, I decided to let him give it a try.

I lubricated Timmy, got into position and waited as he guided his long stiff dick into my anus. It did not really hurt at first, just felt kind of weird. After he started pushing his dick into me I felt the pain and a lot of pressure. At the same time I liked the sensation of his thin penis penetrating me and let him do his thing until he pulled his dick out and shot his load on to my buttocks. He cleaned me off with a towel and said there was no blood when I asked, so I asked him how he liked it?

Timmy said he really liked doing that to me and just as I was about to get dressed to go downstairs he asked me if I would take a turn on him? I could hardly believe this kid! Most boys hated anal sex, especially when they were on the receiving end of it. I lubricated my penis and

accommodated him. Before long I was shoving my penis into Timmy and loving it. His freckled buttocks, back and body drove me crazy and made me twice as horny as I might normally be.

Timmy took my penis really well and although I was sure he must have felt some pain, he did not show it. After I pulled my penis out and shot my load on his buttocks, we cleaned up and laid back on the bed to relax for a few minutes. Before I knew it we were making out. This boy was like a carbon copy of me in many ways and I loved it. The only thing I really worried about was the age difference.

The rest of the day flew by and before long it was time for some fun with the twins. While Robin was shacked up with Jeannie, Timmy and I brought the twins up to my room where we all got naked. We began by taking turns sucking off John and Jerry. There were nervous because after seeing the size of his penis they knew that one or both of them would soon be getting it shoved into them.

Timmy really liked messing around with the twins. He Frenched with them, sucked both boys off and had them suck his dick. We traded twins and enjoyed both of them. Finally, Timmy went at John with his dagger-like penis. I warned him not to try and shove it all the way into either of them and he followed my instructions. While Timmy did John, I went at Jerry. Watching my freckled friend screw John really made me horny and this time I did not hold back. I pushed my penis all the way into Jerry.

Jerry was able to take my entire penis, but not without a lot of pain. Timmy and I agreed to stop short of shooting our loads so that we could switch places. The twins were whining, but we just pushed them down on the bed and began doing our thing. By the time we got through they both had tears in their eyes, so I had them shower and clean up. After I got them settled on cots in the recreation room, I had yet another nasty idea.

I threw a bathrobe on and went to knock on Jeannie's door. I asked Robin and Jeannie if they wanted to join Timmy and I? I knew what that meant, but I trusted Timmy and knew that once he found out about Jeannie he would never out her. He was too worried about people discovering the truth about his own perversions.

The girls smiled, put on robes over their naked bodies and followed me up to my room. As soon as Jeannie dropped her robe to the floor Timmy was wide eyed and probably could not believe what he was seeing. I explained the situation to him, swore him to secrecy and had him make out with Robin while he adjusted to the situation.

I made out with Jeannie and it felt really good to be with her again. We began having intercourse while Timmy was getting a blow job from Robin. Before I shot my load I asked Timmy and the girls if they wanted to switch places? They all said they did, so while Timmy made out with Jeannie I had sex with Robin. Once he felt comfortable with Jeannie, Timmy shoved his penis into her and she loved it.

After we both shot our load and cleaned up, we tried different positions and switched out again. Jeannie allowed the both of us to jack her off. She was able to shoot a load both times! Seeing

she was turned on by everything we were doing and that Robin was eyeing her penis, I asked Jeannie if she would like to screw Robin? She said she would and Robin agreed as well.

As the girls went at it Timmy was amazed and really turned on by what he saw. His penis got hard and even though I was really tired by that time, I took the opportunity to suck him off. Before long he shot his load into my mouth while the girls finished up. I laid back on the bed while Jeannie and Robin whispered something to each other.

Robin threw on her bathrobe, asked us all to get cleaned up a bit and then wait for her to come back. After a few minutes she returned with a vert naked Laura. Seeing her nude re invigorated all of us and before long Timmy was giving Laura the shaft. I was content to screw around with Robin and Jeannie, but soon found myself switched off and inside of Laura. We ended up by watching Jeannie push her penis into Laura. She was too tired to shoot another load and eventually just stopped, but it sure was fun to watch while it lasted!

Our first real group sex event had been amazing. The only one missing was Kathleen, but that could be remedied in the near future. We were all spent so after the girls put on their robes and headed back down to Jeannie's room, Timmy and I cleaned up and went to bed. Once again I enjoyed sleeping next to Timmy. We talked for a while because Timmy was still on a high from all that had happened and amazed at what he experienced with Jeannie. I could tell he liked messing around with her and that was fine by me. I knew she was mine exclusively and would only have sex with guys or girls with my permission.

The next morning I woke up with the thought that I may have created a monster, but I also knew that Timmy had a great fear of exposure and that I could use that to control him. As long as he played my game my way we would be good with each other. He went home after breakfast and said he would come by again on Monday after school. I told him that would be fine and hoped I could connect him with Greg. After all, Greg was the one who brought me this very special present and I thought it only fair to share it with him.

Sunday was the perfect day for an outing with Jeannie. Ingrid was spending time with Diane, Laura was visiting her mom, Terry was busy with something or another, Robin and the twins were at a family gathering and Kathleen was spending time with her family. The house was surprisingly quiet by lunchtime, so Jeannie and I decided to go out early for our date.

We went to the mall for lunch, then saw a movie. We held hands and cuddled in the theater. We talked for a while after the movie while I drove to my dad's hotel. I suspected that by that time my parents were home and no one was using the suite. We changed into the bathing suits we brought with us and hit the beach. Jeannie always attracted a lot of attention, but not for the reason you might think.

She had a clever way of hiding the outline of her penis using some cloth stuffed into her swimsuit. It was her perfectly shaped and freckled body that attracted people's attention. After you looked at her body, her perfect face sealed the deal and you were smitten. Ingrid already asked her if she would consider modeling some of her clothes, but Jeannie was shy about her looks. I was working on that.

Today we know that at least some successful female models are closet hermaphrodites because they tend to look younger than they are and have androgenous-type bodies with smaller breasts and just the kind of perfect shapes that photographers love. In those days all I knew was that Jeannie was beautiful and despite her unique physiology, she was all girl. I made it my mission to get her to model for my cousin.

We swam around, laid on the beach for a while and then went back up to the suite to change and dress for dinner. I brought Jeannie to the supper club in the shopping center for a great meal and show. Afterward we walked down by the boat dock and talked for a while. I was amazed how well Jeannie and I got along. We had similar interests and shared a desire to be with each other.

After we got back to the suite Jeannie dropped a bomb on me. She said that she enjoyed being a part of our core group and did not mind occasionally playing around with the girls, but she also made it clear that she wanted to be with me exclusively. She would no longer allow guys to make out or have sex with her. The only group sex she was interested in was with me and other girls, no other guys. I understood her feelings and said that was no problem.

It was obvious that Jeannie and I had become a lot closer than I thought would be possible. At that point we were basically in love. That would normally be really good news for a guy like me, but it could also be a game changer for our group and my close relationship with Robin. This was a real problem and not something that would just work it self out over time.

To avoid making a mountain out of a mole hill, I changed the subject and encouraged Jeannie to model for Ingrid. She knew it would mean more money for her, but she was afraid that people would discover her secret. I promised that I would be at every photo session I could and that Ingrid would use only photographers she trusted implicitly. I explained that the fashion world was filled with people who had secrets. I also made it clear that from what I had observed so far, everyone who worked in that world had a desire to keep those secrets.

Jeannie knew that modeling would be a positive step for her and with my assurance of complete privacy as far as her anatomical uniqueness went, she was ready to give it a try. With that settled we went into the bedroom I used at the suite, got naked and made love. What we did that night was a lot more than just have sex. We both experienced a closeness and intimacy that sunk into our souls.

Chapter Seven: Things Get Messy

It was never easy for me to balance all the relationships I had. Using the group approach where we were all equal made things a little easier, but they were still bumps in the road like my commitment to Robin. Now that Jeannie and I were a definite item I would have to deal with a more complicated emotional dynamic within our group. I knew this kind of thing would happen and was coming. My hope was to bury it within my overall relationship with all the girls.

There was some good news on the horizon. As summer and my graduation approached Laura had renewed and clarified her relationship with her mom. She planned to move back home as soon as school ended. That not only gave Jeannie the opportunity to have a better room in our house, but it took some pressure off me. Laura would be too far away to remain an active member of our group. As much as I liked her I knew that meant one less complication.

What was not going so well was my situation with Timmy. He and I were getting along really well, but it turned out that he had a ravenous sexual appetite that rivaled my own. He eventually made it with all the girls in our group. Even though he liked Jeannie the best, she had cut herself off from all males accept for myself. His second favorite was Kathleen. She enjoyed doing it with him the first couple of times. After that she began to feel like a pin cushion. His long thin dick jabbed at her in a way that became more annoying than satisfying. Robin felt the same, so both girls stopped letting him have sex with them.

The one girl that was able to take Timmy's long shaft and enjoy it was Laura. Now that she was leaving that meant I had no more girls to offer him. The pool of boys willing to mess around with Timmy was also becoming depleted. He and I used Greg up to the point that he stopped coming around. The twins made it clear that Timmy was too intense and big in the cock for them. That left Mitchell and I.

I loved having sex with Timmy. Fortunately, he liked getting my dick in his anus more than he did giving me his in mine. The same was not true for the other boys. He had really reamed them all good and even done some damage. The only one who was still able to take his long shaft and like it was Mitchell. However, as much as Timmy and Mitchell enjoyed having sex together they also argued a lot.

Mitchell had a big thick penis and loved shoving it into Timmy's anus as much as I loved shoving mine into both of them. Timmy was annoyed that every time they got together Mitchell wanted to have anal sex with him. Mitchell was annoyed that all Timmy wanted to do with screw him in the buttocks and get sucked off in return. He looked at the situation as unequal and unfair. I managed to keep the peace between the two most of the time, but it was obvious they were like oil and water. Things were coming to a head between them and I did not want that to happen in my house.

The solution to my Timmy problem was to find some more players that would be willing to take his long shaft and love it. That was a tall order and with a very limited number of players available, not an easy one to fill. I did have one girl in mind. I met her at school and if I could get her into my game, they would probably take care of my Timmy situation for the most part.

Marianne stood about five foot ten. She had dark shiny hair, a cute freckled face, a nice body that was neither thin or stocky, well formed breasts that were not overly large and pale skin. We had a couple of classes together and although she was cute, she was also a little strange. She had a lot of pet peeves and that turned me off. The good news was that she was as against smoking, drinking and drugs as I was. The bad news was that she seemed to have a lot of personal issues.

I began talking to Marianne during lunch. She had few friends and tended to sit with a girl named Deb until she transferred to another school just after the holiday break. Since then she began sitting with me. By that time my girls had different lunch periods. The one thing I did like about Marianne besides the fact that she was kind of cute was that she loved good conversation. The downside of that was that she was always complaining about any number of things in her life.

Marianne and her family were from Long Island just like me. The family moved to Florida a few years ago after her dad got a terrific job offer from the company where he was already working in New York City. With just Marianne and Maureen still living at home and her dad nearing retirement age, the move made good sense.

The more I got to know Marianne, the more I understood where her pessimism came from. She began to confide in me after a while and share more details about her life. Marianne was the youngest of four sisters. The others did not live at home and only one lived nearby. Her parents were older just like Jeannie's. They were practicing Catholics and attended services on a regular basis. Marianne was less enthusiastic about his parent's religion and thought her sisters made bad choices as far as their men went.

Despite having conservative parents, two of her older sisters hung out with hippie types that Marianne was sure used drugs or smoked pot. The exception was Maureen. She was around twenty two at that time and married to a guy who worked as an administrator for the local Parks and Recreation Department. Although Marianne had less problems with him as far as his personal choices went, she also had nothing really good to say about him either.

After a while I found out that her sister Maureen had recently given birth to a baby. The last part of her pregnancy was rough and she had to spend two weeks in the hospital. During that time Marianne volunteered to stay at her sister's house to take care of their small dog and cook dinner for her brother-in-law Jack after school. Sadly, her act of kindness was not rewarded in kind.

She told me that during her second week at her sister's house and just before Maureen gave birth, Marianne was sitting on the living room couch and finishing up her homework one evening after dinner. Jack came and sat next to her and the two started up a card game. Before long Jack wanted to turn their game into strip poker. Marianne figured it was all in fun.

In the past she played strip poker with her sister and brother-in-law and the most anyone ever took off was their shoes and socks. After a few hands it was obvious that jack had something else in mind. He lost the first two hands and each time he took something off. At first it was just his shoes and socks, but the next time he took off the tee shirt he was wearing leaving him bare chested.

Marianne was not really comfortable sitting next to her brother-in-law that way. She did not like the fact that he took off his shirt. When she lost the next hand, he told her to take off her shirt. She had no shoes or socks on because she was relaxing on the couch, so it was not an outrageous request considering that she was only wearing a shirt, jeans and underwear.

Marianne cautiously played along even though she did not sitting there with Jack in just her bra, jeans and panties. When she lost the next hand, Jack leaned over and began unhooking her bra. She was shocked and upset, but being young and having never been intimate with a guy she really did not know how to handle the situation.

She let Jack remove her bra, but covered her breasts with her blouse after he got a good look at them. Her brother-in-law made fun of her for covering herself up, so she put her blouse down and sat there nude from the waist up. After losing the next hand, Marianne was really nervous. Jack said that she did not have to take anything else off, but that he wanted her to make out with him.

Marianne felt like she was living a nightmare. It was a NO WIN situation. Before she knew what was happening Jack was leaning over her. He forced her to French Kiss with him and started fondling her breasts. Marianne was sickened by his touch and tried her best figure a way out. She made out with him for a while hoping that he would eventually be satisfied with kissing and fondling her and stop, but it did not.

Before long Jack was trying to open her Jeans and get his hands inside them. At that point Marianne (who was no tiny or weak girl) pushed him off of her, grabbed her bra and top, and bolted into the bedroom she was using during her stay. She locked the door and hoped he would leave her alone. He did. Just to be safe she pushed a desk chair up against the door and went to bed.

The next morning Jack was apologetic before he went to work and she left for school. He said that he just got carried away because he missed his wife and had not had relations with her for some time due to the fragile nature of her pregnancy. Marianne looked away from him, said nothing and decided to leave and go back to her house. She packed up the few things she brought with her, dropped them home and went off to school.

Not wanting to create a nightmare situation for her sister or the family, Marianne told her parents that she was homesick and that it was hard to study at Jack and Maureen's house. They accepted her reason for coming back home a few days early. At that point her sister was giving birth and would be back home in less than a week anyway. Although she originally planned to stay around a few extra days to help Maureen with the new baby, the incident with Jack made that impossible.

There was no way that Marianne would be able to be around Jack for any length of time. After visiting her sister and the new baby in the hospital, Marianne used studying for exams as an excuse for avoiding her sister at her house. I felt sorry for her because I had been in what seemed like NO WIN situations myself. I told Marianne that I admired her courage and decision to keep her brother-in-laws ridiculous behavior a secret.

I felt there was more to Marianne than met the eye. I suspected that once she became sexually active, she would be all in and the perfect lover for Timmy. I decided to test my theory by asking her out so that I could see how far she would let me go with her. We had become friends, so I

had no idea how she might feel about a date. I did not yet want to fully expose her to the other girls in my group. That would not be easy with my girls always fluttering around me at school.

Another problem I had was that the Senior Prom was coming up. I knew that taking all the girls as a group was out of the question and just choosing one would make the others upset, so I came up with a better idea. We had a core group meeting at my house that night. I told the others about Marianne and what had happened to her. I made it clear that I wanted to get her together with Timmy, but that would take some time and finessing.

I suggested that after all she had been through and because she did not have a date for the prom, I take her as my date. That would eliminate the jealousy problem over taking one girl or another from our group, help Marianne out and get her closer to me so that I could get her closer to Timmy and the others. The girls saw the logic in what I had in mind and although they were not thrilled at not going to the prom with me, it was the right choice and we all knew it. Secretly, I think they were also hopeful that finding a lover for Timmy would get him off their backs.

The next day I asked Marianne if she would like to go to the prom with me? She seemed surprised at my invitation, but accepted. She knew I had a lot of girls hanging around me so she was probably very flattered when I asked her. Like myself, Marianne was graduating from high school a year early. She also had plans to attend the same Junior College that I was going to attend in the fall, so the situation made sense. If I managed to get her into our group I could keep a close watch on her. If not, we could still be friends.

It was time for Marianne to meet the family now that the girls were on board with my plan to get her involved with Timmy and our group, so I invited her over to go swimming in my pool. Before she arrived I read the riot act to everyone. There would be no fooling around in front of Marianne until after I sealed the deal with her and she became a part of our group. If things did not work out, she would be none the wiser about what we were up to at the house.

As soon as she met her Ingrid thought Marianne was really nice and instantly liked her. She asked if Marianne had a prom dress? With just a week until the prom she said she had not expected to go until I asked her, so she was going to do some last minute dress shopping that weekend. Ingrid very generously offered to bang one out for her.

Having seen some of the wonderful clothes my cousin designed, she excitedly accepted the offer and said she would gladly pay for it. Ingrid would hear none of that and said I did so much for her that it was as much a gift for me as it was for her. I left the room while Marianne stripped to her underwear to be measured by Ingrid. I imagine my cousin enjoyed that as well!

Marianne was growing on me, but I kept my eyes on the prize. I did not need another girl friend, I needed one for Timmy and perhaps a new member for our group. He was not over that day so I did not have a chance to see if Marianne would eye him. I did notice that Marianne gave all the girls in the pool a good look which tended to cement my theory that their was more to her than met the eye.

After being measured for her dress, Marianne changed in the bathroom and joined Robin, Laura, Jeannie, Kathleen and myself in the pool. She got along really well with the other girls. I hoped that was a sign of good things to come. Because it was Friday and the girls already had plans to go out with me that night for dinner and a movie, I decided to take a shot and invite her along. I knew that Marianne wanted to fit in with us, so it was no surprise when she accepted.

I thought about inviting Timmy to go along with us. Instead, I decided not to move things along that fast. I needed time with Marianne to get her acclimated to myself and our group before I let my horny friend meet her. Technically, this group outing was our first date. The girls knew I needed to seal the deal with Marianne, so they were not jealous when we held hands and even kissed a few times during the movie. After it was over we all headed back the house.

My parents were home, so after I introduced Marianne to them we all grabbed our bathing suits and headed off to the hotel suite. I already told Marianne about the suite and guessed she felt safe going there with me since all the other girls were also coming along. I changed in the bathroom while all the girls changed in my room. As we headed down to the hotel pool for a private swim since it was technically closed to hotel guests for the night, Robin took me aside and said that Marianne gave all the girls a good look while they were naked. That gave me an idea.

I told Robin that after we were all in the pool for a while, she and Laura should go off in a corner and play around with each other a little. Nothing too shocking, just some playful kisses and maybe some light tittie touching which meant they would each slide their hands inside one another's bathing suit tops to cop a feel.

Robin and Laura got to work while I pretended not to notice. Marianne stared at them from across the pool, but did not say anything or seem all that upset. After a few minutes I made believe that I suddenly saw what they were doing and went over discreetly to tell them to stop. After a few more minutes we all headed upstairs to the suite, changed and went for some ice cream in the hotel cafe.

It was time to head back, so I dropped the girls off at the house and started to drive Marianne home. She surprised me by asking if I wanted to park at the beach for a while? There was an area that was quiet, secluded and perfect for making out near Pass-A-Grille. I parked there and we got out of the car. We took off our shoes and walked on the beach holding hands.

As we walked I apologized to Marianne for Robin and Laura. Marianne offered a playful laugh in response. She said that girls were often curious about their bodies and admitted to being that way herself. As we walked she told me that when she was twelve a friend the same age was sleeping over her house. The girls were neighbors and had known each other for years, but now that they were both showing obvious signs of puberty Marianne was curious about her friend's body as compared to her own.

For one thing, Marianne said that she wondered if her friend had as much pubic hair down there as she had? The other girl also seemed curious about the changes to their bodies. Marianne asked her friend if she would like to shower with her so that they could get a good look at each other

and compare their bodies? Her friend accepted her invitation and the two girls giggled as they stripped naked and entered the shower together.

While they soaped up they stared intently at each other noting that they both had well formed breasts and pubic hair by that time. After they got out of the shower Marianne admitted that she was fascinated by her friend's body and suggested that they both get into bed naked. Her friend was not quite as adventurous as Marianne, but agreed to stay naked and soon the two girls were both laying next to each other in bed comparing each other's bodies some more.

By that time Marianne said that she had discovered something else. She said, "I sometimes moved around on the bed...laying on my stomach...in a way that felt good to me." That led to some experimentation with touching herself down there and even inserting a small soda bottle into her vagina. At some point she accidently broke through her own hymen while using the bottle. Despite having done that, she continued to use the bottle for some time until she was just too fearful of getting caught by her mom if she found out about it.

As the two girls laid in bed, Marianne said she began touching her friends breasts and eventually got up the nerve to finger her as well. Her friend laid still and chose not to actively participate, but she let Marianne have her way and do as she liked. At some point Marianne told her friend about the bottle experiment, how good it felt and asked her friend if she wanted to give it a try?

Marianne's friend was not particularly thrilled with the idea of having her friend shove a soda bottle into her, but she eventually let Marianne do it after admitting to having had intercourse with a neighbor the week before. They both figured that since she was not a virgin anyway, what damage could be done? Marianne inserted the bottle and her friend seemed to really enjoy the experience. She even took a turn by pushing the bottle into Marianne.

The neighbor her friend had sex with was a boy who was three years older and well known in the neighborhood as a stud with a large penis. Marianne said she was also tempted to give the boy a try, but she knew her folks would kill both of them if they were caught doing it. She had already gotten into trouble after getting a slight infection down there from the bottle play and did not need any more hassles.

When Marianne went to the doctor and her folks found out she was no longer a virgin, she explained it away as having damaged her Hyman as a result of active participation in sports at school. The doctor took her side saying that young girls active in sports sometimes suffer from a damaged or pierced Hyman as a result of that participation. He probably knew better, but went with that explanation knowing how strict her folks were with her.

After a while the two girls hugged and moved around on the bed gently touching each other's breasts, taking turns with the coke bottle and fingering each other. However, everything came to a screeching halt when Marianne suddenly got her period in a big way. The girls remained friends, by after that mess there were no more sleep over sexual adventures between the two.

I was amazed at Marianne's story. Once again I met someone who was a lot like me and the girls. It was like we were all somehow attracted to one another and experienced some sort of

bizarre instant recognition; and considering the story she told me I was certain that Marianne had me pegged as well. After her confession, she asked me if I did anything like that with my friends? I smiled at first saying nothing until she said, "C'mon, you must have done the same thing with some of your friends?"

I finally admitted that I did and began to tell her the story of my doctor game. At that point I was not afraid of what she might think and I felt better after telling Marianne my own bizarre tale. I also told her about the girls, the boys and our core group. Given what she told me, I was certain that she would make an excellent member. Marianne was definitely interested, so I said that we should get together first, than have a session with the others.

At that point I was thoroughly turned on by Marianne. I still planned to get her with Timmy, but I wanted first dibs. We went back to the hotel suite, went into my bedroom and got naked. Before long we were making out in bed. I loved Marianne's pale skin. My only disappointment was that all the freckles on her face stopped there. There were none on her body below her neck. She did have nice soft skin and a very interesting vagina.

Marianne had more pubic hair down there than any other girl I had ever had sex with. She also had a massive opening. After we made out and I shoved my penis into her for the first time, she seemed to feel every thrust and honestly admitted, "I never knew it could feel that good!" However, I could barely feel my dick inside of her. To make things even more interesting, she also got wetter in there than any other girl I had ever been with.

Looking at the massive amount of dark shiny pubic hair Marianne had turned me on. It even extended to the the insides of her legs! Her huge hole was a bit of a turnoff because I think that only a man with a horse-sized penis could enjoy it. I did like her enthusiasm and appreciated her willingness to have sex with me instead of just pleasuring herself with a soda bottle! I could tell that I was probably the first guy to enter her from the way she acted. Despite not really getting much of a sensation from intercourse with her, I soon found another way to enjoy my new lover's body.

Marianne was fascinated by my penis and wanted to jack me off. She hated the idea of sucking dicks, so that was out. Instead, we sat facing each other and she jacking me off as I felt her breasts and fingered her a bit. She loved having me shoot my load on to her pubic hair and abdomen for some reason and I liked it too. After she gave me those hand jobs, it was my turn.

I had her lay back on the bed with her feet on the floor in position to be eaten out. I ate her out for a while, but she was so huge down there that practically my entire face fit inside of her hole! I finally decided to push my hand into her and feel around. At some point I must have found her sweet spot because she began moving around slightly and moaning. I could hardly believe that my entire hand fit inside of her, almost with room to spare!

I moved my fingers around inside of her until a wash of warm fluid flooded her insides and covered my hand. I guess it was an orgasm, but whatever it was it sure made a mess. The liquid was all over my hand and even came out of her opening on to the bed. Despite the mess, it was

not nasty and I actually loved the idea that I could get her to do that. After the hand bath I was instantly tuned on, got up and shoved my penis into Marianne again.

I loved the feeling of wet which surrounded my dick and I guessed that Marianne was enjoying our session. She began moving around a little on the bed and before long more warm fluid gushed forth. After I shot my load we cleaned up, then went at it again. This time I managed to fit both hands into her, although not all the way. Just enough to bring forth yet another flood.

After our session we cleaned up and I drove Marianne home. She was definitely the oddest sex partner I ever had in terms of the size of her hole and the way we were able to pleasure each other. Don't get me wrong; I didn't mind doing those things with her, they were just different and messy. As I drove home I knew that this girl would be perfect for Timmy. I was less certain if she would fit into our group. I doubted that the other girls would be able to deal with her.

I had found Marianne just in time. Timmy was getting too attached to me. He kept coming over and wanting to spend the night. Even when he didn't sleep over we had a lot of sex together. I loved having sex with him, but I knew from experience that too much of a good thing could get us both in trouble. For example, I stopped letting him put his dick into me because he kept trying to shoot his load into me. When I penetrated him, he practically made me shoot my load into him. That was something that a doctor would certainly notice if he had to go to one for any reason.

The only thing that kept me coming back to Timmy was his amazing body and terrific personality. We had become seriously involved, although we never spoke about it. We made out and had sex in the dark. The rest of the time we acted like normal friends. I was fine with that and preferred it. The only problem was that sometimes Timmy acted like he wanted more. When we went to the movies he always opened his pants and wanted me to jack him off after the picture started. When we went to the beach and were out in the water by ourselves he liked to have me pull down his bathing suit and jack him there as well.

I did not mind doing stuff like that, but worried about being caught and eventually told him that we needed to save that stuff for my bedroom. Still, he was hard to resist. I loved his freckled body and huge dick. I loved the way he pumped what seemed like gallons of semen into my mouth when I sucked him off and enjoyed shooting my load into him despite the obvious hazards.

I decided to wait to get Marianne with Timmy until after the Prom. When Prom night came my girls teased me ceaselessly. They were present to see me dressed up and looking like an idiot. None of them were going to the Prom. That was either because they were not seniors, or just did not want to bother. That included Terry who preferred to spend his time at the house with my cousin. Despite the popularity of Proms today, the only ones really interested in going in those days at my high school were the popular girls and boys, jocks, student government members and ass kissers.

Marianne looked great in her custom designed prom dress. She and I were the unofficial hit couple of the night thanks to my cousin's design talents. For me the evening was a drag. I had

never fit in well at school and the fact that I was graduating a year early with a class of kids that barely knew me and who were mostly older than I was did not help the situation. I felt like an outcast and could not wait for the evening to end.

I did my best to put on a brave face for Marianne and tried to help her enjoy the evening despite my own reservations about the event. We danced, socialized and did all the things you're supposed to do at a prom. While we were there I ran into some classmates I knew, but the biggest surprise of the night was that a guy named Aaron decided to spend a lot of time talking to me.

Aaron was on the football team and was also an important member of the student government. We had a few classes together and used to talk at lunch once in a while. I kind of became his father confessor. Despite his popularity and involvement with just about everything at school, his friends were the kind that would rather discuss football scores or school policies than personal matters or issues. If you had any problems, they did not want to hear about them.

Even when we talked I felt like Aaron was just using me as a sounding board. We were not really friends, just classmates and maybe buddies at school when he needed one. After he got elected to the student government he sat at their lunch table. He was polite and greeted me or asked how I was doing every so often, but if we ever friends at all that was over with.

Despite his popularity, things were not going well for Aaron. He showed a lot of promise when he began playing football last year. However, his senior year on the team was unspectacular. He managed to get a less than stellar football scholarship and only accepted it because he had few other options. His parents were working class people who both worked hard and made decent money, but no where near what was needed to send him to a decent college.

As we talked and Aaron told me his tale of woe I could see he was deeply upset. Having been there myself, there was no way I would not take the time to listen to him while Marianne made the rounds to show off her dress to classmates. The more I listened, the more I became convinced that I was not missing out on a thing by graduating early and not being more involved with school activities.

Aaron was a year older then me and well built. He was tall, muscular and cute. He had blond hair and was hung like a horse. I knew that because he was in my p.e. class. Despite his good looks, he was too hairy for me and not really my type. The girls loved him and that's why it was no surprise that the one he decided to bring to the prom was stunning.

Rose was as tall as he was, big breasted and extremely pretty. She had natural blond hair and perfect skin. While modeling or a rich husband were definitely in her future; Aaron was not. The two had been dating since the start of Senior Year, but after his somewhat disappointing performance on the football field she was giving him the cold shoulder so often that they decided to break up. The Prom was to be their last hurray. They only came together to save face and keep the gossips from tongue wagging about them.

As we talked I sensed an opportunity to be gracious to him and maybe help Marianne find real sexual satisfaction. I saw Aaron eyeing Marianne all evening. He was obviously as interested in her as I was in boning his date, so I decided to invite the couple to come to the hotel suite with Marianne and I after the prom. To my surprise, Aaron accepted. Rose was less enthusiastic about the idea, but went along with him for appearances sake.

When the prom finally ended I breathed a sign of relief and could not get to the parking lot fast enough with Marianne, Aaron and Rose. They followed us to the hotel in his car. Once we got up into the suite, I could see that Rose was impressed. Her whole attitude changed and I guessed she smelled money after she found out that my dad ran the entire property and that I was a partner in my cousin's business.

I ordered some room service snacks and beverages. We all sat, listened to music, talked for a while and looked out on the Gulf. It was both romantic and confusing. After what for me was a boring night of too much nostalgia and not enough tail, I made a bold suggestion. I said that there were two bedrooms we could use, the one I used and the one Ingrid used. The suggestion was obvious, but I was not done yet.

I said that since Prom Night was all about fun and new beginnings, we should switch partners for a while. Realistically, no one expected any of us home before three or four in the morning or later. Even Marianne's strict parents had no illusions about her being in by eleven on that night. Everyone acted shocked at my suggestion, but I knew they secretly wanted to give it a try.

To break the ice, I explained the DO's and DON'T's of the suite, which bathrooms to use, then got up and grabbed Rose by the hand. She took my cue, got up and walked to my bedroom with me. As I was closing the door I saw Marianne and Aaron move closer to each other on the couch and instantly knew they would soon be busy in the other bedroom. Business was picking up and for me, this was what I enjoyed most about my Prom Night experience.

I knew that Rose was a bit of a gold digger, but I did not care. She was a year older than me, very cute and worth the trouble. Besides, if Marianne and Aaron got together that would be a good fit for both of them. Certainly better than Marianne and Timmy over the course of time. It would also eliminate the need for me to go hand swimming in Marianne's huge hole each time we had sex.

Rose stripped to her underwear without saying anything, so I followed suit. We laid on the bed and made out. She was a little taller than me, but thin, beautiful and fragile looking. Although she French kissed like a pro, Aaron had told me he was her first lover and broke her cherry. Well, I did not mind seconds or even thirds or more as long as it was worth it and Rose was certainly worth it!

Before long our clothes came off and I found my dick being handled by Rose. She was surprisingly gentle and soon worked me into a position to have intercourse with her. Just staring at her long blond hair, adorable face, large shapely breasts with sharp tips and very blond pubic hair made me hard as a rock. I penetrated her and was surprised that such a tall girl had a relatively tight pussy.

After Marianne I was thankful to be inside a girl's vagina that I could actually feel my penis going in and out of. Considering her small interior, I was amazed that she could take Aaron's huge penis. I found out later that they only had sex about three times, despite his urging for more. She confided in me that his huge penis was just too painful for her and ended up being yet another reason for the demise of their relationship. Even my own decent sized penis appeared to give Rose some discomfort, but she handled it well.

We really went at it changing positions, making out again and enjoying every second of it. Rose had become a kind of blow job expert being forced to satisfy Aaron in that way as opposed to letting him stick his massive dick inside her. She gave him at least two or three blow jobs a week, so by the time she got my dick in her mouth she was a real pro who managed to swallow every drop of what I deposited down her throat.

What began as a roll in the hay became something else. Rose really got into making out with me and after an hour of sex, we put on our bathing suits and took a late walk on the beach behind the hotel. We talked for what seemed like hours and I could feel a new relationship blossoming. Aaron had similar success with Marianne. So much so that he later took her home while I dropped off Rose. It turned out that she only lived four blocks from me, which was also a nice surprise.

I offered to walk Rose to the door, but she thought better of that and said that might wake up her folks. She was in no mood to explain to them why she left for the Prom with one guy and returned from it with another at after five in the morning. Instead, we exchanged phone numbers in the car and I invited her to come over that weekend for my graduation party. She accepted, got out of the car and disappeared into her yard preferring to enter her house through the kitchen door.

Once again I was confused and unsure of myself. Rose was a trophy and I knew that once Ingrid saw her, she would want her to model her clothes. That was all fine my me, but what about Jeannie and Robin? I did not want to hurt them anymore than I wanted to try and develop a meaningful relationship with someone like Rose who I assumed was a little on the shallow side as far as her choice in guys went.

As I had predicted, Marianne called me the next day to say what I great time she had with Aaron. After he got my number from her, Aaron also called to be sure I was alright with him seeing Marianne. I said it was fine as long as he was alright with me seeing Rose. The deal was done and the switch was made.

My parent's were kind enough to make themselves scarce for the coming weekend. They knew I was having a graduation party and probably preferred not to have to deal with a bunch of kids having a wild time. Our house was already full enough. They attended my high school graduation ceremony on Thursday afternoon where I introduced them to Rose, then they headed to a four day weekend getaway paid for by my dad's bosses who were making more money than ever thanks to my dad's meticulous and wise oversight of their hotel property.

I decided to keep the graduation party guest list to a minimum. I did not want to have a bunch of kids over who I barely saw anymore or have the event end up as some kind of a high school nostalgia or echoes event. This party would be about moving forward. I invited Laura, Jeannie, Robin, Susan, Timmy, Terry, Jimmy, Tommy, Greg, Timmy, Kathleen, Diane and even Mary who got special permission to attend.

This party would be more about current friends, family and our core group, with the exception of Rose. Aaron had his own party going and I had no problem with Marianne attending his instead of mine. That made things easier because I did not have to involve her with the girls in my group. As far as Rose went, I was not exactly sure how to handle her situation. I was still not even sure what she was to me, but I figured that my graduation party might be a good opportunity to find out.

My girls handled most of the details and supplies for the party with the help of my cousin. Not wanting to just throw her into the melee, I decided to call Rose and see if she wanted to come over to hang out with me that Friday night before the party on Saturday. Laura was already getting ready to leave. She would be going back to stay with her mom on Sunday.

As much as I hated to see her go, it was probably for the best over the long term. Laura had family issues that really needed to be worked out in order for her to be really happy. Just hiding from them at our house was not the answer. Jeannie would be moving into her room right after she left. That would give her more room and make it easier for us to sneak in and out of each other's rooms at night, being just up the hall from one another.

I went over to pick up Rose and got a chance to spend a few minutes with her family. We met briefly during the graduation ceremonies, but there was no real time for meaningful conversation at that event. They were originally from Virginia and her parents seemed like a nice couple from a very rural background. She had an older brother and sister that no longer lived at home, but were in town for her high school graduation that week. Even though Rose was the youngest, she also seemed a lot more intelligent and sophisticated than the others.

Her parents were immediately impressed with me and I got the impression they wanted their daughter to marry someone who would treat her right. She would be eighteen in a short while just around the time I was turning seventeen, so they extended her a lot more freedom than most teens living at home would have. Besides, she took care of her own needs.

Rose worked as a part time tourist adviser at The Pier in downtown St Pete to pay her own way since her folks were retired and living on fixed incomes. It was a good paying job that offered salary plus some commissions for selling tour packages. With her looks she managed to sell lots of tour packages to single guys visiting town with their with girlfriends, husbands and businessmen!

After meeting her family and seeing her situation, I understood my new girl a little better. Maybe she was not really a gold digger, just a girl looking for a better life with someone she really liked? Our talks the other night revealed that she had deeper feelings than I thought she did, but

that she also felt trapped by her looks. Because of her beauty she was expected to date a jock, be a cheerleader, or both. She hated cheer leading, so she dated Aaron.

Aaron turned out to be a bit of a sex addict and a drinker, so imagine how hard it was for Rose to avoid his huge tool or follow her own no-alcohol rule? Even worse, she felt forced into their first sexual encounter and every one after that. She did managed to avoid drinking, but hated having to smell the alcohol which always seemed to be in Aaron's breath. Me being me, I was in no position to judge Aaron or Rose regarding those things. I did find out that she worried a lot about appearances.

Rose admitted to having sex with me that first night at the suite at first because she did not know me and thought I might go away and tell everyone she was a cock tease or prude if she did not. We would both be attending the same junior college that fall and everyone knew gossip was as much as weapon as a gun or a knife. After we got into making out, she said that she felt differently and began to have a real attraction for me. I tended to believe her considering the situations I had been in over the years, or placed others in.

After we arrived at my house I introduced Rose to everyone. The girls were immediately impressed and rather than jealous, I suspected they wanted a turn with her. For the moment that was out of the question and they knew it. I needed some private time to assess Rose and see how she might react to our group arrangement. I was not even sure if I actually wanted to share her. I knew that was a thought dangerous to my other relationships with Jeannie and Robin, but it was not like I was choosing her over them; I just wanted someone to myself.

We arrived just before dinner, so while Jeannie and Laura were still cooking I gave Rose a tour of the house. After we changed into our bathing suits in my room, we joined Robin and Susan in the pool. Their folks had finally got the relatives helping them with their motel in line which meant that Susan was able to spend more time with us. She was kind of an unofficial member of our group and remained one of my sex partners having recently gotten back together with me. Susan was lonely and seemed unable to easily connect with guys. The twins were with their folks.

After dinner Rose and I sat on the patio talking while the others were in the pool. Ingrid came home from an outing with Diane and as I expected was immediately impressed with Rose as soon as I introduced them. A look passed between us which told me that my new girl was about to become a model if she wanted the job. With that in mind, I took the time to try and explain the complicated situation of people living at our house and my cousin's business without actually lying to her or letting the cat out of the bag about our relationship dynamics.

She had been approached about modeling on prior occasions, but neither she nor her parents trusted the people making the offers. After meeting my cousin and seeing some of her work, Rose felt comfortable accepting an offer to model part time for Ingrid. With things getting busier for my cousin and the loss of Laura as a worker, Ingrid and I also hoped to get Rose to come on board as a full time employee for the summer and part time after she started college in the fall.

I did not want to rush things with Rose, so I told my cousin to give me a week to get to know her better before I tried to bring her on board as a full time worker. I knew that I would eventually have to tell her the truth about myself, but if she was going to be in the house everyday for any length of time she would find out anyway. Being honest and telling her everything up front would be the better way to go.

Later that evening Rose excitedly called her folks to let them know she was fine and to tell them about her new modeling job. She also told them she would be staying overnight to get to know Ingrid and her work better. After Rose got off the phone she said her folks liked the modeling idea. Ingrid went over to meet them briefly with Rose and seal the deal. She was always good with everyone else's parents, just not her own.

I could tell from my time with them that her parents trusted their daughter implicitly. Rose was responsible and mature for her age and they knew it as much as I did. That made me want to be honest with her even more than before about my situation with the girls and my game. That was something I wanted to do before we had sex again. There was no way I was going to use this girl after all that she had already been through with Aaron.

After speaking with the other girls, we agreed that telling Rose the truth was the best thing to do. With that mandate in mind, I waited for Rose and my cousin to return. After grabbing a few things she needed at her house for the sleep over while Ingrid was there, the two girls came back to the house with the good news that Ingrid had made a terrific impression on Rose's parents. The model deal was done. Now I had my own deal to seal with her.

I invited Rose to go to the hotel suite with me for the night. I said that we would have more privacy and it would allow me to tell her a little more about myself. She was all in with my suggestion, so we drove there in my car. After we arrived and stowed our stuff in the suite, I treated Rose to a show at the night club across the street. She loved it and afterward we stopped at a small ice cream store in the shopping center for a treat.

We took a slow walk back to the hotel suite holding hands. People stared at us probably trying to figure out what a sweet dish like her was doing with an average guy like me. I was still trying to figure that one out myself. Once back in the suite we changed into some comfortable clothes and I asked Rose to sit on the couch with me.

I guess she thought I wanted to make out, but before that I said that I needed to clear the air. As we sat with music playing quietly in the background I told her the truth about myself, my game, my cousin and the other girls. I made it clear that working for my cousin or being with me did not mean she had to be a part of what we did or have a relationship with me unless she wanted one. It did mean she had to know what was going on and understand that I was involved with the other girls in a way that should not make her jealous or concerned about any relationship I might have with her.

Rose listened attentively trying to digest everything. After I finished speaking she sat for a while, then asked what I thought the future had in store for our relationship? I said that I really liked her and as long as she could deal with who and what I was, I would be there with and for her. At that

point I made it clear that was all I could promise. I also challenged her to ask the other girls how I treated them. After all, we were not a cult or commune. Just a bunch of young people trying to enjoy each other in ways most others would not.

Although she was apprehensive about what I told her, I sensed that Rose was willing to put aside the conventional lifestyle she was used to be with me and the girls. She liked them and saw that we got along really well with each other. Their was no jealousy or back door sneaking around, just honest love and sexuality. I asked her to give it a try with just me for a while. If she was not comfortable with the situation, she could still work for my cousin with no hard feelings on the part of anyone.

As far as the girls went, I pointed out that she did not have to be involved with them at all apart from just being cordial. If she wanted to be friends with them that was fine. If she wanted less or more with them, that was also fine. I explained that we did not really have any rules in our group apart from being honest with each other. We were a kind of bizarre family of young people that no one else could deal with or wanted to, which was one reason we were all so close.

Even my revelation about having sex with boys did not really upset Rose. She admitted to being occasionally attracted to girls she knew in a way that was more then friendship, but less than love. She just never acted on those feelings for fear of being discovered or labeled a Dyke. Rose had always been afraid of boys because of her looks. As far as she was concerned, all they ever wanted from her was sex. Just the fact that she ended up with someone like Aaron as her first real boyfriend and lover easily justified her fears.

After our long conversation, we undressed and went into my bedroom. Having decided to stay at the suite all night I called home to let my cousin know what I was up to, then joined Rose naked in bed. We kissed for the longest time and then made love like it was the first time we had ever done it. No fancy positions, no blow jobs or anal sex. Just gentle intercourse that brought us closer together.

On Saturday I took Rose to the mall to buy her a friendship ring. She was surprised because Aaron had never bought her much of anything, and certainly not a ring. Unlike many jocks, he did not even allow her to wear his school ring or football team jacket. I could not imagine treating a beautiful girl like her so shabbily, but that was just me. Needless to say, Rose was completely stunned by my generosity and appeared to be on board with our relationship.

Saturday was a great day. With school over, my graduation party looming and a new relationship with a wonderful girl began, I could not have been in a better mood. Since Rose was also graduating, I said it was her party as well. As far as I was concerned it was actually everyone's party. Any excuse to have fun at my house was a good one. I just had to be sure that the fun stayed on track and did not get out of hand.

During the afternoon we all hung out on the patio with music playing in the background, went in the pool and enjoyed a terrific barbecue. The boys hung out with the girls and Rose got to know everyone better. The more I listened to her conversation, the more I was convinced that she would be a huge asset to my cousin's business if I could just pry her away from her current job.

Late in the afternoon I asked Rose how attached to her job she was? I explained that she could earn much more working with my cousin and I not only as a model, but in the office. She was excellent at dealing with people and could easily take over the work that Laura had been doing. That involved a lot of incoming and outgoing calls and such. She could easily make double or even triple what she was bringing home from the other job and Rose was bright enough to see that.

It did not take a lot of convincing to steal her away from the other job. She was tired of being stared out by horny young male tourists and dirty old men as she tried to sell them tour packages to earn a few extra commission bucks. Besides, she had to use her parents car to get back and forth to work each day from where she lived all the way downtown. That car was old with air conditioning that did not work. Working with Ingrid would soon give her the cash she needed for her own car.

When I told Ingrid that Rose agreed to come to work for her, my cousin was extremely happy. She knew having Rose around would free me up to deal with the books and paperwork necessary to keep things moving forward. I didn't mind that work because sitting in a comfortable chair, at a nice desk, in front of a window with a view of palm trees and lush plant life, with music playing in the background and all in the comfort of central air conditioning was a lot better than running errands in the summer heat and humidity.

Another perk of my job was being able to watch Ingrid, Jeannie, Diane and my cousin parade around looking as cute as ever. Now with Rose on board being in the office with all those girls would be an even better experience. I though about that and many other things as our party began to wind down. With Laura leaving the next day, she spent her last night with Robin, Kathleen, Mary, Jeannie, Jimmy and Tommy. They all slept together and had some last minute fun in Laura's room. Terry slept with Ingrid, while Diane went home to spend the night at her own place.

Mitchell, Greg and Timmy shared Jeannie's room since she was sleeping in Laura's room. The three boys had begun to get close to each other during the party. Although he was not particularly into Mitchell during their previous sexual encounter, Timmy began to warm up to him and that was good news for me. I figured that if I could keep Timmy, Mitchell and Greg busy with each other, Timmy would start backing off from me. That would give me time to develop my relationship with Rose and decide where I wanted to go with it.

Rose slept in my room that night. For the first time in a long time I was not involved in some group sex encounter during one of our infamous sleep over parties. I wanted it that way so that Rose would feel welcome without a lot of pressure to participate in whatever sexcapades the girls and boys planned for each other. I sensed that she was definitely not ready for any of that and there was no way I was going to shove our group thing down her throat, or let anyone else do it either.

Once again Rose and I enjoyed each other. We made love without all the frills. That experience made me wonder if Rose was taming me? Even if she was, maybe I needed that in my weird life.

If anything was certain it was that all the madness eventually had to end anyway, and I figured if that was true it should end on a high note.

Chapter Eight: I Needed A Lot Of Aspirin

Now that high school was over for me, I needed to get busy helping my cousin run her business. I was now doing the lion's share of the management work. That involved a learning process, but thanks to having spent time with my dad and learned from him I was able to figure things out quickly and free up my cousin to create her fashions and bring them to market.

Now that Laura was gone Rose took over the majority of her duties. As I expected, she was a fast learner and huge asset to my cousin and I. She made both of our jobs easier and was a great salesperson for Ingrid. Between her and Jeannie, my cousin had the perfect models for her teen oriented clothing, swimsuits and sports wear.

I liked Rose a lot, but I also felt extremely close to Jeannie and Robin. Once again I found myself lost in some bizarre love triangle that I was sure would not end well. I knew that at least two of the girls would eventually find love with a normal guy. Jeannie was the exception. She was special and in many ways I was the perfect mate for her, but a good relationship needed to be based on more than that.

Rose and the girls got closer during her first month working and hanging around our house. Jeannie was now staying in Laura's room. Terry, Diane, Kathleen, Robin, Susan and the twins spent a lot of time at our house, while Patty, Marianne, Jimmy and Tommy had moved on to greener pastures. Timmy, Mitchell and Greg were now a threesome always looking for new boys to join their fun. Worrying that their fun would end up getting us all in trouble, I banned them from the house. They were spending more time at Mitchell's place anyway. If I felt the itch to be with boys, there were always the twins.

Sadness crept into out lives when we all found out that Diane planned on suddenly leaving us. She was dealing with depression and some personal problems that made her want to move to another state to attend college and live with some relatives. Within a week she was gone. We not only lost a good friend, but a wonderful worker and asset to my cousin's business. Fortunately, Jeannie and Rose stepped up and did a good job taking her place.

By this time Ingrid was sending out most of her sewing and pattern work so Diane's loss was not as big a blow to the business as it could have been. She used a local group of very talented seamstresses to cut out and assemble her designer clothing. These young to middle aged women had a small shop in downtown St Pete. They were all from Italy, related and mostly widowed or never married. They did fast, reliable work for a fair price.

The seamstresses credited my cousin's business with saving their shop which was was not very busy during those times of everything being bought off the rack and businesses like dry cleaners getting less and less clothing in for alterations or repairs. Susan and Terry made daily runs back and forth between their shop and our house every day during the work week. Ingrid's talents

provided work for a lot of people including myself and my friends. That was a fact I never forgot and always appreciated.

Despite my cousin's success and my own enrichment from it, I was beginning to feel the stress of being responsible for so much of the management end of the business. Between trying to keep up with everything necessary to keep Ingrid's business running smoothly and the challenges of maintaining so many relationships, I began getting a lot more headaches and taking a lot more aspirin. I needed a break and began to think of ways to ease the stress which came more from my complicated love life than anything else.

Whether I liked it or not, Rose and I were now an item. I still fooled around with Robin, Jeannie and Kathleen some nights when she was not around, but for the first time I began to feel guilty about those sexual liaisons. As much as I really liked Rose, I also felt very close to the other girls. The best answer for me at that time was to try and get Rose more involved with the others. She was now friends with the girls, but nothing more. If I wanted there to be more I would have to be the catalyst behind that and find an ice breaker to see if Rose was into it.

Once again the 4th of July holiday was coming around and just a few days away. And once again my folks would be out of town, so that meant a holiday sleep over party for us! Jeannie, Robin and Rose planned our shindig and began shopping for it, while I procured the necessary fireworks. Before long we were ready and the day arrived. Rose was now the proud owner of her own car. She drove over to my house around ten that morning to help the rest of us get ready for the party. After she arrived I said that I had an unusual surprise for her. I refused to elaborate at that moment.

By previous standards this sleep over affair would be a lot less raucous then previous ones. Only Rose, Terry, Robin, Susan, the twins, Jeannie, Kathleen, Ingrid and I would be there. I could probably have found a few more guys to match up with the girls, but I had something else in mind. By lunchtime we got the barbecue started and had music playing out by the pool. Before anyone could dive in, I suggested we try skinny dipping.

The girls were all in with my plan and quickly got out of their swimsuits and into the pool. Terry and Ingrid joined in, but took their time getting naked. Rose looked at me, so I told her participation was optional. Not wanting to be the odd one out, she began taking off her swimsuit after I got naked. We jumped into the pool together and I began organizing a game of naked volleyball.

Rose was very self conscious for the first few minutes she was naked in front of the others, but after she saw that none of them were embarrassed about their nudity she began to relax. As our volleyball game progressed Rose got used to being naked and fit right in. Seeing that she had adjusted to the situation and was even eyeing the other girls, I decided to take things a little further.

After the game we all got out of the pool and had some beverages and snacks. We remained naked which surprised Rose. I had her sit with me on a back yard swing my folks had recently bought located just off the patio and still well out of eye range of any neighbors. It had a colorful

canvas canopy which kept the sun off of us. After Robin came back from a bathroom run I asked her to join us. She sat next to me on one side, while Rose was on the other.

After we finished our drinks and snacks, I invited Rose and Robin to come upstairs with me. Robin jumped up ready to go. Rose got up more slowly wondering what I was up to? I told her not to worry and took both girls hands in mine while I walked them into the house. After we got up to my room, I closed the door behind us and laid on the bed. Robin jumped on the bed and laid next to me. I told Rose to join us. She sat down on the other side of me near the edge of the bed.

Noting her apprehensive, I asked Rose to lay down with us if she felt comfortable about it. She slowly did and that's when I dropped the bomb shell. I asked Robin to switch places with me, then I suggested she make out with Rose. I reminded Rose that she told me that she had occasionally wanted to try being with a girl. I pointed out that this was the perfect opportunity to give it a try. Robin was cute, a friend, willing and would never out her to anyone outside of our group.

The girls took things slow. Robin began by holding Rose's hand and gently squeezing it. She smiled, then carefully hugged her new friend. Robin began kissing Rose on the cheeks until she worked her way towards her mouth. At some point the two began French kissing as I watched wondering what would happen next? Before long the girls began petting each other's breasts ever so slightly. Robin took the additional step of kissing Rose's breasts, then pulling her mouth towards her own.

Rose kissed Robin's breasts, then Robin returned the favor again. They petted each other some more until Robin started to pet and hug her way towards Rose's vagina. Then she began to gently finger Rose's tight pussy. Robin was really turned on by Rose, and I was turned on watching the two girls play around with each other. Rose started fingering Robin and was having a good time doing it whether she was willing to admit that or not.

I suggested the girls sit in front of each other to make the fingering easier for both of them. They did and while Rose fingered Robin, Robin gently petted Rose's breasts. Rose got really turned on by what she was doing and asked Robin to finger her. Robin began moving her fingers quickly in and out of Rose while Rose rubbed Robin's breasts. Robin was always more aggressive then the other girls.

Before long they pulled me into their fun. Rose got me on top of me and begged me to push my dick into her. While I did, Robin passionately kissed Rose. The two switched places after a bit and, together, we tried various positions. Robin took a turn on top of me and forced my dick into her, while Rose kissed me leaning over in a way which allowed me to finger her at the same time.

I shot my first load into Robin, then after about another thirty minutes of fun I shot another one into Rose. After we cleaned up Rose hugged me, kissed me and thanked me for the surprise. I smiled and told her that the fun was just beginning. At that point I knew I had Rose hooked on

the girls. Before the end of the night I would be sure she pleasured herself with Jeannie and Kathleen as well.

Susan and I had sex in the now empty downstairs spare room while Jeannie and Rose went at it in my room. I figured that since Jeannie had a penis as well as a vagina, those two did not need me in the mix. Anyway, I liked doing it with Susan and had not done so for a while. Later, I paired Kathleen with Rose and joined the two for some more amazing fun. Even though I was all but spent, I managed to bring some extra enjoyment to the mix. Rose seemed particularly turned on by Kathleen (and who would not be?).

Jeannie later told me that Rose and her got it on really well. I had briefed Rose on Jeannie's anatomy the night I confessed the truth about everything to her at the hotel suite. I wasn't sure how Rose might react to actually being alone with Jeannie for fun, but I guess my concerns about that were not justified. Jeannie said the two did just about everything together. The only thing that Rose objected to was being screwed by Jeannie, although Rose did suck her cock and did a great job from what I was later told.

More fireworks took place in my house that night then at the local parks department holiday display. Still, we all went to watch and had a great time together after a terrific barbecue and all that sex. That night was special to me because Rose officially became a part of our group and, more importantly, she was apparently happy about it. The only ones who did not sleep with her were Terry, Ingrid and the twins.

Terry and Ingrid were being exclusive to each other with the exception of me. I still had sex with my cousin at least once a week with their blessing and even got Terry into bed with me during a weak moment a few days before my prom adventure with Marianne and Rose. I knew he would never tell my cousin about our indiscretion and although I hated keeping secrets from Ingrid, sometimes my libido just got the best of me. That was not the last time I took a piece of Terry.

The twins were also regulars with me. The morning after our holiday sleep over I came down to the kitchen and found them eating breakfast with my cousin. After they finished, I smiled at Ingrid and took them up to the recreation room. I was always the most horny in the morning. I sucked them both off on the couch, then had anal sex with John and Jerry. They hated that, but I loved it.

With the holiday over, it was back to business. Now that Rose was a member of our group I no longer had to pussyfoot around with her and the girls. Over the next few weeks I had sexual encounters with Rose alone, Rose and Kathleen, Rose and Robin, Rose and Jeannie and a mix of the girls at different times. Rose did not mind messing around with the girls, but as far as guys went she was exclusive to me.

By that time the only guy around the house more often then myself was Terry. He was with Ingrid, so that was not an issue anyway. I did have some side drama going on with Timmy. Even though I had officially banned him, Mitchell and Greg from the house as a group, Timmy was a hard boy to give up and he still liked me as much as I liked him. We got together at least once a week for a sleep over and sex.

Marianne was another sex partner on the side. I was more than a little surprised when she started calling me and asking me to go out with her. When I did it was not just companionship she wanted. Although she was dating Aaron, I guessed that he was not as adventurous as I was when it came to sex. She loved the way I stuck my hands into her until she made that hot water flow! We meant at the suite on a fairly regular basis for sex and enjoyed every minute of it.

Rose, the other girls and I became really tight. We dated as a group, but I also spent some alone time with Robin, Jeannie, Kathleen, Rose and even Susan. Despite my best efforts I was now actually dating and very close to all the girls. On top of that I was also unofficially involved with Marianne and Timmy. It was ridiculous and made very little sense overall.

After a long conversation with my cousin whose advice I always appreciated, I decided to cut my ties with Timmy and Marianne for a start. Timmy's age could get me in trouble and Marianne had a boyfriend with a big cock and did not really need another for sex. If he could not fill the bill for her, she needed to look elsewhere and forget about me. I also stopped having sex with the Terry. I also left the twins alone, but still played around with one of them.

I really liked Jerry and needed that balance between boys and girls. He also seemed to like me enough to do just about anything I wanted when we slept together. He still hated anal sex as much as his brother, so I only did that to him once in a while. What I really liked was sucking his smaller dick and having him jack me off while I jacked him off. I figured that he was a safe bet at least until I could wean myself off of him and I planned to do that by the fall.

Trimming the boys and girls on the side was easy, trying to make some sense out of dating five girls individually and collectively was a lot harder. Instead of cutting back, I had actually added Susan to the mix. My perversive ways demanded that I have Susan and Robin together in bed with me on a regular basis and that was what I did. I loved doing sisters, especially at the same time! That would be something difficult for me to give up.

In many ways I had the perfect mix of girls. Each one had something or even several things that I specifically liked about them. I was extremely attracted to all my girls and even the thought of giving just one up was not an easy thing to consider. However, I was now almost seventeen years old, running a business and starting college in the fall. Things would only get more complicated, not less and dating the girls that were younger than me could mean big trouble even though we were very close in age and I was not yet eighteen.

By mid-August I knew that I had to make a decision to bring the insanity to an end. I was worn out physically and emotionally, as well as concerned about the future. I was actually beginning to crack. A good example of that was when Robin, Susan and Kathleen brought a new girl over to the house that they knew from school and had run into at the mall.

Jackie was a pretty fifteen year old with dark shiny hair, perfect skin and a great body. She had been in some of Robin's classes and knew Kathleen from church. She was no more religious than Kathleen, but her folks were and they insisted she attend church with them. Jackie lived some distance from the mall and used buses to get there and back, but Susan volunteered to drive

her to her house so that she could get permission to hang with the girls at my house and pick up her bathing suit.

After a stop at Jackie's house and a quick meeting with her mom, they were off again to my house. Her mom happened to know about Ingrid having actually bought a few of her things for Jackie to wear to school during a teen fashion event. When Robin and Susan told her mom that they knew my cousin, lived right across the street from her and wanted to bring Jackie to Ingrid's house, she was fine with the idea. Especially since the group also included Kathleen whom she immediately recognized from church.

It was a hot and humid afternoon when Jackie arrived at our house with the girls. Ingrid, Terry, Jeannie and Rose were off somewhere getting ready for yet another fashion shoot for Ingrid's latest designs. I was in the pool relaxing after a busy morning working for my cousin. As soon as I saw Jackie I knew what the girls had in mind. She was as tall as me, cute, on the thin side and well built.

By that time Robin and Susan were spending as much time at my house as their own. It was tourist season in Florida and that meant their motel was always full. Their parents would not be around on a regular basis until things slowed down in late September, so even when they did not sleep over the sisters spent a lot of time with us. Robin was now also helping my cousin for the summer and doing a nice job.

Jackie was polite, a little shy and a straight shooter. Just like the rest of us, she did not smoke, drink or do drugs. After I met her, the girls took their new friend into the house to change into her bathing suit. After a quick tour, they used the spare room downstairs to get changed. That was where Robin and Susan slept whenever they stayed overnight. I'm sure that they got a eyeful of Jackie and as soon as they emerged in their two piece bathing suits I got my own eyeful.

Looking at Robin, Susan, Kathleen and Jackie getting into the pool made me realize how lucky I was in some ways, but also had me concerned about where I was going with my game? Was I going to sit still for the girls going trolling for new converts at the mall or who knows where else? Was that my future? Had I become their pimp or enabler?

No one understood better then I did the need to fulfill the desires that stirred inside of all of us. However, I also knew that meeting those needs could never come at the cost of compromising secrecy or acting in a manner that would bring attention to our game. I worried that the girls had become a little too enthusiastic about bringing new people into our group, especially after I had already asked them not to.

The girls argued that since I always seemed to be adding to our numbers, they should also be able to do that as well. The difference was that they had turned that activity into a kind of sport, while I did it mostly out of necessity. At least that was what I told myself. I guess they were right in a way, but it all had to stop before we were all busted and my cousin's business was ruined.

I liked Jackie instantly. She had a quiet cool that I admired. After the girls steered her towards me and she began to open up a little and talk with me, we shared stories about school and our

lives. She loved the clothes that Ingrid designed and could not wait to meet her. I was certain that even though she seemed like a bit of a groupie, I was fairly certain that my cousin would take to her as quickly as I did. If Ingrid needed any more models, this girl would certainly be able to fill that position.

In a way I hoped that Ingrid would not even entertain that idea. If she did then Jackie would be yet another informal member of our household and easy candidate for our game. I was sure the girls had already come to that conclusion before they even invited her over. Only time would tell, so I invited Jackie for dinner to be sure that she would still be around when Ingrid, Terry, Jeannie and Rose returned.

Robin and Susan volunteered to make dinner while Kathleen, Jackie and I stayed in the pool. The girls were obviously going out of their way to get Jackie and I closer. Just before dinner Ingrid, Terry and Jeannie returned from their outing. They dropped Rose home because she had some family event to attend that evening. As I expected, Ingrid was instantly impressed with Jackie who heaped praise on my cousin for her designs.

Once again fate was laughing at me. With Rose out of the way and Jeannie having been informed about Jackie by Robin, Susan and Kathleen, the stage was again set for bringing a new group member into the fold. Ingrid and Jackie talked all through dinner and by the time the sisters were cleaning up afterward and doing the dishes with the help of Jeannie and Kathleen, my cousin had already made a pitch for Jackie to model and work for her.

Jackie was all in with my cousin's offer and agreed to help with the everyday work of Ingrid's business. Even with all of the part timers she had working for her as full time for the summer, she barely kept up with orders and had difficulties getting out her new catalogs and such. Before I knew it Ingrid was off to Jackie's house to get her mom on board with Jackie's new job opportunity. Kathleen needed a ride home anyway, so she, Robin and Susan went along for moral support. Jeannie and I mused over the situation while they were gone.

It was no surprise when Ingrid, Jackie, Robin and Susan returned two hours later with Jackie toting an overnight bag. My cousin managed to convince Jackie's mom to allow her to model and work for her. She also got permission for Jackie to stay over for a few days to train for her new position and be fitted for some clothes to model. We placed her in the spare room downstairs. At that point Susan and Robin were not sleeping at their house anyway so they could do some house cleaning and such at theirs.

My parents came home later that night from a dinner date and met Ingrid's new girl. They were also impressed with her. My folks were glad to have her as a house guest and happy that my cousin had found yet another employee. They called Jackie's mom to confirm that everything was on the up and up and being done with their permission. Although my folks would be around that weekend, the girls were already asking me if we could all go to the hotel suite for a Saturday night sleep over party?

Although I was concerned about the situation getting out of hand, I decided to go along with the girls. After all, if Jackie was going to be around for any length of time and working regularly

with Ingrid it would not take her long to see what was going on behind the scenes. At that point I was not in the mood to lie to anyone about us or try and keep the truth from someone who would be working so closely with my cousin.

It was a little tense around the house the next day when Rose came over and found a new chicken in the hen house. She was immediately concerned that Jackie might be a replacement for her, but I explained what she already knew to be true. My cousin needed more help with her business and the other girls had recruited their friend for the job without my blessing after running into her at the mall. I admitted to Rose that they were not just looking for new workers for Ingrid.

Rose knew as well as I did that the other girls had become rabid game players with sexual appetites that rivaled my own. The only difference was that they preferred me as their male sexual partner most of the time and liked to recruit girls for fun. It was also true that Robin, Susan and Kathleen were being occasionally boned by Timmy on the side with my permission. I needed a break from being the only rooster among the chickens and enjoyed watching them do it with each other when that opportunity presented itself. Rose remained exclusive to me.

We all agreed to leave Jackie alone to be trained by Ingrid until the hotel suite sleep over on Saturday, so the first and second day and night of her stay with us went by without anything happening in an official sense. On the second night which happened to be a Friday, Jerry came over to see me. We spent some time in the pool, then I brought him up to my room after everyone else went to bed. We had a pre-planned sleep over most Fridays which allowed me to get my boy fix taken care of.

The next morning Jerry left early to avoid being seen by Jackie, but not early enough. My parents were used to the twins sleeping over, so they never questioned it when one or both slept of them slept in my room with me. By the time I came down for breakfast Jackie was already up and eating some cereal. She gave me an odd look and asked how many people were staying at our house?

I told her that right now Jeannie was the only official house guest, but that any one or all of the girls, Terry or the twins could stay over with little or no notice. The girls had already explained the situation regarding their parents spending so much time at the hotel and she knew that Terry was seeing Ingrid. Jackie was also told that any of the girls that worked for Ingrid might stay over for business or just fun since all of us were also friends. She got that, but wondered if it bothered me to have Jerry sleep in my room with me?

Jackie saw Jerry come downstairs from my room and leave through the front door while she was heading to the kitchen for breakfast. I was not sure what she meant by that question or what her motivation was for asking it, so I remained calm and shrugged my shoulders saying that the twins liked sleeping in my room with me when they stayed overnight and that I did not mind. She did not pursue the matter, but I wondered if she had heard Jerry and I messing around in the room during the night or saw the girls doing something with each other over the past couple of days?

I was not that upset about the whole thing because Jackie would find out about everything that night at the hotel suite anyway. She would either be on board with what we were doing and join us, be against it and just continue to work for my cousin remaining friends with the girls, or freak out and run away. This was what I had been worried about. The law of averages dictated that not everyone we tried to get involved with our group was going to accept what we were doing.

We had been lucky up to that point, but that was exactly why I did not want to tempt fate by trying to add to our numbers despite my cousin's need for more employees. Still concerned about the way Jackie was acting, I got with the girls later that morning to see if any of them had said or done anything to cause Jackie to be suspicious or concerned.

Rose spoke up saying that while Jackie was changing into various outfits to try on for Ingrid, Robin had been helping her. At some point Robin pointed out that the underwear Jackie was wearing was not appropriate for the outfits. After running home to get some skimpier panties, she offered them to Jackie. When Jackie tried to go into the bathroom to change, Robin said she could change right in the work room since it was just her, Rose and Jackie in there at the time.

Jackie was kind of modest and appeared a little embarrassed about getting naked from the waist down in front of Robin, but she explained that Jackie would probably have to change in front of other models showing various body parts during fashion shows and that she should get used to it. Jackie understood and changed in front of Robin and Rose. Rose made the right move by looking away, but Robin stared at Jackie and that may have made her wonder why?

I also found out that Jackie saw Robin dissappear into Jeannie's room the previous night and not come out until the next morning. Jeannie told me about it and said they may have been a bit noisy. None of this was good news. I mean, yea, Jackie was going to find out about everything anyway, but I did not want her to think that we were pressuring her into anything or trying to keep things from her before I had a chance to explain everything.

Jackie did not ask any more questions all day Saturday. I assumed that she knew something was going on, but probably decided to remain quiet about it and go with the flow to keep from putting her job in jeopardy. That was exactly the feeling that I did not want her to have about us and hoped that after I told her the truth that evening she would no longer feel that way.

Although I had done my share of bullying over the years to get what I wanted from some of the people on my list, I was not proud of that and was doing my best to avoid passing that bad habit on to others. If the new girl was going to be involved with us it had to be because she wanted it, not because we forced or coerced her into it.

Jackie already knew we were planning a get together at the hotel suite that night. The girls had talked it up to her as a friendly gathering which allowed us all to take advantage of my dad's perks at the hotel he managed. At lunch that day they also mentioned that we would be going for a late night swim in the interior hotel pool to be sure Jackie brought her bathing suit along. They explained how that my dad had recently given me a key to it and made sure I had permission to use it privately during the hours that it was closed to hotel guests.

Of course Robin had to ramp things up by also telling Jackie that the nighttime swim was clothing optional! I understood why she said it and appreciated her honesty, but I think it would have been better to spring that little surprise on our new friend when we were already at the pool. As soon as Jackie heard the 'clothing optional' line I could see a look of concern come over her face.

I knew that Robin was right to tell her so that Jackie would not feel pressured into taking off her bathing suit at the last minute, but sometimes a little pressure helped someone who had preconceived notions about what we did to get into our game. In the case of most players, once they were involved they were glad they had taken the plunge. Otherwise, how would they know what they were missing out on?

I covered Robin's verbal misstep by telling Jackie that we were all very close as a group and often went skinny dipping together in the pool at my house. I explained that besides the fact that the neighbors could not see us in the pool at the house and that the pool at the hotel was equally excluded from any prying eyes, we did not think of nudity as a big deal.

I pointed out that we all got naked to shower in front of our fellow students of the same sex at school and that unless one of us had not taken health class, I was pretty sure that everyone knew what to expect when they saw people of the other sex naked! That got a laugh from everyone at the lunch table and defused the situation. Jackie appeared less concerned, but I could tell she was still worried about what was going to happen that night.

Our plan was to spend Saturday night at the hotel and stay there all day Sunday with a possible sleep over for Sunday night as well. Ingrid helped me get permission for Kathleen to spend the weekend at our house which included a trip to the hotel for the beach and pool. Robin and Susan were also a go. I did want to bring the twins along because I felt it meant send the wrong signal to Jackie. As my personal boy toys they were not really a part of our group. They would be staying with my cousin at the house.

Just to keep things a little more even I decided to invite Timmy along for the fun. I knew he would keep Robin, Kathleen, Jeannie and Susan busy in bed giving me time to break in or initiate Jackie into our group. I figured that having at least one other boy with us would make us all look like the group of friends we were to Jackie, instead of some sort of weird sex cult. Rose had some things to do with Ingrid for her business that weekend, so she would be staying at the house with my cousin instead of joining us for the hotel suite sleep over.

As the evening approached I thought it might be a good idea to for us to eat dinner at the hotel just so that Jackie felt more comfortable about being there. We all headed out with overnight bags in hand around five that evening. Jackie was immediately impressed when she saw the suite, but also concerned about the sleeping arrangements. I explained that between the three bedroom and pullout sleep couches in the suite there would be plenty of room for all and left it at that.

We went to dinner in the main restaurant and enjoyed some music courtesy of the live Dixieland Band that was playing that night in the lounge which opened up on to the dining area when the

music started. The food was fabulous and filling. After we ate we all changed into our bathing suits in the suite and went for a walk on the beach.

We all took a dip in the warm Gulf Of Mexico and horsed around for a while, then hit the shuffleboard court and played a few games of girls verses boys. Needless to say Timmy and I lost, but I figured we would made up the loss later in bed. Oh the sacrifices that guys have to make just to keep getting laid!

On the way to the coin game room we were talked into a session of volleyball by a group of Canadian young people staying at the hotel for few days. The game was kind of a tie, but we all enjoyed playing it and then moved on to the game room where I treated Timmy and the girls to pinball and the other games in there.

Dinner and the activities we took part in had helped to loosen up Jackie's attitude and quell her fears. By the time we headed back to the suite she was laughing and giggling with the girls who had spotted a few Canadian guys they thought were cute while playing volleyball. Timmy and I also saw some extremely pretty girls among the Canadians, but my mind was focused on the problem at hand and I knew better than to ever try to get involved with hotel guests or let anyone in my group do that.

The last thing I wanted to do was to reward my dad's kindness of allowing us to use the hotel suite and facilities with a betrayal by messing around with the guests. There was always the possibility that they could say something to someone or make a complaint. Before my dad began managing the property there were regular incidents of the help getting involved with guests and many of those did not end well. As a result, such contact was forbidden and I had no intention of breaking that rule or allowing any of my friends to break it.

Once back in the suite I opened the drapes wide to reveal that beautiful and romantic view of the Gulf which always tended to help when I needed to explain myself and my game to a new potential player. Everyone changed into shorts and tee shirts so that our bathing suits could dry for the late night dip in the indoor pool later that night. The girls put on some music and we sat around talking.

I was glad that Rose and Jeannie were not with us. It was already five against one if Jackie chose to see it that way. Thinking about that made me wonder how I had let the girls talk me into even considering another member for our little group which was not so little anymore. Being involved with so many young people in the manner that I was had its obvious perks, but it was also a lot of responsibility since what we were doing had to be done in secrecy.

The girls were giving me looks that indicated they wanted me to tell Jackie what the deal was while we were all sitting around. I felt that it would be better to wait until we went skinny dipping in the hotel pool. Since I was going to be the one doing the telling, it was my way or the highway. I called and ordered some hot snacks from room service for us and tried to keep Jackie as relaxed as possible.

A little over an hour later we all decided it was time to go to the indoor pool and changed into our bathing suits. Once we were in the pool area, I locked the glass door behind us and pulled down a shade which had some printing on it to tell hotel guests that the pool was closed. Just past the glass door was a short hallway which lead to the pool. There were no side windows in that room, just some murals with tropical scenes painted on the walls. The roof was glass and offered a beautiful view of the day or night sky.

I distributed towels to everyone and started things off by slipping out of my bathing suit. Timmy followed my example, then we both jumped into the pool. The girls began giggling and took off their swimsuits. While Jackie slowly removed hers, Robin, Susan and Kathleen mocked Timmy and I by alternatively showing us their breasts and covering them up with their hands. I told them that we had already seen those melons and that they looked nice and ripe to me.

Once Jackie was naked I could see that she had nicely shaped breasts that appeared larger without anything clothes to confine them. Her tall, slim body made her look like a goddess of the sea as she swam around in the pool. She shaved her legs and under arms and had no other body hair to speak of except for a nice dark and shiny bush. She also had a terrific buttocks. It was perfectly shaped and very feminine looking compared to some girls who had asses like twelve year old boys.

Timmy and I set up the volleyball net the hotel kept in a side storage area by the pool. We all played pool volleyball for a while, then everyone took turns in our stupid diving contest. Each person got one chance to use the diving board and dive into the pool in a way which was as stupid as possible. Timmy won with a weird backwards dive that landed him right on his butt in the water.

Despite the fun we were having I was nervous. I had no idea how to tell Jackie about our group. Everyone was having such a good time that I began to wonder if that was really the right time to drop the bomb, or if anytime was the right time? Maybe inviting Jackie into our game was an all around bad idea? I took Robin and the others aside as the opportunity presented itself to see if they still wanted her to join us.

The girls were set on having Jackie join our game, while I was concerned that it could backfire and cause her to bolt, quit working for my cousin and avoid us all from that point on. She could also rat us out or start rumors about us that could do a lot of damage. She did not seem the type to do any of those things, but I really did not know her well enough to be sure.

I needed some personal time with our new potential group member to be sure that she did not feel pressured into anything, so I again took Robin aside while Jackie used the restroom in the pool area and told her that I planned to explain everything once we got back to the suite. I wanted Robin to take Timmy and the girls to the cafe or hotel store on the pretext of getting us some more soda and snacks. While they were gone I would use that time to explain things to Jackie.

Robin was with my plan and after Jackie rejoined us, we all agreed it was time to head back to the suite for the night. We got back into our swimsuits, cleaned up the pool area after ourselves

and went on our way. Once we were back in the suite Robin said that she was going to get us some soda and snacks. The hotel cafe and shop were open late on weekends, so she took everyone but Jackie with her and left. I asked Jackie to stay behind so that we could talk privately for a few minutes.

I'm sure that Jackie had no idea what to expect from our conversation, but she sat down on the couch next to me without being too close and got ready to hear what I had to say. I began by telling Jackie that it meant a lot to all of us that she had begun hanging around. I also said that we appreciated her help with my cousin's business. I explained that Robin, Susan, the twins, Kathleen, Rose, Jeannie, Timmy and I were like a family and that we wanted her to be a part of it.

I explained that as a family we were all a lot more than just close friends, we were intimately involved. I said that we would all like for her to be involved with us in that way, but that was a choice she would have to make. If she chose to be just friends with us, that was fine. If she wanted more, we were on board with that as well. Either way, there was no pressure and any decision she made would have no affect on her work with Ingrid.

Having opened the door, I went on to explain enough about our game to give her the big picture about our sexual adventures and enough information to made a decision. Jackie had a look of shock on her face and I feared the worst. She told me that she had no idea we were into those sorts of things and was not sure that she wanted to be a part of them. I said that I understood completely, but asked her not to judge us too harshly.

Jackie calmed down a bit and said she was not judging us, it was just that she was caught off guard by what I had to say and did not really know how to react to it. I appreciated her honesty, but did not really know where to go from there? I felt a little out of control at that point and wondered how the girls would react to her objections to our sexual experimentation. I worried they would blame me.

The truth was that Jackie was just being polite. Having gotten as many people into my game as I had by that time gave me a kind of six sense about how to gauge their reactions. I knew that Jackie was probably horrified by what I told her and wanted no part of what we were into. She had looked at Timmy, me and the others girls naked with curiosity, but not in a way that told me she wanted to be with any of us sexually.

At that point I had two choices: Give up on her, or force her into something she did not want to do. Neither was really acceptable to me, but then again I was so frustrated and tired of having to deal with all the girls and everything else that I suddenly came up with another idea. I told Jackie that I was emotionally spent from all the pressure that my cousin's business and the people involved in our game put on me.

I explained to her that it was not that I did not enjoy having sex with the girls and boys or that I did not want to help my cousin run her ever growing business, but I was just tired of everyone always asking me to do more or looking at me as a perpetual problem solver. It was too much for

any teenager to deal with. She said she understood, but I told her that I needed her help and that she probably would not like what I was going to ask her to do.

I told Jackie that I could just tell the girls that she was not really into doing the kinds of things we did and leave things the way they were, but I was not going to do that. Instead, I was going to give her a choice that was as unfair to her as the pressure that I felt daily was to me. I said that she could either get into our game, or get out of our lives. It was that simple.

I looked Jackie in the eye and said that she seemed smart and ambitious enough to know that my cousin could make her a lot of money and do a lot to help her get started in life, but there would be a price to pay. If she wanted the benefits of working for my cousin she would have to surrender her body to me and the girls.

Timmy was not really a part of our regular group so I told her she could ignore him if she liked. She could also avoid Susan and Rose who were not really into girls. But she would have to have sex with me, Robin, Kathleen and Jeannie individually and as a group. I did promise that if she went along with us I could protect her and try to divert the other girls attention from her whenever that was possible.

Jackie looked away from me trying to remain composed, but I could see tears streaming down her cheeks. I guessed that she really wanted the opportunity that my cousin offered her, just not the additional requirements that came with it. She told me, "I have never been with a boy and I don't think I can do that kind of stuff with girls. I never tried it and I don't really want to." At that point I had another idea, a very bad idea.

I told Jackie to play along with me when the others got back to the room and made some small talk with her until the others finally returned with the soda and snacks. After we chowed down on junk food and drank up the soda, I began to separate everyone into two groups. At that moment Robin and the girls knew I had achieved some sort of success or compromise with Jackie and smiled at me.

I sent Susan, Kathleen, Jeannie and Timmy into my cousin's room to enjoy each other any way they pleased. I knew that Timmy's big dick and endless supply of energy would keep those girls busy until they got too tired to continue. I told Robin and Jackie to join me in my bedroom. As we all stood up to go our separate ways, Robin took Jackie's hand and lead her into my bedroom as I followed.

Once we were in the bedroom I closed and locked the door behind me. Jackie stood near the bed looking at Robin and me wondering what was going to happen next. I told Robin that Jackie felt like she might not be able to do the kind of things we did together. I suggested that we all get naked just to keep things equal and that she watch Robin and I play around with each other.

Jackie reluctantly removed her clothing and sat in a comfortable chair near the bed. I got on the bed with Robin and started making out with her. After a while I asked Jackie if she ever made out with a boy? She said she did, but never with her clothes off. I told her to come over to the bed and once she was close enough pulled her down into the middle of Robin and I.

Jackie was flustered and asked, "What are you doing?" I told her that I was going to make out with her and pulled her close to me while Robin gently rubbed her back. Jackie resisted at first, but eventually gave in and made out with me. As we kissed I gently felt her breasts while Robin massaged Jackie's back and buttocks.

I had Jackie turn around and face Robin, then told her to try making out with her. Before she knew what was happening, Robin was in her face and kissing her. Jackie pulled back, but I pushed her face back into Robin's until the two were kissing. I could see that Jackie really did not want to give making out with Robin a chance, so I began massaging her back and buttocks the way that Robin had done to try and settle our newest player down.

Jackie was not a happy camper, but forced herself to kiss Robin. I could almost feel the stress coming through her body as I touched her, so I told Jackie to turn back around and I started making out with her again. Robin tried fingering Jackie, but that got her upset and almost made her jump out of the bed.

At that point I had enough. I tried to be gentle and make things work, but Jackie was being a bitch and a prude. I got up off the bed, lubricated my penis, pulled Jackie down to the edge of the front of the bed and had Robin sit next to her and hold her hand. I spread Jackie's legs and lifted them up so I that could get ready to penetrate her.

Jackie got really upset and tried moving out of the position I had her in, so I stopped what I was doing and asked her straight out, "Do you want to do this or not?" I did not need to state the obvious. Jackie knew that if she did not have sex with me and Robin she would not be able to continue her job with Ingrid and that being around us would just be uncomfortable for all involved.

Jackie said, "Go ahead and do it!" I immediately penetrated her opening which was average sized. As I pushed through her Hyman she shuttered and took a deep breath, then began quietly crying. Robin tried comforting her as I moved my penis in and out of Jackie. It was not like I was raping her! I gave her a chance to decide if she wanted me to have intercourse with me and she chose to go ahead with it.

I was still kind of angry that Jackie was being such a baby, so I turned her over and did it with her doggie style until my penis finally exploded inside of her. After I shot my load Robin walked Jackie into the bathroom to clean up while I wiped myself off with a towel I had ready. When the girls came a while later I saw that Jackie had bathed, so I had her lay back down on the bed and ate her out.

At some point I let Robin take a turn eating Jackie. Robin loved it! Tears till occasionally flowed down Jackie's face, but Robin and I were determined to get her into what we were doing. After we ate her out I laid down on the bed and had Robin show Jackie how to give me a blow job. Robin forced Jackie's face down on my dick and held it there when I was ready to shoot my load.

way. Jackie had been converted and was enjoying herself. We did it for a long time, then cleaned up and got into our bathing suits.

Before we left the suite to join the others Jackie said that she did want to be a part of our group. All she asked was that I kept Timmy or any other boys away from her and that if the girls wanted to play around with her she be allowed to refuse sex with Jeannie's penis. That really freaked her out and she did not want Jeannie inside of her again. I said all that was fine and we left things there.

Chapter Nine: The End Is Near

We decided to spend Sunday night at the suite and return home Monday morning. Now that Jackie was a part of our little band of sexual rebels, I had her and Kathleen join me in my bedroom that night. I loved having sex with Kathleen and so did Jackie. I was surprised at how well she seemed to bond with Kathleen. After I had intercourse with both of them, they made out with each other for a long time. That was followed up by fingering and even oral sex.

Watching Jackie eat Kathleen out was a real turn on for me. Before long all three of us were having sex in every way we could think of until I was totally exhausted. Once again I had created a monster. More the proof was that Kathleen actually went and got Robin from the other bedroom to join her and Jackie while I was showering.

After I cleaned up I sat up for a while to watch TV. After Jeannie feel asleep in the other bedroom, Timmy came out and joined me having had his fill of boning the girls. Seeing him always turned me on, so as he sat there in his underwear I pulled him close to me and pulled down his underpants. He knew better then to resist because he was now officially my Number One Boy Toy and had to do whatever I liked for continued access to the girls.

I played with his penis, sucked him off and then had anal sex with him on the couch. He was the one boy I was able to shoot my load into. After so many sessions his anus was stretched and easily accommodated my penis. It was also easy for him to sit on the toilet and let my semen drip out of him. Each time I shot my load into him most of it ended up on the outside anyway as my dick slipped out of his anus while I was ejaculating.

I loved making out with my beautifully freckled boy and we did that for a long time. Even he had gotten used to it. Whether either of us admitted it or not, we were lovers and enjoyed each other's company a lot. We were both very much bisexuals and loved getting it on with each other and the twins as much as we did with the girls.

The next morning we all returned to our houses, our lives and work for those who helped out my cousin. There was a lot to do, but I made time to visit the mall with Jackie late Monday afternoon. I bought her a beautiful friendship ring to seal the deal of her joining our group and before long she was having sessions with me and Rose as well as the other girls.

Whenever things were going really well in my life I knew it was time to watch out. Something bad was bound to happen and usually did. I never felt closer to the girls and enjoyed my relationship with Timmy and my fun with the twins. My cousin's business was doing really well and it seemed like there was no end in sight. The only problem was that whenever you involve yourself with a group of people in anything at least one of them ends up screwing everything up. Such was the case with Robin.

Even though I may not have always have mentioned it in my writing, I used condoms and was careful with the girls. When Timmy or the twins had sex with the girls I insisted they used condoms as well. However, Robin was a loose cannon. She really got into having sex with girls and boys and lost control to the point that she was even screwing Terry without me or Ingrid knowing it.

Terry was used to having sex with Ingrid. My cousin had found out a short time ago that she could not get pregnant. Terry and I knew about it because we were very close to her, but we kept that fact to ourselves since it really was not anyone else's business. Terry started having sex with Robin a short time after summer vacation began and was not using condoms or being careful.

One day not long after Jackie joined our group I came back to the house to find a huge argument going on between Ingrid, Terry, Robin and Susan. It seems that Robin was pregnant and Terry was the one responsible. Even though I had sex with Robin a lot more then Terry did, I used condoms. Terry did not and Robin confronted him with the news right in front of Ingrid.

To make matters worse Susan also admitted to having sex with Terry several times, but she claimed it was only because Robin insisted on doing a threesome on those occasions. Luckily, Susan had not allowed him to shoot his load into her. Robin had always taken his semen in her vagina or sucked him off when he was ready to ejaculate.

This was not something that could just be swept under the rug. This was a full blown disaster that could take us all down and I knew it. The first thing I did was to try and get everyone to calm down and see what could be done. Even though this was not my fault and really did not involve me apart from my own relations with Robin, I did not want to abandon her in her time of need.

After discussing it amongst ourselves, I told Robin and Terry that they would have to own up to what they did and tell her parents. I said that if they left the rest of us out of it, I would go with them and try to help as much as I could. I knew that Robin would not rat me out because there was no way she wanted her folks to know how many guys she was screwing. The same was true of Susan. We would just leave her out of the picture entirely and the same with the twins.

That night I told my folks about Robin and Terry. They were disappointed in Terry because they thought he was being exclusive to Ingrid, and in Robin because they said they thought she was smarter than that. Imagine what they would have thought if they knew all that I was up to? My folks wanted me to stay out of the business between Terry, Robin and the Jensens, but I said that both Terry and Robin were my friends and that I felt partially responsible for the mess. After all, I had brought everyone involved together.

We planned to tell Robin's parents about the situation when they got home that evening, but she jumped the gun by going to her parent's motel and telling them there. I do not know exactly what happened, but Robin called me and said that she was grounded. The good news was that she had kept me and the others out of it. Only Terry was named and as far as the Jensens were concerned, they never wanted to see or hear from him again.

From that point on Robin, Susan and the twins were banished from our house and any contact with their friends. The Jensens called my folks and told them that they were not blaming me or any of us for what happened, they just did not want their kids to be around any of their previous friends. They had enough trying to figure out what to do with the mess that Robin and Terry had made.

Just like that Robin, Susan and the twins were gone from our lives. The family moved less than a month later saying they wanted to live closer to their motel, but it was obvious they also wanted to get their kids away from us. I felt really bad and knew this was a sign that it was time to make some serious changes. Ingrid agreed and made the first one herself. Terry was history. She kicked him out of her business and her life.

It did not bother her that Terry had sex with Robin and Susan, after all she knew that he and I had also been together and she and I still had sex on a regular basis. What upset her was that he had tried to sneak around her back instead of just telling her he wanted to bone some of the girls. There was a trust thing going in our group. Terry, Robin and Susan violated that trust and destroyed all that we had built together.

Robin eventually gave birth, but the child was adopted by a friend of the family. I did not see any of the Jensen kids from that point on and noticed that even their hotel was under new ownership a few months after they moved out of our neighborhood. Right after the Robin mess came to light things began to fall apart quickly. Terry was now completely out of the picture and after Kathleen's folks heard about what happened with Robin they barred Kathleen from seeing any of us.

Jackie got cold feet worrying that she might somehow get pregnant or in some other trouble with us. She modeled and worked for Ingrid until the end of summer, but our relationship and any contact between her and the others came to an end long before her job did. Before long it was just Jeannie, Rose, Timmy and I. That list got even shorter after Rose got a modeling gig in New York City thanks to her work with Ingrid and moved on.

By the time I started Junior College that fall Timmy was also gone. Even though we got along great and had something special between us, he could not cope with the pressure that his peers were putting on him and stopped coming by. As soon as he returned to school he was immediately associated with the Robin mess and word got out that he had messed around with her and the twins. Fortunately, my name somehow managed to avoid being mentioned.

I cannot say that I was sorry to see things end between me and most of the others. Our group had always been an accident looking for a place to happen. I was just lucky that things ended without

me or my cousin being blamed or worse. The only problem was that Ingrid lost all of her employees except for Jeannie and me. I felt responsible for that and quickly found a solution.

There was a small fashion design class of sorts at the Junior College. It was not huge, but there were probably close to twenty five full time students. I placed some flyers in the foyer outside that class advertising for paid interns to work with my cousin. Most of the people who responded to the flyer knew about my cousin. She had become known as a local wunderkind and anyone interested in the local fashion scene probably heard of her.

This time I did it smart. With Jeannie and Rose, my cousin had the models she needed for her catalogs. What she really needed now were a few very reliable workers. I interviewed eight of the twelve students who called. The others were not available for the hours we needed them to work. As it was I could only attend the Junior College part time at night in order to keep my cousin's business afloat. The good news was that kept me out of trouble since most of my fellow students were older.

I ended up hiring four paid interns from all the students who applied. I started them one at a time over a month so that there would be time to train each of them. They all had their own transportation and could work either in the morning or afternoon. Jeannie and I covered things the rest of the time. All four were guys and they were all gay. Ingrid, Jeannie and I stayed to ourselves.

After the disaster with Robin and Terry, Ingrid was in no hurry to get involved with another guy. Instead, she and I got really close and had sex at least twice a week the way we used to before all the others came along. Jeannie and I also began close. We started dating seriously and grew to love each other very much. There were obvious advantages to being intimate with Jeannie, but that was not why I enjoyed her company or having sex with her. I was genuinely in love with her.

By Christmas everything was again right with the world. The new employees were not only doing a great job, but they were really happy to be working with a creative person like my cousin. Ingrid began seeing a guy named Jerry who was her age and lived nearby. They met through a mutual friend who was one of her photographers.

I was very happy to see my cousin dating again. Jerry was attending a law college nearby and was as smart as he was charming. Even with them dating my cousin and I still got together for sex once in a while. Jeannie and I had become soul mates and hung together tightly. Most other people could not deal with us anyway, so our relationship was a natural.

It might surprise you to find me ending the story here, but that is what I choose to do. I may write more later if I feel the need. As it is I feel I have opened my heart enough for now. I have allowed my story to flow out so that you can learn from my mistakes and accomplishments alike. I believe that my story was one worth telling and hope you enjoyed reading it.

Check in with me at http://gothicmoods.tripod.com/misplaced.html

If there is to be more, I will place on it on that web page. Peace and love to you all.